AGRICULTURE IN IRON AGE ISRAEL

AGRICULTURE IN IRON AGE ISRAEL

by
Oded Borowski

Eisenbrauns
Winona Lake, Indiana
1987

First printed 1987
Reprinted by the American Schools of Oriental Research, 2002
This paperback edition by Eisenbrauns, 2009

Library of Congress Cataloging-in-Publication Data

Borowski, Oded.
Agriculture in Iron Age Israel.
Initiated as a Ph.D. dissertation at the University of Michigan.
Bibliography: p.
Includes index.
1. Agriculture—Palestine—History. 2. Iron age—Palestine.
3. Agriculture in the Bible. I. Title.
S425.B67 1987 630′.933 86-24237
ISBN 978-0-931464-27-0 [original hardback]
ISBN 978-1-57506-174-0 [paperback reprint]

The paper used in this publication meets the minimum requirements of the American National Standard for Information Sciences—Permanence of Paper for Printed Library Materials, ANSI Z39.48-1984.⊗™

In memory
of my good friends
Shamai Kaplan and Avraham Raʿanan (Frischer)

Table of Contents

Abbreviations

AASOR	Annual of the American Schools of Oriental Research
BA	*Biblical Archaeologist*
BAR	*Biblical Archaeology Review*
BASOR	*Bulletin of the American Schools of Oriental Research*
EAEHL	*Encyclopaedia of Archaeological Excavations in the Holy Land*
EB	*Encyclopaedia Biblica* (Jerusalem)
EI	*Eretz-Israel*
HTR	*Harvard Theological Review*
HUCA	*Hebrew Union College Annual*
IEJ	*Israel Exploration Journal*
JBL	*Journal of Biblical Literature*
JNES	*Journal of Near Eastern Studies*
JSS	*Journal of Semitic Studies*
PEQ	*Palestine Exploration Quarterly*
PJB	*Palästina Jahrbuch*
QDAP	*Quarterly of the Department of Antiquities in Palestine*
RB	*Revue biblique*
VT	*Vetus Testamentum*

List of Illustrations

The cooperation of the copyright holders is gratefully acknowledged for providing illustrations and/or the sources for the drawings which appear in this book.

List of Tables

Acknowledgments

This study was initiated as a Ph.D. dissertation at the University of Michigan and benefited from the advice of my committee. I would like to take this opportunity to thank Drs. Kent V. Flannery, George E. Mendenhall, Matthew W. Stolper, and especially Professor David Noel Freedman, chairman of the committee, for their help. I also would like to thank Drs. Lawrence E. Stager and Sy Gitin for reading the manuscript and offering many valuable comments. Needless to say, however, the opinions expressed, and errors which remain, are solely my responsibility.

I owe special thanks to the Memorial Foundation for Jewish Culture for a grant which enabled the study and to Emory University for a research grant which enabled me to prepare the study for publication.

Introduction

For a long time students of the Bible and biblical history have maintained that "agriculture was the basis for the economy of most countries in antiquity including Palestine. Not only villagers but many 'city dwellers' made their livelihood from agriculture, and farmers were the majority and the backbone of the population" (Aharoni 1967:13). Statements such as this one were made without being supported by a comprehensive study dealing with all aspects of agriculture and demonstrating the versatility and efficiency with which the farmers of ancient Israel practiced their livelihood. A survey of scholarly literature shows that most works concerning ancient agriculture in the Near East deal with prehistoric times. These studies have been devoted mostly to research on the domestication of plants and animals and to the development of agricultural methods and tools (e.g., Harlan 1972, 1975; Harlan and Zohary 1966; Renfrew 1973; Zohary and Hopf 1973; Zohary and Spiegel-Roy 1975, 1978). In addition, some scholarly interest has been directed at the material remains of agriculture in the Roman-Byzantine period in the Negev (e.g., Kedar 1956, 1957a, 1957b, 1957c, 1967; Mayerson 1956, 1960). But only a few studies have been devoted to agriculture in Iron Age Israel. Most of these studies deal with one aspect or another of agriculture during that period (Galil 1968; Galil and Eisikowitch 1968; Goor 1965, 1966a, 1966b, 1967a, 1967b; Evenari et al. 1971). Some works concerning biblical agriculture, which supposedly are comprehensive, are deficient because they were undertaken by people who were not able to deal with the Hebrew text or did not have the necessary background in archaeology (e.g., MacKay 1950; Shewell-Cooper 1962). Other works are too general and without documentation (e.g., Avitsur 1972, 1976) or are outdated (Dalman 1932–35; Löw 1924–34). Many works are devoted primarily to the identification of plants and do not present any other aspect of agriculture (e.g., Moldenke and Moldenke 1952; Anderson 1957; Andrews 1964; Balfour 1857; Callcott 1842; Cook 1846; Goldsmith 1960; Jerusalem American Colony 1907; King 1941, 1948; Peelman 1975; and many articles in several languages).

The purpose of the present work is to produce a picture of agriculture as practiced in Iron Age Israel, from the time of the settlement to the destruction of the First Temple. This study describes the different types of field crops and fruit trees cultivated by the Israelite farmer and the methods and implements used in cultivation. It includes a survey of the end products of the agricultural effort and the installations used for processing and storing foodstuffs. Other agriculturally related matters, such as land ownership, land use, restoration of soil fertility, pests, and diseases, are also included here.

Information was gathered from literary and archaeological sources. Most of the literary evidence was gleaned from the Old Testament (OT), where agricultural data can be found in narratives, law codes, parables and allegories, prophecies, and other genres. However, this evidence is very sketchy, and the OT does not present a complete picture of Israelite agriculture at any point in history—nor should we expect it to. At no time was it the intention of the biblical writers and compilers to systematically describe daily life in Israel. For example, the law codes include several laws related to agriculture, but they do not cover all aspects of agriculture—only those that were of interest to the compilers at that time. Much of the biblical evidence related to agriculture has to be gleaned from the material dealing with other topics, where agriculturally related information is presented in passing or used symbolically. For example, some narratives dealing with historical events mention agricultural subjects. Another example is that of the prophets, who used agricultural terminology in their speeches because it was part of the daily vocabulary with which their audience was familiar. These are some of the limitations imposed on the present work by the nature of the biblical evidence. They could not be overcome with the help of extra-biblical sources because of the scarcity of written documents from Iron Age Israel (see below).

The result, for the most part, is that the picture presented here is not one which shows progress and development, but rather is a still picture. In certain instances, this situation is remedied with the help of material culture recovered in archaeological excavations. Whenever archaeological information is available, e.g., implements and installations, it is used not only to illuminate biblical references, but also to show development and change. It should be mentioned here that since the biblical material is limited, our most important means of broadening our knowledge of Iron Age agriculture is archaeology and the intentional effort to retrieve related information.

Information gathering for the present work was conducted along two lines, literary and archaeological. As stated earlier, most of the literary information came from the OT. The steps involved in using the OT as a source of agricultural data were as follows:

1. Identification of all terms relating to agricultural activities;
2. Definition of each of these terms on the basis of context and etymology; the latter was done with the help of dictionaries and other scholarly works;
3. Division of the terms into categories on the basis of subject matter;
4. Selection of categories to be dealt with in the present work; the selection provided the framework for the study.

To supplement the biblical evidence extra-biblical sources related to agricultural topics were sought. The sources identified as pertinent to the present work are very few and include the Gezer Manual, the Samaria Ostraca, and the letter from Meṣad Ḥashavyahu. Additional inscriptional material includes seals and stamps, such as the *lmlk* jar-handles.

Archaeological data were collected by surveying scholarly literature, including preliminary and final excavation reports. This part of the investigation produced information pertaining mainly to implements, installations, and plant remains. Other scholarly works dealing with special topics and problems were also consulted. This brought to the fore work that had already been done, and it was integrated into the present work.

Information gathering was followed by integrating the evidence into as complete a description as possible of all aspects of agriculture in ancient Israel. The biblical information served as a foundation upon which the other evidence was added. Data collected from the OT offered descriptions and terminology for the agricultural subjects dealt with here. They were further illuminated by archaeological finds. Artistic representations, mostly from Egypt, are cited to illustrate certain practices such as plowing, reaping, and wine making. In doing this I have made the assumption that since Egypt exerted some cultural influence on Palestine, it is likely that this influence extended to certain agricultural practices. Some Mesopotamian artistic representations were also chosen for the same reason. Of course, each case had to be considered individually.

In the absence of information from ancient sources, modern conditions and practices are also taken into consideration. The assumption is that certain present conditions and processes have not changed much since the Iron Age.

The results of the investigation are presented here in eleven chapters that deal with specific topics, a chapter devoted to the impact of agriculture on life in ancient Israel, and another chapter summarizing the conclusions. Biblical terminology is introduced either to illustrate and clarify certain points or to show how the topic under discussion is reflected in the Scriptures or to try to explain the passage in light of the discussion. One of the contributions of the present work is the increase in our understanding of passages using agricultural terminology and metaphors.

As for geographical terms used in the present work, Canaan is employed in reference to Syria-Palestine before the conquest and settlement of the region by the Israelites; Eretz-Israel is the term used to define geographically the land after the conquest. Palestine is used as a geographical designation without any reference to a specific historical period.

Part I
The Land

1

The Place of Agriculture in Ancient Israel

Eretz-Israel was regarded by the OT as "a land flowing with milk and honey" (Exod 3:8). A more detailed description of its agricultural richness and mineral resources is presented to the Israelites with the words

> For YHWH your God is bringing you into a good land, a land of brooks of water, of fountains and springs, flowing forth in the valleys and hills, a land of wheat and barley, of vines and fig trees and pomegranates, a land of olive trees and honey, a land in which you will eat bread without scarcity, in which you will lack nothing, a land whose stones are iron, and out of whose hills you can dig copper (Deut 8:7–9).

Although some of the details in this description are idealized, the portrayal of the agricultural versatility of Palestine is accurate, as evident from historical documents and archaeological discoveries.[1]

Egyptian sources from the Old, Middle, and New Kingdoms concerning Canaan supply ample information about the agricultural resources available in this region. At first, the Egyptians did not take advantage of Canaan's agricultural richness but devastated the land, as reported by Uni, commander of the Egyptian force in the reign of Pepi I (ca. 2315 B.C.E.) on the first recorded Egyptian campaign into Canaan: "This army returned in safety, (after) it had cut down its [the land's] figs and its vines" (Breasted 1906, 1:143; see also Pritchard 1950: 228). A detailed description of the agricultural wealth of Canaan in the time of the Middle Kingdom is recorded in "The Story of Sinuhe,"[2] the account of an Egyptian nobleman who was forced to flee Egypt for political reasons and found shelter in Upper Retenu (Canaan) with a sheikh named Ammi-enshi. After marrying the sheikh's daughter, Sinuhe received land which "was a goodly land

[1] See chaps 8–10.

[2] The story opens with the death of Amenemhet I (ca. 1970 B.C.E.) and continues during the reign of his successor, Sen-Usert I (ca 1970–1928 B.C.E.). This tale survived in many manuscripts from the late Twelfth Dynasty (ca 1800 B.C.E.) to the Twenty-first Dynasty (ca. 1000 B.C.E.); see Pritchard 1950: 18.

named Yaa; figs were in it and grapes. It had more wine than water. Plentiful was its honey, abundant its olives. Every (kind of) fruit was on its trees. Barley was there, and emmer.[3] There was no limit to any (kind of) cattle" (Pritchard 1950: 19).

As time went on the Egyptians learned to exploit Canaan's agricultural resources. This was accomplished through countless military campaigns into the land under the leadership of several Pharaohs of the New Kingdom. The most detailed accounts were recorded by Thutmoses III (1490–1436 B.C.E.) on the walls surrounding the holy of holies in the great temple of Amon at Karnak. The greatest feat of his first campaign in 1468 B.C.E. was the capture of Megiddo. The spoil included "1,929 large cattle, 2,000 small cattle, 20,500 white small cattle" (Breasted 1906: 2. 187). Since the campaign was conveniently conducted during harvest time in Canaan, the Egyptians carried away the harvest of Megiddo, which amounted to "208,200 (+x) fourfold heket grain, besides that which was cut as forage by the army of his majesty" (Breasted 1906: 2. 189).[4]

Subsequent campaigns by Thutmoses III into Retenu exhibit the same policy of exploitation. In his second campaign he carried away among other things "823 (*mn*-) jars of incense; 1,718 (*mn*-) jars of honeyed wine" (Breasted 1906: 2. 191), and in his third campaign he brought back samples of flora and fauna found in Canaan. The results of this campaign are depicted in a long series of reliefs accompanied by an inscription reading in part: "Plants which his majesty found in the land of Retenu. All plants that [grow], all flowers that are in God's-land [which were found by] his majesty when he proceeded to Upper Retenu" (Breasted 1906: 2. 193).

One of the places despoiled by Thutmoses III in his sixth campaign was the land of Djahi (presumably a region in northern Canaan), where "their gardens were filled with their fruit, their wines were found remaining in their presses as water flows, their grain on the terraces.[5] . . . It was more plentiful than the sand of the shore"

[3] Erdman (1966: 19) translates 'wheat' in place of 'emmer'; Breasted (1906: 1. 238) translates 'spelt'. I suggest that the reference could be either to wheat, *Triticum durum* Desf. (hard wheat), or to emmer, *T. dicoccum* (Schrank) Schuebl., biblical *kussemet*, but not to spelt, *T. spelta*, which was not cultivated during that period in Canaan; for details see chap. 8.

[4] According to Breasted's calculations this equals 112,632 imperial bushels, and at twenty bushels per acre (which is too much for that period) he assumes that the harvest covered an area close to nine square miles (Breasted 1906: 2. 189). J. A. Wilson (in Pritchard 1950: 238) reads "207,300 (+x) sacks of wheat," which according to him amounts to 450,000 bushels. All these figures are probably too high.

[5] Wilson (in Pritchard 1950: 239) translates here 'threshing floors', which seems better from context.

(Breasted 1906: 2. 196). In the tribute from this expedition Thutmoses lists "incense, oil, 470 (*mn-*) jars of wine . . . 616 large cattle, 3,636 small cattle, loaves, . . . clean grain in kernel and ground. . . . All good fruit of this country" (Breasted 1906: 2. 196–97). Similar results are recorded from the seventh, ninth, fourteenth, and sixteenth campaigns in Retenu and Djahi (Breasted 1906: 2. 200, 206, 211, 213).

The exploitation of Canaan during the period of the New Kingdom was achieved by political pressure exerted by the Egyptians as a result of their military superiority. During the Late Bronze Age, Canaan was divided into city-states whose petty kings were vassals of Pharaoh. These semi-independent political units, which were heavily fortified and were engaged in a constant power struggle among themselves, were situated in the fertile plains and near major trade routes. They formed a political network, whose influence extended over all, or most, of the agricultural land. The geographical distribution of these city-states is known from the Amarna letters, from archaeological excavations, and from traditions and historical accounts in the books of Joshua and Judges (Aharoni 1967: 157–73, maps 11, 15). The Egyptians maintained their presence in Canaan with military garrisons stationed in several cities. The existence of these garrisons is attested in the Amarna letters.[6] Some of these garrisons, such as the one in Beth-shan, were manned by Philistine mercenaries who, in some cases, remained in the heartland of Canaan throughout the reign of Saul (1 Sam 31:10, 12) until the capture of these cities by David.[7]

The Canaanite cities, according to the OT, were heavily fortified and possessed war chariots (Jos 17:16, 18; Judg 1:19; 4:3, 13). Most of these cities were situated in areas where they controlled large tracts of agricultural land. The Israelites, who wanted to conquer the land but lacked the military might to do so, were obliged to develop an economic base in the fringe areas which were unoccupied by the Canaanites.[8] In spite of the harsh conditions, and with the help of land-use innovations (see below), the Israelites managed to become agriculturalists and created for themselves an economic base from which they could conquer the land. From that time on agriculture dominated Israelite daily life.

[6] See in Pritchard 1950, especially letters EA 137, RA 100, EA 234, EA 244, EA 286, EA 287, EA 289, EA 290, EA 292.

[7] For the Egyptian presence in Beth-shan during the twelfth century B.C.E., see James 1966: 13; for the Philistines in Beth-shan, see Negev 1972: 52.

[8] The exact date of the Israelite conquest and the methods by which it was achieved are not discussed here; for details see Aharoni 1967: 174–253; Bright 1971: 105–75; Mendenhall 1962; B. Mazar 1981; Callaway 1968; Miller 1977; Weipert 1971; Yeivin 1971; Albright 1956.

In ancient Israel agriculture had an impact on almost every facet of daily life—economic, social, and cultural. From the beginning, Israelite settlement depended heavily on successful adaptation to natural conditions and available resources. In spite of Canaan's agricultural versatility, the political situation left the Israelites with only limited resources since the Israelite tribes could occupy only previously unsettled land in the Ephraim and Judean hill-country and in the mountainous regions of the Galilee. These regions had been left unsettled because they were heavily forested and lacked suitable agricultural land. The scarcity of water sources added to the difficulty of agricultural settlement in these regions.

These conditions did not deter the Israelites, and as reported in Jos 17:14–18, they started with the task of clearing the forests. For the creation of agricultural land, the Israelites employed terraces, a method heretofore not widely used in Canaan. By terracing the sloping hills the Israelites created plots of leveled land which were utilized for agricultural purposes.[9] Near these terraced fields small villages were established and occupied by the clans and families owning and cultivating the land. The initial phase of settlement shaped Israelite society and attitudes in generations to come.

Another innovation in land use which took place during the Iron Age is that of runoff farming in the Negev. Studies show that during the Iron Age there were three phases of settlement in the Negev, and they were each dependent on runoff farming. The earliest phase is dated to the end of the tenth/beginning of the ninth century B.C.E.; the second phase is dated to the eighth century and the third to the seventh century B.C.E. While the first phase might have been related to the Solomonic commercial and copper-mining activities in the south, the second and third phases were probably connected with periodic expansions by the Judean monarchy, possibly under Uzziah and Josiah, respectively. What is important to note is the fact that during all three phases the Judean monarchy relied not only on isolated fortresses but also on agricultural communities to maintain its presence in the south.[10]

There were other agriculturally related developments which took place during the Iron Age and influenced Israelite daily life. One important change was the use of iron for tool making. Although at the beginning of the Iron Age the Israelites continued using bronze for tools, it was slowly replaced by iron.[11] The use of iron for tool making resulted in the production of better tools, which led to the creation of

[9] For details see chap. 2.
[10] For details see chap. 2.
[11] For details see chap. 5; see also Garbini 1978.

agricultural surplus, which, in turn, led to the introduction of new types of storage facilities, such as the pillared storehouses.[12]

A very important agriculturally related innovation, which now can be dated safely to the Iron Age, was the beam-press used in olive-oil production. Archaeological discoveries at Beth-shemesh, Gezer, and Tell Dan show that beam-presses were used as early as Iron II.[13] The use of beam-presses enabled production of large quantities of oil. Oil surplus was another factor behind the construction of larger and better storage facilities. The surplus created by these innovations shaped the economy of the country and led to changes in the structure of the state (see below).

Once the Israelites settled, they became quite versatile agriculturalists, as suggested by some of the references in the book of Judges and in early Hebrew poetry. In addition to the herding of large and small cattle (Deut 32:14; Judg 4:19; 5:16, 25; 6:25), the Israelites cultivated cereals (Deut 33:28) and a variety of fruit trees. Although wheat was cultivated (Deut 32:14; Judg 6:11; 15:1; 1 Sam 6:13), in the early stages of the Israelite settlement the most important cereal was barley,[14] which was used for making bread (Judg 7:13) and beer (Judg 13:7, 14). In addition to wheat and barley, paleobotanical studies reveal that broad beans, lentils, bitter vetch, and chick-peas were also cultivated during this period.[15]

The most prominent fruit-bearing plant, judging from the number of OT references to it, was the grapevine, the fruit of which was used mainly for wine making.[16] The second most important fruit tree, by the same criterion, was the olive, with the product of its fruit, oil.[17] Other fruit trees cultivated by the Israelites were fig, pomegranate, date, sycamore, and various nut-bearing trees.[18]

There is no evidence that the Israelites introduced any new species of domesticated plants. The Israelite farmer inherited from his predecessors a large variety of field crops and fruit trees to choose from.

[12] See chap. 7.

[13] Previously, it had been maintained that beam-presses were introduced during the Hellenistic or Roman period; see chap. 9.

[14] This fact can explain the interpretation of 'barley bread' in the dream of the Midianite soldier (Judg 7:13–14), in which the 'barley bread' is identified with Gideon and Israel. Barley achieved a prominent place in early Israelite agriculture because of the necessity to settle fringe areas and barley's tolerance of harsh conditions; for details see chap. 8.

[15] See chap. 8.

[16] Gen 49:11–12; Deut 32:14, 32–33; 33:28; Judg 6:11; 9:12–13, 27; 13:7, 14; 19:19; 21:20–21; for details see chap. 9.

[17] Deut 32:13; 33:24; Judg 9:8–9; for details see chap. 9.

[18] See chap. 9.

But it seems that the major contribution to agricultural methodology, crop rotation, was made as early as the Iron Age by the Israelite farmer.[19] Crop rotation, together with organic fertilizing and fallowing, resulted, no doubt, in larger crop yield and created a surplus of produce.

While Israelite society remained mostly agricultural throughout its history, agriculture aided in the development of a multifaceted economy, which included commerce and crafts. Agricultural surplus, which was the result of the innovations I mentioned above, was used by the monarchy to pay for imported goods. One such example is Solomon's payment of oil, wheat (1 Kgs 5:25), and wine (2 Chr 2:9, 14) to Hiram of Tyre for cedar wood.[20]

To facilitate the use of agricultural surplus for payment for imported goods and for the support of the growing bureaucracy and urban population, a tax-collecting system was initiated and developed by the monarchy. Scholars suggest that David was the first to divide Judah into twelve administrative districts (de Vaux 1961: 136; Bright 1974: 201). This system was inherited by his son Solomon, who expanded it by dividing the north into twelve districts (1 Kgs 4:7–19; Cross and Wright 1956: 224–25). After the division of the monarchy, the administrative system in the south remained in use and included the territory of Benjamin (2 Chr 11:12, 23); a final reform of this system was made under Jehoshaphat (ca. 873–849 B.C.E.) as recorded in 2 Chr 17:2, 12–13. The outcome of Jehoshaphat's reforms of the administrative districts can be seen in the boundary lists in Jos 15:21–62 and 18:21–28 (Cross and Wright 1956: 226). (Alt [1925] and Noth [1966: 98–99] date these lists to the time of Josiah.)

The information about the northern kingdom is much scantier. It seems that after the division Jeroboam attempted a certain reform, the nature of which is unclear. The only detail given in the OT is that Jeroboam changed the date of the *ʾāsîp* festival.[21] This move could have been related to reforms in the tax-collecting system since taxes were probably paid in kind at the end of the ingathering season. This reform might have been necessary to balance the loss of the territory of Benjamin and to support the cult centers rededicated by Jeroboam.

It should be pointed out that the source of agricultural surplus was not limited to the small farmer; the monarchy was also a large agricultural producer. The united monarchy, and later the northern

[19] See chap. 11.

[20] Solomon was engaged in many other commercial endeavors (1 Kgs 9:26–28; 10:11, 15, 22, 28–29) and must have used agricultural surplus to pay for imported goods.

[21] See chap. 4.

and southern monarchies, owned large royal estates where many agricultural activities were carried out.[22]

In addition to its crucial role in the economy, agriculture influenced the social structure of ancient Israel. Although during the time of the monarchy there were Israelites living in urban centers, where they were employed in the state bureaucracy or as artisans, small village communities continued to exist until the fall of Jerusalem (587/6 B.C.E.).[23] The agricultural character of Israelite society was not disturbed by the deportation of the urban population by the Babylonians (2 Kgs 25:12; Jer 52:16).[24]

Agricultural concerns were also the driving force behind some social movements. One such movement was the uprising led by Jeroboam against Rehoboam, which resulted in the secession of the north from the united monarchy (ca. 922 B.C.E.). As the OT describes the event, the people of Israel requested Rehoboam to abolish the corvée, an institution established by his father, Solomon.

> King Solomon raised a levy of forced labor out of Israel; and the levy numbered thirty thousand men. And he sent them to Lebanon, ten thousand a month in relays; they would be a month in Lebanon and two months at home; Adoniram was in charge of the levy. Solomon also had seventy thousand burden-bearers and eighty thousand hewers of stone in the hill country (1 Kgs 5:28–30 [5:13–15]).

An agrarian society cannot survive when a large portion of its labor force is engaged in activities away from home and is not available to attend to agricultural activities which have to be performed daily. The hardships caused by conscription for corvée probably led to changes in land ownership. I suggest that the rebellion against Rehoboam and the killing of Adoniram, who was in charge of the forced labor (1 Kings 12), stemmed mainly from the fear of the Israelites that they would become landless.[25]

Another social uprising which had its roots in agricultural concerns was Jehu's purge (ca. 842 B.C.E.) of Jehoram and the Omride dynasty. As the OT describes this event, it was instigated by the prophetic circles of Israel, led by Elisha. The Omride dynasty was

[22] See chap. 3.

[23] See chap. 3.

[24] For details see Bright 1974: 330; see also Jer 40:10, 12; Neh 1:36–40; 13:5, 12.

[25] The only request the Israelites presented to Rehoboam was the alleviation of the corvée burden. I believe that one of the main reasons for Israelite hatred of the corvée was the interruption of agricultural activities. It seems that Jeroboam, whose early reforms included a new date for the celebration of Sukkot, was more sympathetic to Israelite agricultural needs.

opposed by the prophetic circles for several reasons, one of which was the execution of Naboth the Jezreelite and the confiscation of his vineyard (1 Kings 21).[26] The importance of the Naboth incident in causing the rebllion is demonstrated by Jehu's statement when he left Jehoram's body in Naboth's vineyard: "As surely as I saw yesterday the blood of Naboth and the blood of his sons—says YHWH—I will requite you on this plot of ground" (2 Kgs 9:26).

Besides being the dominant factor in the economy and social life, agriculture influenced ancient Israel's ideology through religion and laws. The basic premise that the land belongs to YHWH, who gave it to his people, is reflected in many aspects of Israelite daily and spiritual life. Many of the stipulations included in the covenant between YHWH and Israel related directly to agriculture.[27] The observation of the covenant assured Israel's prosperity through YHWH's intervention in nature, which is spelled out in agricultural terms in the blessings and curses.[28] YHWH's punishment of Israel for breaking the covenant is always described by the destruction of the agricultural economy in addition to the physical destruction of the people.[29] The restoration and prosperity of Israel are also described in agricultural terms.[30] The rule bestowing all the family land, *naḥălâh*, on the eldest son does not have to be regarded as insensitive to the plight of the other sons of the family, nor must the rule lead to the creation of a landless class of people, if we assume that the inheritance laws were composed at the time of the settlement and that land was still available for settlement and farming. The younger sons were expected to create their own *naḥălôt*.[31] This is consonant with the idea that the promised land belongs to YHWH and individuals share the land by the process of conquest and settlement.[32] Each member of the family who did not inherit land could become a landowner by participating in the process of conquest and settlement in his own generation.[33]

[26] This was probably not an isolated incident; compare the confiscation of the land of the Shunamite woman (2 Kgs 8:3–6).

[27] For example, see Exod 22:4–5; 23:10–12; Lev 19:19a, 23–25; 25:2–7; Deut 14:22–23, 28; 15:14; 20:6, 19–20; 22:9–10; 23:25–26; 24:19, 21; 26:1–2, 12.

[28] Blessings: Lev 33:3–5; Deut 11:14–15; 28:1–14. Curses: Lev 26:19–20; Deut 11:16–17; 28:15–18, 22–24, 30b, 33, 38–40, 42, 51.

[29] See, for example, Isa 7:23; 24:7; Jer 5:17; 8:13; Hos 2:14; Joel 1:7, 12; Hab 3:17.

[30] See, for example, Hos 14:8; Amos 9:13–15; Mic 4:4; Hag 2:19; Zech 3:10; 8:12; Mal 3:11; Ps 128:3.

[31] See chap. 3.

[32] See chap. 3. The law in Deut 21:15–17 seems to reflect a specific case. Dividing the land among all sons, generation after generation, would have created a landless society within a very short period.

[33] This concept of land acquisition is derived directly from the covenant, where everyone who becomes a member of the covenant shares in the common history of Israel, e.g., coming out of Egypt; see Bright 1974: 146.

Part of the moral code imposed by the covenant on the Israelites was the care of the socially and economically weak, defined by the OT as the poor, the sojourner, the orphan, and the widow. Being an agrarian society, Israel could fulfill this obligation mostly by using her agricultural resources. There were several ways by which the unfortunate could be helped: (1) allowing them to participate in harvesting the seventh-year growth (Exod 23:11; Lev 25:6); (2) leaving for them a *pēᵓâ*, 'corner, side', of the field unharvested (Lev 19:9a; 23:22); (3) allowing them to glean in the fields, *leqeṭ* (Lev 19:9b; 23:22), the vineyards, *ᶜôlēlôt* (Lev 19:10; Deut 24:21), and olive groves (Deut 24:21); (4) leaving for them in the vineyards the *pereṭ*, 'small bunches' (Lev 19:10); (5) allowing them to have any sheaves which had been forgotten at the end of the day (Deut 24:19); (6) paying a tithe for their support (Deut 26:12).[34]

The cultic calendar was also influenced by agriculture. The three most important festivals, *šālōš rěgālîm*, were celebrations of the beginning or ending of certain agricultural activities. *Pessaḥ/maṣṣôt*, celebrated in the beginning of the month of *ᵓābîb*, marked the beginning of cereal harvesting, and *šābūᶜôt*, celebrated seven weeks afterward,[35] marked the completion of this task. The third festival, *sukkôt*, was celebrated at the end of the year and marked the end of ingathering fruit. This festival also marked the beginning of the sowing period.

The support of the cult centers and their functionaries relied heavily on agricultural surplus. Although it seems that during a certain period the Levites owned property,[36] it is very likely that those serving in the central shrines depended mainly on gifts and donations extended by the populace. Helping the Levite was a covenant stipulation (Deut 12:19; 14:27, 29; 26:12–13), and the nature of this responsibility was spelled out in detail in Num 18:8–32 and Deut 18:1–9, where the Israelites were commanded to donate the first fruit and a tithe for the benefit of the Levites.[37] To what extent this responsibility was actually discharged is not known, but it was adhered to, to a certain degree, in the time of Samuel (1 Sam 9:23–24), and it was clearly a part of the reforms instituted by Hezekiah (2 Chr 31:4–21) and Nehemiah (Neh 10:36–40).

Israel's closeness to the soil and her dependence on it are evident in the use of agriculturally related terminology as metaphors throughout her literature. Proverbs and allegories, blessings, prophetic

[34] This last provision applied also to the Levites. There was also a special provision made for freed slaves (Deut 15:14).

[35] For details see chap. 4.

[36] See chap. 3.

[37] See also Exod 34:26; Lev 19:24; 27:30–33; Num 5:8–10; 6:20; 15:19–21.

speeches, and psalms use agricultural symbolism extensively. Gideon (Judg 8:2), Jotham (Judg 9:8–15), Samson (Judg 14:8), and Nathan (2 Sam 12:1–4) use agricultural allegories when trying to clarify a problem. Israel was likened by the prophets to a vineyard (Isa 5:1–8), a grapevine (Jer 2:21; Ezek 17:6–10; Hos 10:1), a night shelter in a cucumber patch (Isa 1:8), and a threshing animal (Hos 10:11; Mic 4:13). When Jeremiah wanted the people of Judah to repent of their iniquities, he said, "Break up your fallow ground, and sow not among thorns" (4:3; see also Hos 10:12). The Latter Days were described by the prophets as a time of peace when all people "shall beat their swords into plowshares, and their spears into pruning hooks" (Isa 2:4; see also Mic 4:3). In these days "they shall sit every man under his vine and under his fig tree" (Mic 4:4; see also Zech 3:10).[38] Since the public to whom the prophets addressed their speeches included many urbanites, it appears that not only Israelite farmers were closely acquainted with agricultural practices and terminology.

Israelite art was not very well developed during the Iron Age. Most art works recovered from this period were either imported or executed by foreign artists (Ussishkin 1969). Nevertheless, local artists did express themselves by creating art objects which were mostly functional and used agricultural motifs. One of these objects is the *kernos*, a cultic vessel decorated with little, three-dimensional, hollowed representations of animals and fruit, the most popular of which was the pomegranate (cf. Amiran 1963: 366, fig. 358).[39] An architectural feature influenced by agriculture is the *timōrâ*, a pillar capital whose shape was modeled after the date palm (Shiloh 1976, 1977). Agricultural motifs were also prominent in the decoration of the Tabernacle, the High Priest's clothes (Exod 37:17, 21; 39:25–26), and the Solomonic Temple (1 Kgs 6:18, 29, 32, 35).

Israel's relationship to agriculture is also underlined by the use of place-names derived from agricultural themes. There is a possibility that some of these place-names originated before the Israelites settled in Eretz-Israel, but there is no doubt that the perpetuation of this tradition is due to the fact that Israel was basically an agriculturally oriented society. Listed below are some Israelite place-names of agricultural origin and some possible identifications.[40]

Beṭen, 'pistachio': Jos 19:25; city in Asher. Kh. Ibtin(?) = Ḥ. Ivtan.
Bĕṭōnîm, 'pistachios': Jos 13:26; city in Gad. Kh. Baṭneh.

[38] This is only a *very* small sample of the material available.

[39] See also the *rimmôn*-bowl found at Tell Halif, in Seger and Borowski 1977, photo on p. 166.

[40] Some of the identifications with modern sites are based on Aharoni 1967, Appendix 2.

Bêt-haggan, 'place of the garden': 2 Kgs 9:27.
Bêt-hakkerem, 'place of the vineyard': Jer 6:1; Neh 3:14. Kh. Ṣaliḥ = Ramat-Raḥel.
Bêt-leḥem, 'place of bread': Ruth 1:19; 1 Sam 20:6; city in Judah. Beit Laḥm.
Bêt-leḥem, 'place of bread': Jos 19:15; city in Zebulun. Beit Laḥm = Bet Leḥem Haggelilit.
Bêt-tappûaḥ (also *Tappûaḥ*, Jos 12:17; 15:34), 'place of the *tappûaḥ*':[41] Jos 15:53; city in Judah. Taffuḥ.
Ba^{c}al-tāmār, 'possessor of date palm': Judg 20:33; near Gibeah.
Goren-nākôn (also *Goren-kîdon*, 1 Chr 13:9), 'threshing floor of Nakon': 2 Sam 6:6; in Judah.
Gat-haḥēper, 'winepress of digging': 2 Kgs 14:25; home of the prophet Jonah. Kh. ez-Zurra^c = T. Gat Ḥefer.
Gat-rimmôn, 'press of the pomegranate': Jos 19:45; in Dan. T. Jarisheh(?) = T. Gerisa.
Gittāyim, 'two presses': 2 Sam 4:3; in Judah. Rās Abū Ḥamid.
Dimnâ, 'compost place': Jos 21:35; in Zebulun.
Har-hazzêtîm, 'mountain of olives': Zech 14:4. Mount of Olives.
Ḥaṣăṣōn-tạmār, 'Ḥ.(?) of the date palm': 2 Chr 20:2. ^{c}En Gedi.
Yizrĕ^{c}e$^\supset$l, 'God sows': Jos 15:56; 1 Sam 25:43; in the Negev of Judah.
Yizrĕ^{c}e$^\supset$l, 'God sows': Jos 19:18; 2 Sam 4:4; in Issachar. Zer^{c}in = T. Yizre^{c}e$^\supset$l.
Karmel, 'garden-land, plantation': Jos 15:55; in Judah. Kh. el-Kirmil.
Lĕbônâ, 'frankincense': Judg 21:19; near Shiloh.
Madmēnâ, 'compost place': Isa 10:31; in Benjamin.
Madmannâ, 'compost place': Jos 15:31; in southern Judah. Kh. Umm ed-Deimneh.
Ma^{c}alēh-hazzêtîm, 'ascent of the olive trees': 2 Sam 15:30.
Nahalōl, 'pasture, watering place': Judg 1:30; in Zebulun.
Naḥal-$^\supset$eškōl, 'wadi of the (grape) cluster': Num 13:23–24.
Naḥal-śōrēq, 'wadi of the *sōrēq*-vines': Judg 16:4. Wadi Sarar = Naḥal Sorek.
Sela^c-rimmôn, 'rock of the pomegranate': Judg 20:45, 47; near Bethel.
Sansannâ, 'fruit-stalk of the date': Jos 15:31; in southern Judah. Kh. esh-Shamsaniyat = Ḥ. Sansanna.
^{c}Ên-gannîm, 'spring of gardens': Jos 15:34; in the Shephelah of Judah.
^{c}Ên-rimmôn, 'spring of the pomegranate': Neh 11:29; in post-exilic Judah. Umm er-Ramammin = Ḥ. Rimmon.
^{c}Ên-tappûaḥ, 'spring of the *tappûaḥ*':[42] Jos 17:7; between Ephraim and Manasseh. Sheikh Abū Zarad.

[41] For the identification of this fruit see chap. 9.
[42] See n. 41.

ᶜ*Îr-hattĕmārîm*, 'city of date palms': Judg 1:16. Jericho.
Rimmôn, 'pomegranate'; Jos 15:32; in southern Judah. T. Khuweilifeh = T. Ḥalif.
Tāmār, 'date palm': Ezek 47:19; 48:28. ᶜAin Ḥuṣb = Ḥaṣevah.

From the preceding discussion it is apparent that agriculture was the backbone of ancient Israel throughout her history. Israel lived off the soil, which nourished her economic as well as her spiritual life. Her relationship with the soil is exemplified by the OT description of the Judean king Uzziah, "he loved the soil" (2 Chr 26:10).

2
Land Use

The availability of agricultural land in Eretz-Israel is limited by topography, climatic conditions, and water sources. In times of population expansion, especially with the arrival of newcomers, e.g., the Israelites, new agricultural lands had to be found. In ancient Israel a solution to this problem was found by the development of two land-use systems, terracing and runoff farming. Both systems enabled farmers to use land never before cultivated and became highly developed, influencing future agricultural practices.

Terracing

The date and place of the origin of agricultural terracing are still unknown. Although it has been suggested that the art of terrace building was invented by the early Phoenicians and then diffused into Eretz-Israel (Reifenberg 1955: 39; MacKay 1950: 202), there is no archaeological evidence for such a claim. Archaeological investigations have determined that agricultural terraces had been used to a limited extent in Canaan by the Jebusites around Jerusalem in the Late Bronze Age (Hakar 1956: 193; Ron 1966: 115–16; de Geus 1975: 68–69). The extensive use of terracing in the hill-country as means for creating agricultural land was introduced and practiced by the Israelites since the early days of their settlement in this region.

When the Israelites arrived in Canaan at the end of the Late Bronze Age, they found that the fertile lands in the valleys were controlled by strong Canaanite cities (Aharoni 1967: 139). Realizing that they could not overpower the city-states and confiscate their agricultural lands, the Israelites started settling regions previously unsettled or sparsely occupied, such as the Judean hills (Mazar 1981), Mount Ephraim (Kochavi 1972; Garsiel and Finkelstein 1978), and the Galilee (Aharoni 1956). These regions were heavily forested and needed clearing before settlement could take place. Memories of this process can be found in Jos 17:14–18, where the people of the House of Joseph were told by Joshua: "Go up to the forest, and clear there ground for yourselves . . . the hill country shall be yours, for though it

Fig. 1. Ancient terraces in the Judean hill-country

is a forest, you shall clear it and possess it to its farthest borders." This situation continued throughout the period of the Judges.[1] Although the reference in Joshua is localized, "the general picture reflected here is one of inability to penetrate the Canaanite plains and the necessity to create sufficient room for occupation in the hilly regions by the cultivation of waste lands and clearing the natural forest" (Aharoni 1967: 218). The process of preparing the land for agricultural use involved the clearing of the forest and then the construction of terraces, since settlement in the hill-country could not have been achieved without both of these activities.

A similar picture appears from the results of a survey conducted in the Galilee by Aharoni (1956). The earliest settlements with distinct Israelite pottery were founded in regions previously unsettled, where

[1] The name *ḥărōšet haggôyim* (Judg 4:2), Sisra's home base, is interpreted by B. Mazar and Y. Aharoni as 'the forest of nations', showing that the area was still forested during the period of the Judges (Aharoni 1967, 201, 203). It seems that the forest-clearing operation was also the background for Deut 19:5: "When a man goes into the forest with his neighbor to cut wood, and his hand swings the axe to cut down a tree, and the head slips from the handle and strikes his neighbor so that he dies—he may flee to one of these cities and save his life." Remains of almond wood in Fortress III (eighth to seventh century B.C.E.) at Tell el-Fûl suggest that by that time most of the coniferous forest had disappeared; see chap. 9.

topographic conditions made their defense possible for the newly arrived settlers. According to Aharoni, the small size of the unfortified villages suggests that they were occupied by small groups, such as families or clans (Aharoni 1956: 56–64; Aharoni 1967: 176–77). Only after establishing themselves in these regions and gathering strength could the Israelites face the Canaanite might as described in several narratives in the books of Joshua and Judges.

Extensive terracing in the hill-country has been practiced continuously from its introduction by the Israelites at the beginning of the Iron Age till the present day. Its utilization by the Israelites made possible the settlement of the mountainous regions and shaped not only the terrain but the course of history. In his study of terraces in the Judean hill-country, Ron (1966) points out that the success of terracing depended on the farmer's becoming familiar with factors such as topography, lithology, and water management. Terracing affected the shape of the slopes by controlling erosion, and the shape of stream channels and their courses. In historical terms, terracing affected the course of roads and paths and dictated the sites for settlement and the direction for their expansion, since, for the most part, only uncultivable land was used for these purposes (Ron 1966: 121–22). But above all, terrace-culture enabled the Israelites to maintain their presence in Canaan while developing strength to overpower the Canaanites. Later, in the time of the divided monarchy, terracing was the cornerstone of Judean agricultural economy (Dar 1980: 99–100; Edelstein and Kislev 1981: 54), because most of the agricultural land in the plains belonged to the northern kingdom.

The OT uses two terms that can be interpreted as 'terrace'. The term *madrēgâ* (pl. *madrēgôt*) is used in Cant 2:14 when the coming of spring is announced; in this passage the term is part of the description of an orchard or a vineyard. The term is used also by Ezekiel in the description of the Latter Days:

> The fish of the sea, and the birds of the air, and the beasts of the field, and the creeping things that creep on the ground, and all men that are upon the face of the earth, shall quake at my presence, and the mountains shall be thrown down, and the *madrēgôt* shall fall, and every wall shall tumble to the ground (Ezek 38:20).

The second term, *šĕdēmâ* (pl. *šĕdēmôt*), is used several times and only in a specialized way. Twice it is connected with the region around Jerusalem and the Kedron Valley (2 Kgs 23:4; Jer 31:39);[2] once it is

[2] In Jer 31:39 the Ketiv is *šĕrēmôt*, but the Qere is *šĕdēmôt*, which is preferable; in Isa 37:27 the Ketiv is *šĕdēmâ*, but the Qere *šĕdēpâ* is more appropriate (see chap. 12).

mentioned in connection with Gomorrah (Deut 32:32); and once with Heshbon (Isa 16:8). In the last two cases and in Hab 3:17, the term *šĕdēmâ* is closely related to vineyards and orchards, signifying a special type of field or place of cultivation, the most likely interpretation of which is 'terrace'. Since archaeological investigations show that the Kedron Valley was terraced, at least since Jebusite times, the term *šĕdēmâ* in this context apparently describes this agricultural structure.[3]

Runoff Farming

Until the extensive study conducted in the Negev by Evenari et al. (1971), it had been maintained that runoff, or flood, agriculture was introduced and developed by the Nabateans during the Roman period. Present information indicates that the beginning of runoff farming in the Negev should be dated to the beginning of the Iron II period (end of tenth/beginning of ninth century B.C.E.), the early period of the Israelite monarchy.

Runoff farming in the Negev, which seems to be an offshoot of terracing in the hill-country, was the answer to two constant problems plaguing farmers in this arid region: lack of land suitable for cultivation and insufficient supplies of water. Both problems were solved with the development of water catchment systems, which directed runoff water by walls and channels into cisterns, for drinking and watering animals, and to agricultural terraces, for growing crops and fruit trees. Flooding the terraced fields with runoff water not only complemented the small amount of rainwater falling directly on the fields, but furnished them with a new layer of topsoil eroded from the surrounding hills, which enriched the soil with each flood (Evenari et al. 1971: 127–47).

Survey and excavations in the Negev show four major periods of settlement in this region: (1) Early Bronze II; (2) Early Bronze IV/Middle Bronze I; (3) Iron II; (4) Roman-Byzantine period (Evenari et al. 1958: 231–53; Evenari et al. 1971: 127–47; Aharoni et al. 1960: 23–35, 97–111; Cohen 1979c; Cohen and Dever 1979; Meshel and Cohen 1980). These studies determined that during the third and fourth periods, the settlements were agricultural and depended on runoff farming. The economic basis of the settlements from the two early periods has not been determined yet. Remains of farming communities belonging to three phases in the Iron Age were discovered in these places: (1) Ramat Maṭred (el-Maṭrada); (2) Mishor ha-Ruaḥ

[3] De Geus (1975: 73) suggests that *gēbîm* is the term used for agricultural terraces and that "*yōgebîm* are the workers/owners of irrigated terraces." For recent studies of terraces around Jerusalem, see Edelstein and Gat 1980–81; Edelstein and Gibson 1982 and Stager 1982.

(Sahil al-Hawa) and the Upper Niṣṣana Valley (Wadi ᶜAjram); and (3) the Buqeiᶜah. The first and second groups are located in the Central Negev, and the third is located west of Qumran in the Judean Desert. In addition to these communities, many forts and fortresses dated to the eleventh to tenth century B.C.E. (Cohen 1979a, 1979b) have been recently discovered.

The Israelite community of Ramat Maṭred is one of the earliest agricultural communities in the Negev, and it dates to the end of the tenth/beginning of the ninth century B.C.E. The uniformity of the pottery discovered in the survey and excavations suggests that the settlement was short-lived. The site itself includes several houses dispersed over a distance of 1.5 km, corrals, water cisterns, and terraced fields with water channels. Several of the houses have storage pits. The settlement itself was not fortified; it was defended by four forts, two situated in Naḥal Avdat and two in Naḥal Laᶜana, along the road from the north to Egypt (Aharoni et al. 1960). The settlers depended on the produce of their fields, located close by, and on domestic animals, as the many corrals indicate. The excavators point out that although the relationship between the forts and the settlement is not clear, they were all built at the same time. This fact and the proximity of the forts to the settlement suggest that (1) the forts depended, to a certain extent, on these farms for their food supply, and (2) the soldiers stationed at the forts were part-time farmers. If either or both of these suppositions are correct, then this settlement was established by the central administration of the state.

As for the exact date of the community at Ramat Maṭred, the excavators suggested that it was established during the reign of Solomon and destroyed by Pharaoh Shishak ca. 920 B.C.E. They admit that there is a later possible date for the destruction, ca. 850 B.C.E., during the revolt of the Edomites against Joram, the son of Jehoshaphat (2 Kgs 8:20–22; 2 Chr 21:8–10).

A second phase of settlement in the Negev, possibly by order of the Israelite monarchy, took place at Mishor ha-Ruaḥ and the Upper Niṣṣana Valley. In general, this phase of settlement is similar to the one at Ramat Maṭred, being unwalled and defended by several forts. However, in addition to individual houses and many cisterns, several farmsteads (fields connected with a farm house) were identified (Evenari et al. 1958: 231–53). The pottery is typical of the period 850–600 B.C.E., and the establishment of this community is attributed by the excavators to Uzziah, who "built towers in the wilderness, and hewed many cisterns . . . for he loved the soil" (2 Chr 26:10).

The settlements of the third phase from the monarchical period are located in the Buqeiᶜah, west of the northern tip of the Dead Sea.

In this valley, three forts with associated fields were discovered, one of which was excavated by Stager (1972–1973, 1975, 1976), who dates its establishment to the seventh century B.C.E. and relates it to the expansion of the Judean kingdom under Josiah. The discovery of *lmlk* handles (Stager 1975: 147, 247–48) might also indicate some involvement by the central administration of that period in this settlement.

Organic remains and seed impressions in clay show that all of the three settlements in the Buqei^{c}ah cultivated field crops, such as barley, wheat, and legumes. Experiments conducted in two reconstructed Nabatean farms near Avdat and Shivta in the Central Negev show that settlements in the Negev, with the use of runoff farming, had the capacity to grow fruit trees and grapevines (Evenari et al. 1971: 179–219).

The founding of all of these settlements can be placed in a historical context. The goal was to create agriculturally self-sufficient communities (for which the practice of runoff farming was crucial) that would defend the border areas and the trade routes. The first phase of settlement, the remains of which were found at Ramat Maṭred, was founded along the road from the Central Negev to Egypt. In addition to protecting the road, the community was probably charged with the defense of the southwestern flanks of the Judean kingdom against attack from Egypt. The second phase of settlement, which took place at Mishor ha-Ruaḥ probably during the reign of Uzziah, was initiated to protect the lands taken back from the Edomites after their revolt against Joram. The third phase, which took place in the Buqei^{c}ah during the seventh century B.C.E., is most likely related to the expansion of the southern kingdom under Josiah. This southward expansion can be associated with the Josianic expansion in the west, which is evident from finds at Meṣad Ḥashavyahu. Since the establishment of all these communities can be fitted into plausible political contexts, it is very likely that the central administration was behind the settlement of the frontier (Reviv 1975: 46–55; Stager 1975: 210, 250–58).

The approach of the Judean kingdom to the wilderness was economic as well as political. The desert settlements were charged with the protection of the borders and trade routes, while trying to be economically independent by utilizing runoff farming. The establishment of the settlements in the Negev was probably regarded by the Judean kings, from the time of Solomon on, as a political statement claiming this region as an integral part of their kingdom (Cohen 1970, 1976; Gophna 1966, 1970; Meshel 1976, 1977; Meshel and Meyers 1976; Meyers 1976).

3
Land Tenure

The OT does not systematically present information regarding land tenure. There are no clear answers to questions such as who owned land; how ownership was acquired; how ownership was maintained; how land was purchased. A few laws related to the subject of land tenure are scattered throughout the different law codes. There are several passages where land transactions are described. Here and there, one can find hints or get a glimpse of the prevailing land tenure system. But on the whole the picture is sketchy. Archaeology is not of much help in this matter since the number of documents recovered in Eretz-Israel is small. Only a very small collection, the Samaria Ostraca, is directly related to land tenure in the Iron Age.

Because of the limited number of documents it is impossible to paint a complete picture of land ownership or show the development of a land tenure system in ancient Israel. It is also impossible to show changes that took place through time. Although some of the evidence found in the OT is ideologically biased and the customs described there were probably not practiced in their entirety, it seems that the biblical writers did try to harmonize ideology and practice in their writings. Therefore, the biblical material can be used, with extreme caution, in trying to reconstruct the land tenure system in ancient Israel.

YHWH's ownership of the land is the underlying idea dominating the Israelite concept of land ownership. This idea, which is expressed in Lev 25:23, "The land shall not be sold in perpetuity, for the land is mine," can be traced back to the patriarchal stories and traditions.[1] All three patriarchs were promised by YHWH that the land would be theirs and their children's. One way of fulfilling the promise was by business transactions as recalled in the purchase of the Cave of Machpelah by Abraham (Gen 23) and the land near Shechem by Jacob (Gen 33:19). These transactions were conducted in line with the local

[1] Gen 12:7; 13:14–17; 15:7, 18; 17:8; 24:7; 26:3–4; 28:4, 13–15; 35:12; 48:4. If Thompson (1974, 324–26) is right in suggesting that the historical context of the patriarchal narratives is the Iron Age, then the situations depicted in the conquest and patriarchal narratives are chronologically very close.

customs, but served as a means to achieve the final goal, namely, that of inheriting the promised land. The Israelite conquest of Canaan was another way of achieving the same goal. The connection between the promise to the patriarchs and the Israelite conquest is made very clear in YHWH's promise to Joshua on the eve of his campaign (Jos 1:2) and in Joshua's speech to the Israelites at the renewal of the covenant at Shechem (Jos 24). Promising the land to the patriarchs served as an ideological justification for the conquest and for other ways of land acquisition. Whatever the historical background and date of the patriarchs and the conquest were, continuing the patriarchal tradition in writing strongly suggests that the customs enshrined through the memory of these events and personages were indeed practiced, at least to a certain extent. These traditions served an an ideological justification for daily practices and concepts.

It is possible to recognize in the OT three types of land ownership: (1) private, (2) royal, and (3) priestly. The following discussion describes each of these types and is based mostly on the evidence available in the OT.

Private Land

The right to private land ownership was secured, according to biblical traditions, by participation in the conquest and settlement processes. As described in Jos 13–19, the land was divided among the tribes by lot, and each tribe apportioned its land to clans and families. Scholars believe that this tradition is part of the idealization of the conquest which occurred late in Israelite history, probably during the monarchy (Bright 1974: 127). According to this tradition, the conquest was carried out in one large, swift military campaign under the leadership of Joshua, who personally divided the land among the tribes.[2] Nevertheless, even in some of the early traditions deviating from the official point of view, especially Jos 15:15–19 = Judg 1:11–15 and Judg 1:2–10, where the wars in the south are recounted, land is acquired by individuals through their participation in the conquest and settlement.

The family inheritance, *naḥălâ* or *ʾăḥuzzâ*, was guarded zealously, as the story of Naboth (1 Kgs 21:1–3) shows. The many inheritance laws found in the OT provide for the *naḥălâ* to stay intact within the family or clan. The fundamental law was that only sons had the right to the inheritance. The eldest son had the privileged right to inherit the

[2] The lists of "the land which was left to be conquered" in the book of Joshua and in Judges 1 show that not all the conquests mentioned in Joshua took place at the same time; for details regarding the conquest and settlement see Aharoni 1967: 174–253.

family possession (Deut 21:17), though he could probably transfer his right to another brother, as illustrated by the story of Jacob and Esau (Gen 25:1–6; 27).[3] A father could not prefer a younger son over the eldest when family inheritance was involved (Deut 21:15–17). When a man died without sons, his property passed to his brothers. If this was not possible, the next in line were his father's brothers, and if this could not be carried out, "you shall give his inheritance to his kinsman that is next to him of his family" (Num 27:11). An amendment to this law allowing daughters to be the first in line for the inheritance when there were no sons was introduced with the precedent of the daughters of Zelophehad (Num 27:1–8) with the provision that they marry within their father's clan to prevent the inheritance from passing to another tribe (Num 36:1–9).[4]

Another law formulated in order to preserve the inheritance within the family was that of the levirate marriage. When a man died without a son, his brother had to marry the widow, and the first son of this union was supposed to receive the family inheritance (Deut 25:5–6). One example of this custom is the story of Tamar the wife of ᶜEr (Gen 38).

Besides death without issue, there were other ways by which a family could lose its inheritance, such as the necessity to sell the land. Selling the land was usually the result of economic hardship caused by factors such as drought or war. Selling the land was the last resort, and a person would first sell himself (Lev 25:39) or his children (Exod 21:7–11) as slaves rather than sell his land.

The OT made several provisions to help return the land to its original owner after the sale. The first provision is the institution of the *gôʾēl*, the 'redeemer', who was the closest kinsman. "If your brother becomes poor, and sells part of his property, then his next of kin shall come and redeem what his brother sold" (Lev 25:25). When the seller did not have a *gôʾēl*, he could redeem his land himself when he could find sufficient means to do so. The selling and redemption prices of the land were calculated according to the number of years remaining till the Jubilee (see below), since in actuality, it was not the land that was

[3] The story of Jacob and Esau is most likely a dramatized account of such a transfer during the Iron Age; probably one of the reasons for the survival of this tradition is that it did reflect a practice acceptable to the Israelites.

[4] Two names in the Samaria Ostraca are similar to names of two of Zelophehad's daughters. According to Aharoni (1967: 325), names appearing in the ostraca belonged to clans of Manasseh. Is the account in Num 27:1–8 and 36:1–9 of an actual case or is it only aetiological? Whatever the reason for the account, the story would not have survived if it were contrary to daily customs. Female names used as clan names seem to corroborate the biblical tradition.

sold but rather the crop yield of that land (Lev 25:15–16). Therefore, when the land was redeemed, the redeemer had to compute the number of years still remaining till the next Jubilee, and the price he paid to redeem the property was supposedly the price for the crops yet to be harvested before the coming of the Jubilee (Lev 25:27).[5]

The practice of *mišpaṭ haggĕʾullâ*, 'the law of redemption', is described in Jer 32:6–14, where the prophet bought the field belonging to his uncle in front of witnesses. Two copies of the bill of sale were made, one of which was left unsealed, and both were placed for safekeeping in a clay jar. Although the transaction was conducted by Jeremiah according to prevailing Assyrian customs, it did not contradict Hebrew law. Furthermore, the terminology used in this account shows full agreement with Hebrew law and with the Hebrew concept of land ownership.[6]

The institution of the *gôʾēl* was closely related to levirate marriage. An example of both provisions practiced at the same time is described in Ruth 4:1–14. Here, after the death of her husband and her return to his hometown, Ruth finds out that Boaz could be her *gôʾēl* if a closer relative would not perform the act. When the relative, who was ready to redeem the field belonging to her dead husband, discovered that he had to marry her, he forfeited his right and Boaz redeemed the field and married Ruth.

The law code makes a distinction between agricultural property and property in a city. A house sold in a walled city could be redeemed within one year; if it was not redeemed within that time, it would belong to the buyer. A house sold in one of the unwalled villages, *ḥăṣērîm*, was considered to be part of the agricultural inheritance and would revert to the original owner in the year of the Jubilee (Lev 25:29–31).

The second provision for assuring the return of land to the original owner is that of the Jubilee, *yôbēl*.[7] After seven occurrences of *šĕmiṭṭâ*, 'a fallow year', the fiftieth year was one in which all land sold

[5] An example will illustrate how the law of redemption was supposed to be carried out. If a man had land yielding crops worth 100 shekels a year, the total worth of the land would be placed at 5000 shekels, i.e., 100 shekels per year over fifty years. If the land was sold immediately after the Jubilee, the price the owner would get would be 5000 shekels. The value of the land would decrease by one-fiftieth each year until the Jubilee. If the land had to be sold or redeemed five years before the Jubilee, the price would be 500 shekels.

[6] Although it is possible that the Jubilee was a post-exilic institution, the institution of the *gôʾēl* appears to be pre-exilic, as the case of Jeremiah indicates.

[7] The original meaning of *yôbēl* is 'ram, ram's horn' (BDB 1972: 385). The fiftieth year was announced by sounding the ram's horn, an act which lent itself to the name of the year, *šĕnat hayyôbēl* (Lev 25:13) or just *yôbēl* (Lev 25:10).

and not redeemed had to return to the original owner (Lev 25:28).[8] Houses sold in unwalled villages had to be returned to their original owner since they "shall be reckoned with the fields of the country; they may be redeemed, and they shall be released in the Jubilee" (Lev 25:31). In spite of the uncertainty regarding the date of the establishment of the Jubilee, and although it is unknown to what degree, if at all, it was practiced, I think that it is important to mention this provision since it is closely related to land ownership.

As is evident from the laws and practices cited above, the OT regarded the land as the property of YHWH, who entrusted the people of Israel with its safekeeping. Land was acquired through the process of settlement, and several laws and customs assured that the land would stay forever within the family. It should be noted here that not all Israelites were at all times landowners. Under certain circumstances some families had to sell their land and even sell themselves. Others had to hire themselves out and work for wages either as day laborers, *śākîr* (Lev 19:13; Deut 24:14), or by the year, *śĕkîr šānâ* (Lev 25:50, 53; Isa 16:14; 21:16; de Vaux 1961, 76). Others belonging to the landless segment of society were mostly non-Israelites and were classified by the terms *gērîm* and *tôšābîm* (de Vaux 1961, 74–76). The landless population, together with the landowner, his family and slaves, constituted the agricultural work force (de Vaux 1961, 80–88).

Private land ownership did not cease throughout the history of the divided monarchy. Evidence for land remaining in private hands in the northern kingdom till the second half of the eighth century B.C.E. is provided by the Samaria Ostraca. This collection of sixty-three receipts for oil and wine was discovered in the royal palace at Samaria. The ostraca are distinctly divided into two groups: one group is dated to years 9 and 10 of a certain king, and the second to year 15 of a certain king. Several scholars have proposed that the two groups belong to the reign of two different kings.[9] Shea (1977) makes a convincing suggestion that the first group belongs to the reign of Menahem and the second group to the reign of Pekah, both of whom

[8] Although the law code does not specify it, I assume that the land returned during the Jubilee must have been returned to the family of the original owner if he were dead. In such cases the original owner was considered to be the family or clan and not the individual. There are other laws related to the Jubilee, such as freeing slaves and canceling debts, which are beyond the scope of the present discussion.

[9] Aharoni (1962; 1967: 324) and Rainey (1970) propose Joash (ca. 800–785 B.C.E.) and Jeroboam II (ca. 785–749 B.C.E.); Yadin (1962, 1–17) suggests that the ostraca belong to the reign of Menahem (ca. 745–738 B.C.E.); Bright (1974: 256) treats the ostraca as an indication for "an administrative system patterned on that of Solomon" instituted, probably, by Jeroboam II.

ruled during the second half of the eighth century B.C.E. Aharoni (1967: 315–27), in a detailed study of the ostraca, concluded that the receipts signify commodities received mostly from private land owners. In some of the ostraca the origin of the commodies is documented as coming from land designated by clan names. Aharoni (1967: 322) traced these names to clans belonging to the tribe of Manasseh, recorded in the genealogy of the tribe (Num 26:30–33; Jos 17:2–3; 1 Chr 7:14–19). It is interesting to note that two clan names, Hoglah and Noah, are similar to those of two of the daughters of Zelophehad (see above). The royal vineyards, according to Aharoni (1967: 324), are represented by only two names. For the purpose of the present discussion the significance of the Samaria Ostraca lies in the fact that land in Mount Ephraim acquired by clans of Manasseh during the conquest and settlement remained in the hands of their descendants till, at least, the second half of the eighth century B.C.E., and probably till the fall of Samaria in 722 B.C.E.

In the southern kingdom a similar picture emerges from accounts recorded in the books of Isaiah and Jeremiah. The warning of Isaiah "Woe to those who join house to house, who add field to field, until there is no more room" (5:8) refers to the accumulation of wealth by a small number of people at the end of the eighth century B.C.E. It is obvious that this process of land accumulation by certain individuals was possible because there were still private landowners who wanted or had to sell their land. But the selling of private land around Jerusalem in the time of Isaiah did not completely eliminate the small landowner. Even in the final days of Jerusalem before its sack by the Babylonians, land tenure laws were still observed, at least to a certain extent. While Jerusalem was under siege, Jeremiah acted within the law of land redemption when he bought his uncle's field, located in Anathoth in the land of Benjamin (32:6–14). Of course there is no way to determine how much land was still left in the hands of the descendants of the original owners and out of the hands of large plantation owners, but the account documented in the book of Jeremiah shows that laws regarding family inheritance were still known and observed in the first quarter of the sixth century B.C.E.

Royal Estates

The law codes of the OT do not mention the royal estates but rather deal exclusively with private land and life in the small villages. The existence of royal estates is documented in the OT historical texts, in accounts and lists derived from the royal archives. The institution of royal estates, or crown lands, can be attributed to Saul, the founder of the Israelite monarchy. Saul's family belonged to the landed segment of Israelite society, but was of only modest means. This situation is reflected in 1 Sam 9:3, where Saul himself is sent to look for the lost she-asses, and in 11:5, where he plows his family's land. By the end of his reign, Saul had a vast amount of property, which was "inherited" by David (2 Sam 12:8), who in turn gave the land to Meribaal, son of Saul (2 Sam 9:9–10). Later, David gave it to Siba the servant (2 Sam 16:4), and finally he divided the land between Meribaal and Siba (2 Sam 19:30).

Saul was, probably, the first to grant land to his officers in return for service, as can be deduced from his speech to his followers against joining with David: "Hear now, you Benjaminites; will the son of Jesse give every one of you fields and vineyards, will he make you all the commanders of thousands and commanders of hundreds, that all of you have conspired against me?" (1 Sam 22:7–8).

There were six ways by which royal land could have been acquired:

1. Military conquest, as was done by David, who conquered Jerusalem and renamed it *ᶜîr dāwid*, 'the city of David' (2 Sam 5:7, 9); in other areas, such as Moab (2 Sam 8:2), Aram Damascus (2 Sam 8:6), Edom (2 Sam 8:14), and the land of the vassals of Hadadezer (2 Sam 10:19), David appointed governors, *nĕṣîbîm*, in charge of collecting tribute for the royal treasury.
2. Taking possession of vacant land, as happened with the land of the Shunamite woman (2 Kgs 8:1–6).[10]
3. Buying, as in the case of Araun's threshing floor (2 Sam 24:24 = 1 Chr 21:22–24), the land of Shemer (1 Kgs 16:24), and Naboth's vineyard (1 Kgs 21:6).
4. Exchanging for other commodities, as between Solomon and Hiram (1 Kgs 9:11–14); or for other land, as between Ahab and Naboth (1 Kgs 21:2).
5. Receiving land and cities as presents, as when Solomon received Gezer from the Egyptian Pharaoh (1 Kgs 9:16); or for services granted, as when David received Ziqlag from the Philistines (1 Sam 27:5–10).
6. Confiscating land from domestic enemies charged with treason, as with the land granted to Meribaal (2 Sam 9:7; 16:1–4) and with Naboth's vineyard (1 Kgs 21); land could also have been confiscated by a king for no good reason, as 1 Sam 8; 12–17 foretells, a warning which must have been based on actual cases.

[10] Henrey (1954, 12) claims that in this case the land was a fief given to the Shunamite's husband, and when she left the land, she forfeited possession. There is no textual support for this proposal.

David also came from a family of modest means, but he managed to build up during his reign a large estate which had to be managed by several overseers, *śārê hārĕkûš* (1 Chr 27:25–31). These officials were in charge of the royal storehouses; the storage facilities in the cities, villages, and forts; the field workers; the vineyards and the storage facilities in them; the olive and sycomore groves; the storage facilities for oil; the cattle in several regions; the camels and she-asses; and the flocks of sheep and goats. David's monarchy became a complex enterprise, as seen by the institution of a cabinet (2 Sam 8:16.18 = 1 Chr 18:15–17; 27:32–34), which later was enlarged by his son Solomon (1 Kgs 4).

Work on the royal estates was carried out by state slaves (de Vaux 1961, 88–90) and Israelite forced labor (1 Sam 8:12), the establishment of which is attributed to Solomon (1 Kgs 5:27; de Vaux 1961, 142–43). The use of forced labor for royal projects was continued after Solomon and is recorded for Asa (1 Kgs 15:22) and Jehoyakim (Jer 22:13). In periods of territorial expansion in the south, as in the days of Solomon, Uzziah, and Josiah, land was settled by order of the central administration, but the details of the relationship between the settlers and the administration are not yet clear. The "Letter of Complaint" from Meṣad Ḥashavyahu, in which a reaper complains to the governor, *śār*, that his garment was confiscated by an overseer under the pretense that he (the reaper) had not completed his work, sheds some light on the nature of this relationship. It has been suggested that the reaper was a serf (Naveh 1960: 135), a tenant (Cross 1962: 46), or a corvée worker (Amusin and Heltzer 1964: 156). Whichever interpretation is correct, it is obvious that the site had a royal overseer and must have been part of the royal estate belonging to King Josiah.[11] It is very likely that the relationship between the settlers of the Negev settlements and the king who settled them was similar to the one implied in this letter.

Further archaeological evidence for the royal estates is supplied by the *lmlk* jar-handles (Lance 1971). Several suggestions have been made concerning the function of these jars, which have handles stamped with the royal designation *lmlk* (*lammelek*, 'belonging to the king') and one of four place-names, *ḥbrn*, *śwkh*, *zp*, and *mmšt*. It has been proposed that the jars were used for the collection of taxes in kind (Paul and Dever 1974: 186), that they were manufactured in the royal potteries (Diringer 1949: 82), that the place-names designated military centers (Yadin 1961: 6–12), and that the stamps were the royal symbols of Israel (the four-winged scarab) and Judah (the two-winged scarab) used by Josiah in his claim for the Davidic empire (Tushingham 1971).

[11] For the date of the site see Naveh 1962, 89–113.

Most of these theories leave several questions unanswered, especially concerning the distribution of the jar-handles i.e., the places where they were found. The most attractive theory, to date, is that proposed by Tufnell and Lapp (Lapp 1960: 11–22): the names of the sites designate royal vineyards in the region of Hebron. The date of the seals has been proven to be the end of the eighth century B.C.E. (Ussishkin 1977: 54–57), which coincides with the reign of Hezekiah. It should be noted that some *lmlk* jars bear in addition to the royal seal a private seal (Ussishkin 1976), and I suggest that the private seals belonged to the overseers of the royal vineyards and olive groves.

The information concerning the royal estates in the northern kingdom is much scantier. In addition to the information supplied by the biblical texts,[12] some of the Samaria Ostraca might relate to crown lands. As Aharoni points out (1967: 322, 324), two vineyards, Kerem Hattel and Kerem Yeḥo-eli, are registered in the receipts without a clan name. His suggestion is that both of them were royal vineyards. Thus, the Samaria Ostraca may describe a situation where royal and private land existed side by side in the northern kingdom during the eighth century B.C.E.

Priestly Land

The matter of priestly land might have been idealized by the OT writers, but nevertheless, the topic should not be omitted from a discussion of Israelite land ownership. Although the OT refers to priestly lands only four times, it seems that their size was not negligible. Jos 21 records the places in which land and houses were allotted by the Israelites to the different priestly families. The total of forty-eight cities which were allotted to the Levites is corroborated by a shorter account in Num 35:1–8. In the latter account the dimensions of the land given to the Levites surrounding each of the cities are one thousand cubits measured from the city wall outward, and two thousand cubits on each side. This document allots the Levites 8,000,000 square cubits of land around each of the forty-eight cities. According to de Vaux (1961: 197), a cubit is ca. 0.5 meters; this means that in present-day measurements the Levites had close to 4,000 dunams around each city, or a total of 192,000 dunams of land (close to 48,000 acres) in different parts of the country. Although with regard to the length of the cubit de Vaux states that "these calculations are in any case rather pointless because there was no official standard"

[12] Buying land from Shemer for the purpose of building Samaria; the incident of the Shunamite woman; the confiscation of Naboth's vineyard.

(1961: 197), the calculations of priestly land are presented here to stress the point that if the documents cited above have any historical value, then the Levites owned a large amount of land in ancient Israel.

As for the lists of the Levitical cities, de Vaux suggests that although the systematization is only Utopian, the lists are based on an ancient document and must reflect a real situation which existed at a certain time. The historical context of these texts, according to de Vaux, is the time after the foundation of the Temple in Jerusalem and the organization of the official cult in Bethel (1961: 367). This would explain why there were no Levitical cities in the immediate area of Jerusalem and in the center of Israel.

According to Henrey (1954: 14), the statement "The Levitical priests, that is, all the tribe of Levi, shall have no portion or inheritance with Israel; they shall eat the offerings by fire to YHWH, and his rightful dues; they shall have no inheritance among their brethren" (Deut 18:1–2) reflects a later situation and was intended to protect the Levites who left the land and moved to the city after the abolition of the local sanctuaries and the centralization of the cult in Hezekiah's reign.

Priestly land was not owned by individuals, but by the priestly community, as implied by the term *migrāš*, 'common land', which is used to describe the land (BDB 1972, 177).[13] This land was probably attached to the local sanctuaries, some of which are mentioned in the OT or have been discovered in archaeological excavations. Priests were also the recipients of land that was vowed to YHWH by private individuals, as described in Lev 27:19–21:

> If he who dedicates the field wishes to redeem it, then he shall add a fifth of the valuation in money to it, and it shall remain his. But if he does not wish to redeem the field, or if he has sold the field to another man, it shall not be redeemed any more; but the field, when it is released in the Jubilee, shall be holy to YHWH, as a field that has been devoted; the priest shall be in possession of it.

When a private house in the city was sold, it could be redeemed within a year (Lev 25:29), but a house belonging to the Levites could be redeemed at any time (Lev 25:32). A Levitical field could not be sold "for that is their perpetual possession" (Lev 25:34).

[13] Except in one instance (1 Chr 5:16), the term *migrāš* is always used in passages describing priestly land holdings. From context it appears that *migrāš* was an open space around the city. According to Num 35:3 and Jos 14:4, *migrāš* was pasture land. There is no evidence that Israelites other than priests and Levites owned *migrāš*-land (except for the enigmatic passage in 1 Chr 5:16). There is no reference in the OT to common land other than that owned by the Levites. There must have been common land used especially for grazing, but the OT neglects to mention it.

4
The Agricultural Calendar

During a prosperous year, one agricultural activity does not end before another starts, as described by the prophet Amos: "'Behold, the days are coming,' says YHWH, 'when the plowman shall overtake the reaper and the treader of grapes him who sows the seed'" (9:13). The same idea is expressed in Lev 26:5. The agricultural seasons correspond to the solar year and depend on temperature, precipitation, and other similar factors, all of which influenced the daily life of the Israelite farmer. Several biblical events are reported to have occurred during a specific agricultural season, e.g., the burning of the Philistines' fields by Samson during the wheat harvest (Judges 15) and the sending of spies to Canaan by Moses at the period of first grapes (Num 13:20).

The OT mentions a number of agricultural seasons and activities: *ḥārîš*, 'plowing' (Gen 45:6; Exod 34:21); *zeraᶜ*, 'sowing' (Gen 8:22; Lev 26:5); *bitḥillat ᶜălôt halleqeš*, 'at the beginning of the growth of the late crop', (Amos 7:1); *qāṣîr*, 'reaping' (Gen 8:22; Exod 34:21); *qĕṣîr śĕᶜorîm*, 'harvesting barley' (Ruth 2:23); *qĕṣîr ḥiṭṭîm*, 'harvesting wheat' (Gen 30:14; Judg 15:1); *dayiš*, 'threshing' (Lev 26:5); *bāṣîr*, 'grape picking' (Lev 26:5; Isa 24:13); *yĕmê bikkûrê ᶜănābîm*, 'the period of first grapes' (Num 13:20); *ᵓāsîp*, 'ingathering (of fruit)' (Exod 23:16; 34:22); *qayiṣ*, '(ingathering of) summer fruit' (2 Sam 16:1; Jer 40:10, 12; Amos 8:1, 2). These seasons are mentioned in different contexts, and no effort is made in the OT to present a complete agricultural calendar. In several verses where agricultural activities are mentioned, a sequence is established, but no determination is made of when each agricultural season starts or ends. It should be remembered that agricultural seasons can vary from locale to locale because of differences in natural conditions. It should also be remembered that with the establishment of a central civil and cultic administration, general dates for the beginning and ending of the agricultural season have to be established to facilitate the collection of taxes and the celebration of festivals related to these seasons. Such a system was employed to a certain extent during the period of the tribal league but became more sophisticated during the time of the monarchy.

One extra-biblical document which helps clarify the sequence of agricultural seasons in Eretz-Israel is known as the Gezer Calendar. A preferred term for this inscription should be the Gezer Manual because the inscription is obviously a list of chores and not a calendar to tell time. The Gezer Manual, discovered during the excavations at this Palestinian site by R. A. S. Macalister in September 1908, has been studied by many scholars who have tried to determine its date and purpose.[1] It contains a seven-line inscription on a small limestone slab, with three letters, *ʾby*, at the lower left corner, possibly part of a personal name, such as *ʾby*[*h*]. The reverse side shows signs of an earlier inscription which was scraped off. The date of the inscription has been established from paleographic and orthographic evidence as ca. 925 B.C.E. (Albright 1943; Cross and Freedman 1952: 45), and the reading, with the exception of the third word in line 5, has been generally accepted as follows:

L. 1 *yrḥw ʾsp/ yrḥw z*
L. 2 *rʿ/ yrḥw lqš*
L. 3 *yrḥ ʿṣd pšt* (or *pśt*)
L. 4 *yrḥ qṣr śʿrm*
L. 5 *yrḥ qṣr* xx*l*(x)
L. 6 *yrḥw zmr*
L. 7 *yrḥ qṣ*

The word *yrḥ* is the early term for the period consisting of one-twelfth of a year, from one new moon to another, later replaced in the OT with *ḥōdeš*. It was also used to describe a month-long period with no relationship to the actual calendar, as in the expression *yeraḥ yāmîm* (Deut 21:13; 2 Kgs 15:13). Since the inscription does not contain twelve names or activities, I suggest that the word *yrḥ* does not apply here to a calendrical month, but rather to a measure of time, and therefore the beginning of a Gezer *yrḥ* does not necessarily occur at the beginning of a calendrical month. The meaning of the word *yrḥw* has been interpreted as 'his two months' (Wright 1955: 50–55) and as 'the two months of' (Cross and Freedman 1952: 46–47); thus the inscription accounts for twelve month-long periods.

Line 1 *yrḥw ʾsp:* 'the two months of ingathering (of fruit)'. This period occurs in the autumn, the beginning of the year in the Canaanite calendar (Langdon 1935: 23–24). Wright translates this line "his two months are (olive) harvest" (1955: 50), which is a reasonable interpretation since the major agricultural activity in this period is harvesting

[1] For extensive bibliographies see Diringer 1934; Cross and Freedman 1952; Cassuto 1954; Wirgin 1960.

Table 1. The Gezer Calendar and its relationship to the early Israelite calendar

spring equinox — autumn equinox

Apr	May	June	July	Aug	Sep	Oct	Nov	Dec	Jan	Feb	March
I *ʾÂbîb* *maṣṣôt*	II *Ziw* *šâbuʿôt*	III	IV	V *ʾâsîp*	VI (Judah)	VII *ʾÊtânîm*	VIII *Bûl*	IX	X	XI	XII
yrḥ qṣr *śʿrm* *maṣṣôt*	*yrḥ qṣr* *wkl* *šâbuʿôt*	*yrḥw*	*zmr*	*yrḥ qṣ*	*yrḥw*	*ʾsp* *ʾâsîp*	*yrḥw* (Israel)	*zrʿ*	*yrḥw*	*lqš*	*yrḥ ʿṣd* *pšt*

Table 2. Sowing season, based on modern agricultural practices in Israel

	Oct	Nov	Dec	Jan	Feb	Mar	Apr
Wheat		x	x				
Barley		x	x				
Oats		x	x				
Peas			x	x			
Chickpeas					x		
Lentils			x				
Vetch		x	x				
Sesame							x
Flax			x				
Millet						x	x
Vegetables				x	x	x	
		yrḥw zr^{c}		*yrḥw lqš*			

olives (table 1). As Talmon notes (1958: 56), olive harvesting in the district of Lydda-Ramleh, which is essentially that of Gezer, takes place between mid-September and mid-October. The allocation of two months for this activity can be explained by assuming that oil pressing, a time-consuming process which was an integral part of the harvest, was included and also by the fact that olives do not ripen all at once.

Lines 1–2 *yrḥw zr*^{c}*:* 'the two months of sowing'. With this activity the actual agricultural cycle begins anew. During these two months the farmer planted cereals, such as wheat and barley (table 2).

Line 2 *yrḥw lqš:* Vincent (1909: 247) suggests that these two months designate the period when plants grow as a result of the late rain, *malqôš*. J. G. Fevrier thinks that this is the time of the *malqôš* itself (Cassuto 1954: 472). Both suggestions appear to be incorrect since they do not describe an agricultural activity, as all the other entries do. Besides, the late rains do not last for two months, and since *yrḥw lqš* starts in late December, neither can it designate a time of plants growing as a result of the late rains which come in February. It seems more likely that *yrḥw lqš* is a period assigned to the late sowing of legumes, such as peas and chick-peas, and vegetables (table 2).

Line 3 *yrḥ* ^{c}*ṣd pšt:* Most scholars read the third word as *pšt* and interpret the activity as 'harvesting of flax with a hoe', *ma*^{c}*ăṣād* (Lidzbarski 1915: 40–41; Wright 1955: 50, 53). There are several ways to show that this interpretation is incorrect because agriculturally it is impossible. According to Löw (1924–34: 2:212), flax was sown during Mishnaic times in Eretz-Israel in Adar, a month which roughly falls

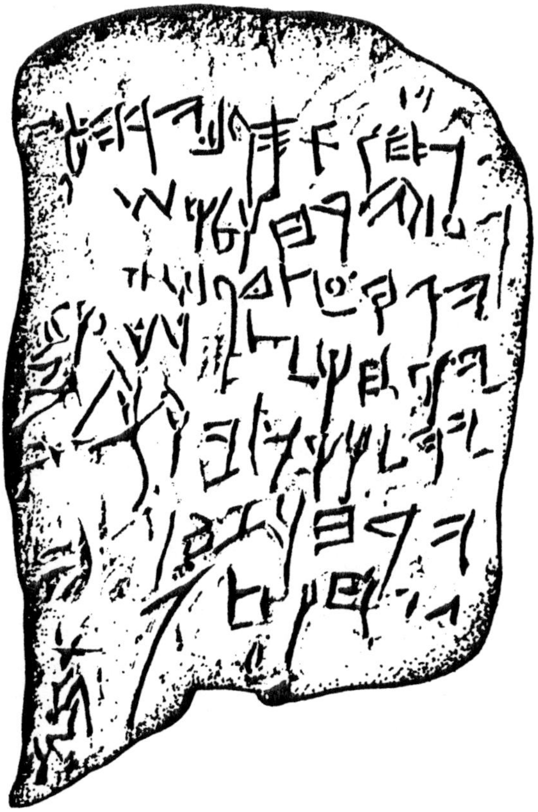

Fig. 2. The Gezer Calendar

within the period designated in line 3. Today, flax is sown in December (Kislev to Ṭevet) and is harvested in July (Tammuz to Av; Irgun Ovdey ha-Falha 1960–61: 16–17; Dalman 1932: 2:298). Neither of these last two periods allows for flax harvesting during *yrḥ ʿṣd pšt.* Zohary (1971: 636) says that flax could be harvested in Adar in the Jordan Valley, but this would have been impossible at Gezer because of its cooler climate.

Tur-Sinai (1947: 44) and Talmon (1961: 199–200) have proposed a better interpretation of the line. They suggest that the third word in line 3 is *pśt*, from the root *pśh* 'spread,' and that it means weeds, grasses, and other plants which grew wild in the fields. Accordingly, the line can be read 'a month of hoeing weeds', which were probably collected, stored, and used as hay. In Palestine, at the beginning of the twentieth century, weeding was observed by Dalman (1932: 2:216–17), who states that the agricultural activity assigned in February at el-Qubēbe is weeding in the gardens, and in March the assigned activity at el-Ṛuwēr is weeding in the fields of winter-sown crops. The time of both activities roughly corresponds to the time of *yrḥ ᶜṣd pśt* (table 3).

Line 4 *yrḥ qṣr śᶜrm:* 'a month of harvesting barley'. The harvest of barley marked for the ancient farmer in Eretz-Israel the beginning of ingathering the fruit of his labor. The beginning of the harvest season was celebrated by the Israelite farmer with the festival of *pessaḥ/maṣṣôt.*

Line 5 *yrḥ qṣr* xx*l*(x). The reading of the third word in this line has generated more controversy than any other part of the Gezer Manual. Although Cassuto (1954: 472) sees a third illegible letter following the *l* and reads the line *qāṣīr wĕtālīm*, most scholars distinguish only two letters preceding the *l* and read them *w* and *k*, respectively. Several scholars read the second and third words as *qṣrw kl* (*qĕṣirô kol*) 'harvesting everything' (Cassuto 1954: 473–74). Other interpretations are as follows: H. L. Ginsberg, *qāṣor wĕkalē[h]*, 'harvest and finishing'; Albright, *qāṣīr wāgīl*, 'harvest and festivity'; N. H. Tur-Sinai and J. G. Fevrier, *qāsīr wāka[yi]l*, 'harvesting and measuring' (Albright, 1943a: 23; Cassuto 1954: 472). The last reading seems to be the correct one in light of the readings proposed by Cross (1962: 42–46) for lines 5, 6, and 8 of the letter from Meṣad Ḥashavyahu. The orthography suggests that the northern dialect was dominant during this period at Gezer, as I discuss below (line 7). The second month of harvest was probably devoted to wheat harvesting and ended approximately when *šābūᶜôt* was celebrated (table 3).

Line 6 *yrḥw zmr:* Most scholars interpret this period as 'his two months are vine-tending' (Wright 1955: 54). This interpretation is incorrect. Langdon (1935: 35) observes that "pruning in Palestine falls in February," and Wright, who suggests that these two months "refer to pruning and cleaning the grapevine which took place in the unoccupied time after the harvest," notes that "in the area of Gezer the grapes begin to ripen in July and continue through the following months" (1955: 54). The latter period partially coincides with *yrḥw zmr*, and therefore cannot be 'the two months of pruning' but 'the two months of grape harvesting', an activity commonly known in the OT as *bāṣîr*. This suggestion has already been made by Vincent (1909: 247), S. Yeivin, and N. H. Tur-Sinai (Cassuto 1954: 472). Tur-Sinai notes the semantic identity between the roots *bṣr* and *zmr*, both of which mean 'power, strength'. I would like to suggest that although the root *zmr* is used in the OT for 'pruning, cutting off', the Gezer Manual employs this root for 'grape harvesting' because the same tool,

Table 3. Harvesting and ingathering, based on modern agricultural practices in Israel

	March	Apr	May	June	July	Aug	Sep	Oct	Nov
Wheat			x						
Barley		x							
Oats			x						
Peas		x	x						
Chickpeas				x					
Lentils		x	x						
Vetch		x	x						
Sesame					x				
Flax					x				
Millet					x	x			
Grapes				x	x	x	x		
Figs						x	x		
Pomegranates						x	x		
Olives							x	x	x

yrḥ qṣr śʿrm	*yrḥ qṣr wkl*	*yrḥw zmr*	*yrḥ qṣ*	*yrḥw ʾsp*

mazmērâ, was used in both activities. This interpretation should also be applied to the OT expressions *zimrat hāʾāreṣ* (Gen 43:11), 'the fruit of the land', and *ʿēt hazzāmîr* (Cant 2:12), 'the time of grape harvesting'.[2]

Line 7 *yrḥ qṣ*. Although the word *qṣ* could mean 'end', as in Amos 8:2, I suggest that the reference in the Gezer Manual is to 'harvesting of summer fruit (*qayiṣ*)', as in Jer 40:10, 12 and Amos 8:1, 2. According to Cross and Freedman (1952: 47), the orthography reflects "the contraction of the diphthong *ay* > *ê*, [and] indicates that the dialect of the Gezer Calendar was North Israelite, as opposed to Judahite." As I mentioned above, the same phenomenon appears in line 5 with the word *kl* (*kayil* > *kēl*). During this month the farmer ingathered the fruit of trees, such as figs and pomegranates (table 1).

As a result of the preceding discussion I propose the following interpretation of the Gezer Manual:

L. 1 two months of ingathering (olives)/ two months
L. 2 of sowing (cereals)/ two months of late sowing (legumes and vegetables)
L. 3 a month of hoeing weeds (for hay)
L. 4 a month of harvesting barley
L. 5 a month of harvesting (wheat) and measuring (grain)
L. 6 two months of grape harvesting
L. 7 a month of ingathering summer fruit

After establishing the general sequence of agricultural activities in Eretz-Israel during the latter part of the tenth century B.C.E., it now remains to be seen whether a more precise dating of the agricultural seasons can be achieved. To accomplish this task one needs to be able to date the major Israelite festivals, *pessaḥ/maṣṣôt*, *šābūʿôt*, and *ʾāsîp/sukkôt*, within the Israelite calendar since each of these festivals marks the beginning or end of an agricultural season. A correlation of the festival dates with the Gezer Manual would help to place the latter within the framework of the Israelite calendar and thus produce a correlation between the agricultural and cultic calendars.

On the basis of textual analysis scholars distinguish three dating systems for the festivals, which were employed at different periods of Israelite history (Morgenstern 1924, 1926, 1935; Auerbach 1958). The earliest system is recorded in Exod 23:14–18 and 34:18, 22–23, 25–26. According to this system, *pessaḥ* and *maṣṣôt* were two separate festivals. *Maṣṣôt* was celebrated for seven days beginning at the new moon of *ʾābîb* (Exod 23:15; Morgenstern 1924: 59; Auerbach 1958: 7).

[2] For a detailed discussion of *zāmîr* as 'grape harvesting' see Lemaire 1975.

Pessaḥ was celebrated on the night preceding the beginning of *maṣṣôt* (Auerbach 1958: 8) as suggested by Exod 23:15 and confirmed by Deut 16:1. Morgenstern (1924: 58–64; 1935: 5) proposes that the beginning of *ʾābîb* coincided with the spring equinox. Harmonizing the beginning of *ʾābîb* with the spring equinox was done by the Israelites, according to Morgenstern (1924: 64–71), by means of a solar calendar which had a very intricate system of intercalation. His theory—which has no evidence, textual or otherwise, to support it—has been challenged by Segal (1957: 253), who rightfully suggests that the Israelite calendar has been throughout its history a lunar calendar. According to Segal (1957: 276, 280–81), the Israelite lunar calendar was kept harmonized with the solar year and the agricultural seasons by intercalation based on the heliacal rising and setting of certain fixed group of stars near the time of the equinoxes. The stars observed for this purpose might have been the Pleiades and the constellation of Orion (Amos 5:8; Segal 1957: 274). According to Segal, evidence for intercalation in biblical times can be found in the change of date for *ʾāsîp* by Jeroboam (1 Kgs 12:32–33) and the celebration of *maṣṣôt* by Hezekiah in the second month rather than in the first (2 Chronicles 30); this is discussed further below.

The same dates for *pessaḥ/maṣṣôt* are maintained by the second dating system (Deut 16:1–4, 8), termed by scholars the Deuteronomic, or Holiness, calendar (Morgenstern 1924: 58–64; Morgenstern 1935: 29–72; Auerbach 1958: 1–5). The system was introduced as part of the Deuteronomic reforms promulgated by Josiah and, therefore dates to no later than his death in 609 B.C.E. Morgenstern (1935:5) says that at this time a transition was made from a solar to a luni-solar calendar, but as Segal (1957: 253) had already shown, such a transition was not necessary because a solar calendar was never used. The material included in Deuteronomy is very old. According to Nicholson (1967: 83), "the traditio-historical investigation of Deuteronomy has revealed that the book has as its basis the sacral and cultic traditions of the old Israelite amphictyony and that it probably owes its origin to prophetic circles in northern Israel by whom these traditions were preserved and transmitted during the period of the monarchy." Therefore, the dates given in the Deuteronomic calendar can be used to a certain extent to corroborate those of the earliest calendar.

The third system, found in Leviticus 23, is very late and was composed during the Exile or in post-exilic times (Morgenstern 1924: 73–75; Morgenstern 1935: 72–148), and therefore it will not be dealt with here in detail.

The second festival is called in the earliest calendar *ḥag haqqāṣîr*, 'the feast of the harvest' (Exod 23:16), and *ḥag šābūʿôt*, 'feast of weeks'

(Exod 34:22), and it marks the completion of the cereal-harvesting season. No precise date is given for this celebration, but it is closely related to *pessaḥ*. The name *šābūᶜôt* is repeated in the Deuteronomic calendar, where it is stated: "You shall count seven weeks; begin to count the seven weeks from the time you first put the sickle to the standing grain. Then you shall keep the feast of weeks [*ḥag šābūᶜôt*] to YHWH your God with the tribute of a freewill offering from your hand, which you shall give" (Deut 16:9–10). The prescription in Deuteronomy states the number of weeks and the commencement time of the counting. The prescription in Leviticus adds that the first sheaf to be harvested, the *ᶜōmer*, should be brought "on the morrow after the sabbath . . . and you shall count from the morrow after the sabbath, from the day that you brought the sheaf of wave offering; seven full weeks shall they be. Counting fifty days to the morrow after the seventh sabbath; then you shall present a cereal offering of new grain to YHWH" (Lev 23:11, 15–16).

Morgenstern (1935: 13, 35, 47) and Auerbach (1958: 11) maintain that the counting of the weeks till *šābūᶜôt* commenced on the day after the completion of the *maṣṣôt* festival. If this was the practice during pre-exilic times, then the celebration of *šābūᶜôt* coincided with the end of *yrḥ qṣr wkl* of the Gezer Manual (table 3). The tradition of counting the seven weeks from the day after the completion of *pessaḥ*/*maṣṣôt* has been observed in various ways by sects removed from mainstream Pharisaic Judaism, such as the Boethusians, the Falashas, the adherents of the book of *Jubilees*, and the Samaritans (Goudoever 1959: 15–29; Bowman 1959).

Pharisaic Judaism celebrates the festivals according to the Priestly calendar developed during the Exile or in post-exilic times. This calendar lost its relationship to Israelite agricultural traditions and celebrates the festivals as historical milestones. As Morgenstern (1935: 15–28) points out, during the development of the Priestly calendar the reckoning of the day changed from that of sunrise to sunrise into that of sunset to sunset, a change which in my opinion also reflects the loss of a relationship between agricultural daily life and the cultic calendar.

The third festival, *ʾāsîp*, 'ingathering (of fruit)', was celebrated at the end of the year, *bēṣēʾt haššānâ* (Exod 23:16; Morgenstern 1924: 22–28). Auerbach (1958: 11) suggests that it was celebrated at the beginning of the year, but the term used for the dating of the festival means 'exit, end' (BDB 1972: 423). The date of this festival was changed in the Priestly calendar to the fifteenth of Tišre, and the name was changed to *sukkôt*, 'tabernacles' (Lev 23:42). Some scholars suggest that the first day of Bul fell immediately after *ʾasîp* and was celebrated as New Year's Day (Morgenstern 1935: 5; Auerbach 1958:

11), coinciding with the autumn equinox (Morgenstern 1935: 5), but as shown in table 3 this cannot be so. The seven-day duration of the festival is prescribed by the Deuteronomic calendar (Deut 16:13, 15). This feast concluded the period of ingathering fruit and signified the beginning of the new agricultural year. As mentioned above, harmonizing the dates of the spring and autumn equinoxes with the festivals was enabled by observations made of heliacal risings and settings of certain stars at the time of the equinoxes (Segal 1957: 267). According to Segal (1957: 275, 280), the Israelites viewed the first nine days of the months of spring and autumn as "days of 'uncertainty'" during which a determination was made whether to intercalate a month or not; but there is no textual evidence for such a practice. Segal (1957: 259) makes the suggestion that the lack of mention of intercalation in the OT is due to the fact that the calendar was kept a priestly secret. This is a very weak explanation. If Segal is right in suggesting that intercalation was the result of star observations, then since it was performed semi-annually, it was not necessary to intercalate a whole month but only a few days at a time. This helps to explain why there is no mention of an official intercalation in the OT.

The celebration of *ʾāsîp/sukkôt* was also the occasion for the dedication of the Temple in Jerusalem by Solomon (1 Kgs 8:65; 2 Chr 7:8). Morgenstern (1924: 36) says that *kĕbôd YHWH* and the fire coming from heaven (1 Kgs 8:11; 2 Chr 7:1–3) are all related to the autumn equinox. It has been suggested by Hayes (1979: 299) that the fall festival was the cultic "day of YHWH," the origins of which go back to the days of the tribal league. According to Hayes, the festival initially lasted only three days, and in the wake of the Deuteronomic reforms it was lengthened to seven days. Nicholson (1967: 60) states that "during the period of the tribal league the traditions seem to have their home at the central shrine where the covenant festival was celebrated from time to time, very probably annually in the autumn." It seems that the non-Yahwistic agricultural festival of *ʾāsîp* was given a Yahwistic character by the Israelites by celebrating the feast as a covenant renewal festival, which later became an annual celebration of dedicating the Temple. Traces of this tradition can also be found in the account of the dedication of the Tabernacle in the desert (Leviticus 16).

In light of these traditions and practices it is possible to understand Jeroboam's act of changing the date of *ʾāsîp* from the seventh to the eighth month (1 Kgs 12:32–33). The date of the fifteenth in the account is most likely a gloss by a later redactor in whose time *ʾāsîp/sukkôt* was celebrated on VII/15. Talmon (1958: 57) says that "Jeroboam readjusted the time-reckoning to actual climatic and agricultural conditions prevalent in the north of Palestine . . . [and] the

Ephraimite peasant acclaimed the change which brought the cultic festivals again into focus with the agricultural seasons," but it should be noted that the differences between the north and the south are not great enough to justify a totally different calendar. Differences between Hebron and the Judean Shephelah are greater than those between the Shephelah and the Valley of Jezreel (Atlas of Israel 1970: IV/3). According to Talmon, Jeroboam changed the dates of all the festivals so that they were celebrated a month after their celebration in Judah (1958: 57).

While the change of the date for *ʾāsîp* is attested in the OT, there is no real proof that Jeroboam totally changed the calendar. Talmon suggests that Hezekiah's celebration of *maṣṣôt* in the second month coincided with the date of the northern *maṣṣôt* festival and was meant to attract northern Israelites (1958: 64). Segal (1957: 257–58) explains the change as an act of intercalation. Actually, there is no reason to look for hidden explanations for this change in date since the OT offers a solid reason for this act, connecting it with Hezekiah's reforms (2 Chronicles 29–30).

The discrepancies in Nebuchadnezzar's regnal years as found in 2 Kgs 24:12; 25:8; and Jer 52:12 and as recorded in Jer 52:28–29 (the last of which Talmon ascribes to the northern calendar [1958: 64]) can be explained as differences resulting from the use of two different regnal calendars, such as Nisan to Nisan and Tišre to Tišre (Thiele 1965: 27). Talmon's suggestion that the Samaritan calendar is a remnant of the northern Israelite calendar has to be examined in light of Bowman's contention (1959: 23–37) that the Samaritan calendar is an old Zadokite calendar. Besides, the example cited by Talmon from Rabbinic sources showing that the Samaritan *pessaḥ* could occur before the one celebrated in Judah (1958: 70) only proves that the Samaritan calendar is *not* a northern Israelite one developed by Jeroboam, lagging one month behind the southern calendar. Also, the Elephantine papyrus known as the Passover papyrus cannot be, as Talmon claims (1958: 70), a response to the inquiry of a Jewish group in Egypt observing the northern Israelite calendar. Rather, it is a product of the period in which the date for celebrating *pessaḥ* was changed from the new to the full moon, because the emphasis in the letter is on the days in which the festival should be celebrated and not on the month. This could have occurred only during the development of the Priestly calendar.

Talmon is right when he states that the redating of the festival of *ʾāsîp* by Jeroboam was a symbolic act of sovereignty, but as scholars have already observed, Jeroboam could not afford to be an innovator; therefore his act could not have been so radical as to totally divorce the northern Israelite calendar from previous practices. I suggest that Jeroboam's act is closely connected with the reestablishment of the cult in Dan and Bethel (1 Kgs 12:29–31). Jeroboam rededicated the old tribal shrines and declared a new date for the old rite, an act which resulted in the new date for the festival of *ʾāsîp* in northern Israel. Jeroboam changed only one date, and he could take this step because he related the new date of *ʾāsîp* to the old rite of covenant renewal which had strong ties with the shrines in the north. And if Morgenstern is right in saying that the Canaanite year started in the eighth month of the local calendar (1935: 5), then Jeroboam did not even introduce a new date, but revived an old one. The report in 1 Kgs 12:32 implies that this was a permanent and not a one-time change. As a result of this move, the ingathering season in northern Israel was officially extended by one month. Since regnal years in Israel were counted on the basis of a Nisan–Nisan year, while in Judah the counting followed a Tišre–Tišre year, it can be understood why Jeroboam could tamper with the date of *ʾāsîp*, which occurred in the middle of the regnal year, and could not change the date of *pessaḥ*, which fell at the beginning of the northern kingdom's regnal year. This is also the reason why Hezekiah could change the date of *pessaḥ*, for whatever reason he deemed it necessary.

The change in date for *ʾāsîp* and the hypothesis that it was not a result of intercalation and thus was a change that lasted as long as the northern kingdom kept its independence can also be supported by an *ex silentio* argument. In Deuteronomy, which according to Nicholson (1967: 98, 106) contains strong northern influences there is no mention of the date for *sukkôt*, while *pessaḥ* is clearly dated to the beginning of *ʾābîb*, and *šābūʿôt* is dated seven weeks after *pessaḥ* (Deut 16:1, 9, 13, 15). It is very possible that the northern contributors to this composition left out the date of *ʾāsîp* (*sukkôt*) purposely because of the discrepancy in dates between the north and the south.

A look at the Gezer Manual shows that it reflects the new northern Israelite order after the change made by Jeroboam. *Yrḥ qṣr śʿrm* (l. 4), which is exactly at the center of the inscription, is the key for a correlation between this list of agricultural chores and the cultic calendar of northern Israel. This *yrḥ* begins at the new moon of *ʾābîb* with a seven-day celebration of *maṣṣôt*. Seven weeks after the close of *maṣṣôt*, the harvest ends with the celebration of *šābūʿôt* coinciding with the end of *yrḥ qṣr wkl* (l. 5). The end of *yrhw ʾsp* (l. 1) coincides with the new date for the celebration of *ʾāsîp*.

This leads me to the following conclusions. (1) It seems very likely that the Gezer Manual, dated by scholars to ca. 925 B.C.E., is a direct result of the changes made by Jeroboam in the cultic calendar immediately following the secession of the north ca. 922 B.C.E. (Bright

1974: 226). The connection between the northern kingdom and Gezer is demonstrated by the use of the northern dialect (as evidenced by the spelling of *kl* and *qṣ*) and by the fact that during the time of the divided monarchy, until the fall of the north, Gezer was never considered a Judahite town. Gezer's status as a northern city is apparent from city lists dated to the time of the monarchy, in which it never appears as a Judahite city. (2) The lack of a date for *sukkôt* in the Deuteronomic calendar leads me to believe that the order of the agricultural seasons in the Gezer Manual was observed till the fall of Samaria in 722 B.C.E. While the Gezer Manual serves as evidence for the agricultural seasons in the north, there must have been a similar order in the south.

Part II

Field Work & Grain Production

5
Plowing & Sowing

The Gezer Manual assigns the second agricultural season to sowing, *yrḥw zr*ᶜ, and the third agricultural season is dedicated to late sowing, *yrḥw lqš*. During the first two months of sowing the farmer, *ʾikkār*, planted cereals, such as wheat and barley, and during the late sowing season he planted legumes and vegetables.[1] Thus, it appears that in the Gezer Manual four months were devoted to sowing. The reason for such a long sowing season, besides the fact that different species are planted at different times, was the need for ground preparation, which was carried out by plowing. However, plowing in biblical times was done for the sole purpose of sowing, as the prophet Isaiah (28:24) observed: "Does he who plows for sowing plow continually?" The relationship between these two agricultural activities was so close that sometimes one term was used in place of the other; e.g., the word for plowing in Gen 45:6 and Exod 34:21 is used in place of that for sowing.

Since plowing was a time- and effort-consuming activity, it is safe to assume that when sowing did not take place, as during the seventh year and the year of the Jubilee, no plowing was performed. Although it is not stated specifically, the laws regarding the seventh year and the year of the Jubilee imply that no plowing could take place during these years. Therefore, when the land was supposed to be left fallow, it was, most likely, left unplowed, contrary to modern practices.

Sowing took place after the first rain, *yôreh*, softened the ground. The farmer had to wait for the first rain because otherwise his plow could not penetrate the ground, which had become hardened by heat, dryness, and the pressure of grazing animals. The timing of the first rain was very crucial for ensuring an optimal period for the plants to grow and mature. If sowing had to be postponed because the first rain was late, the plants did not have enough time to develop and mature before the summer heat would dry them. If the first rain came early and the farmer planted his field immediately afterward, there was the

[1] For details see chap. 4 and table 2.

possibility of a long interval before the next rain would come. In this case the germinating seeds would die, resulting in a complete loss of crops. Therefore, it is understandable why the OT stressed the importance of observing the covenant between the Israelites and YHWH. The blessings and curses attached to the covenant state clearly the obligations and rewards:

> And if you will obey my commandments which I command you this day . . . I shall give the rain for your land in its season, the early rain and the later rain, that you may gather in your grain and your wine and your oil. Take heed lest your heart be deceived . . . and the anger of YHWH be kindled against you, and He shut up the heavens, so that there be no rain, and the land yield no fruit. . . . (Deut 11:13–17)

Plowing

The importance of plowing in Israelite agriculture is attested by the numerous terms used by the farmer to describe the types of furrows he used and their different parts. The term *nîr*, as in *nîrû lākem nîr* (Jer 4:3; Hos 10:12), was used to describe a furrow created by plowing a virgin field. This kind of subsoil plowing was probably performed with a special plow.[2] *Maᶜănâ* was a term applied to the marking-furrows for sowing, as I explain later. *Gĕdûd* was used to describe the deep part of the furrow, the cut in the soil, while *telem* was the term describing the high part of the furrow, the moundlike (*tēl*-like) part. Understanding the various terms used in describing furrows enables us to fully comprehend the meaning of statements such as the blessing in Ps 65:11: "Her [the land's] furrows, upper and lower parts [*gĕdûdêhā, tĕlāmêhā*], saturate with rain, and bless her growth."

In addition to the words discussed above, the OT uses several roots to describe the act of plowing, such as *ḥrš*, *ptḥ*, *plḥ*, and *bqᶜ*.

The Plow

The plow, *maḥărēšâ* or *maḥărešet*, is basically a development of the hoe into an instrument pulled by animals rather than by human hands. From artistic representations and archaeological finds we can see that the basic structure of the plow was not altered from the earliest model known to us[3] to the plow still in use by twentieth-century farmers in the Near East (Dalman 1932: 2.figs. 18–39).[4]

[2] See Akkadian *majjāru*, from *nēru* (Salonen 1968: 29–30, 65–69).

[3] Pictographs of plows from the Uruk IV period—last quarter of the fourth millennium B.C.E. (Salonen 1968: pl. 3:1).

[4] For examples of ancient plows see also representations of plows on Old Babylonian seals (ca. 2850 B.C.E.) in Gressmann 1927: fig. 160, and Salonen 1968: pls.

All parts of the plow (handle, crossbar, etc.) were made of wood with the exception of the plow-point, the part penetrating the soil. Archaeological finds indicate that early plow-points were made of bronze. After the introduction of iron into Canaan in the twelfth century B.C.E., iron plow-points started replacing bronze plow-points. At first this process was slow, and the use of bronze continued along with iron in the manufacture of plow-points and other implements. This can be seen in Iron Age sites such as Beth-shan, where bronze plow-points were found in an early Iron Age context (James 1966: pls. 103:3, 122:14). The slow replacement of bronze by iron in ancient Israel is ascribed to a monopoly held by the Philistines (1 Sam 13:19–22) over metal tool production and service (Bright 1974: 169, 181). The coexistence of bronze and iron plow-points during the period of the Judges and the early monarchy is evident from finds made at Beth-shemesh (Grant 1932: pl. 47:31–32, 40–41; Grant 1939: pl. 53:74–75) and Tell Beit Mirsim (Albright 1943b: 32–33, pls. 61:1–4, 62:1–2, 4). At both sites, plow-points made of bronze and iron were discovered in strata dated to the early Iron Age.

The Philistine monopoly theory has been recently challenged by Waldbaum (1978), who, after a careful study of the replacement of bronze by iron in the Mediterranean basin, concluded that although iron was already known during the Late Bronze Age, it did not gain popularity because of "some reluctance, probably because of its unsatisfactory and unreliable properties" (1978: 70–71). The people of the Mediterranean basin were eventually forced to use iron, according to Waldbaum, because for an unknown reason a shortage of tin for manufacturing bronze occurred, and the people had to resort to iron as a replacement (1978: 72, 73).

Iron plow-points belonging to the time of Saul and the early monarchic period are known from Tell el-Fûl = Gibeah (Albright 1924: 17; Sinclair 1960: 47, pl. 19A), Ain Shems = Beth-shemesh (Grant 1932: pl. 48:31–32, 40–41), Tell Jemmeh (Petrie 1928: pls. 26: 2, 66:5), and Tell Beit Mirsim (Albright 1943b: 78–79, pl. 61:1–7, 14–15). Plow-points dated to the late Israelite period were found at Tell en-Nasbeh = Mizpeh (McCown 1947: pl. 96:1–5), Tell ed-Duweir = Lachish (Tufnell 1953: pl. 61:1–2), Tell Jezer = Gezer (Macalister

---

3:2–4, 4:1–4; a wooden model of a man plowing with a two-handled plow drawn by two yoked oxen (Sixth to Eleventh Dynasty, ca. 2350–2000 B.C.E.) in Pritchard 1954: fig. 84; an Egyptian plow drawn by slaves (relief, Eighteenth Dynasty, ca. 1550–1350 B.C.E.) in Pritchard 1954: fig. 85; a Mesopotamian plow with two handles and a seed-drill (ca. 1320–1295 B.C.E.) in Pritchard 1954: fig. 86, and Salonen 1968: pl. 6:1; a Mesopotamian plow with one handle and a seed-drill (stele of Esarhaddon, 680–669 B.C.E.) in Pritchard 1954: fig. 88.

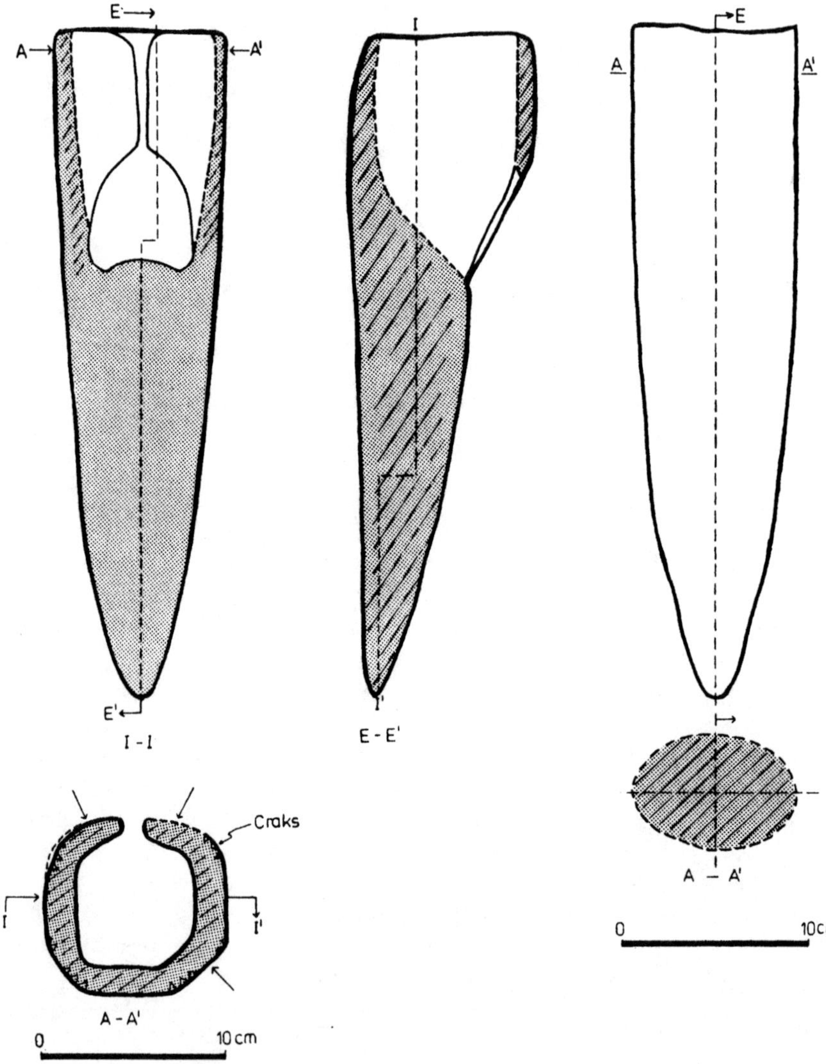

Fig. 3. An iron plow-share from Beer-sheba

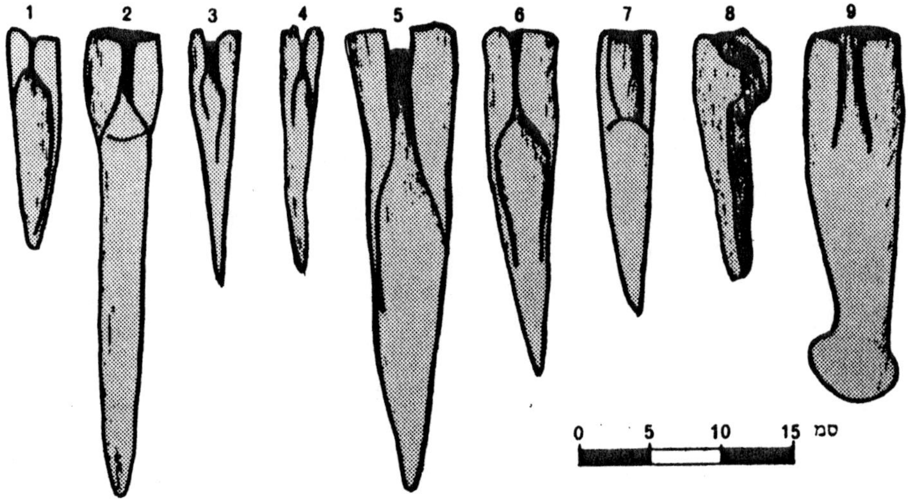

Fig. 4. Ancient plow-shares from Tell Beit Mirsim (1,5): Megiddo (2); Tell en-Nasbeh (3,4); Lachish (6,7,9); Tell Qasileh (8)

1912: l.pl. 128:1–2), and Beer-sheba (Aharoni 1973: 34, pl. 31:2). Other recently discovered plow-points dated to the Iron Age but not yet published are known from et-Tell = ᶜAi, Bethel, Dothan, and Khirbet Radana.

The plow-point was an elongated tool, 20–30 cm long, with a pointed tip for soil penetration. The other end was shaped like a pipe, ca. 8–10 cm wide. A wooden shaft, which was part of the plow-handle, was inserted into this end. Unlike the Mishna, the OT does not describe the plow nor list its parts in a clear manner. Therefore, it is hard to describe the biblical plow except from information gleaned from extra-biblical sources. From artistic representations[5] we know that the plow had either one or two handles to apply pressure on the point to facilitate soil penetration. The plow was pulled by a team of animals, *ṣemed*, or by a single beast of burden.

Animals Used in Plowing

Pulling the plow was done usually by a team of oxen (Pritchard 1954: figs. 84, 86, 91; Gressmann 1927: figs. 161, 165) connected to the plow with a yoke, *kĕlĕ habbāqār* (2 Sam 24:22; also *môṭ*, Nah 1:13; *môṭâ*, Jer 27:2; 28:10, 12–13; and *ᶜōl*, 1 Kgs 12:4; Hos 11:4). Yokes

[5] See above, nn. 3 and 4.

were usually made of wood.[6] Iron yoke, *ᶜōl barzel* (Deut 28:48), is probably used figuratively and does not refer to an implement actually used in plowing or any other work, since an iron yoke would constitute an unnecessary burden. The animals pulling the plow were attached to the yoke, which was placed on the back of their necks, with ropes, *môsērôt* (Jer 2:20; 27:2; also *ʾăguddôt môṭâ*, Isa 58:6). The yoke itself was attached to the crossbar, which was part of the plow. In the absence of a crossbar, the yoke was attached to the plow with ropes, *ᶜăbôt* (Ps 129:4; Job 39:10).[7]

The term *ṣemed*, 'a pair of animals', came to be used as an area measurement meaning 'an area which can be plowed in a day by a team of animals, e.g., oxen' (BDB 1972: 855), and it is so used in 1 Sam 14:14, *ṣemed śādeh*; 1 Kgs 19:19, twelve *ṣĕmādîm*; and Isa 5:10, ten *ṣimdê kerem*.

In several instances in the OT the general collective term *bāqār*, 'cattle', is used to describe the animals made to draw the plow (as in *ṣemed bāqār*; 1 Sam 11:7; 1 Kgs 19:20–21; Job 1:14). The more specific term *šôr*, 'ox', is used in Deut 22:10 in the prohibition against the use of an ox and a donkey, *ḥămôr*, in the same team. Although the *šôr* appears frequently in the OT as the principal beast of burden, this is the only time it is directly related to plowing. Deut 22:10 is also the only place where the donkey is mentioned as an animal used for plowing.[8] Another animal used for plowing was the *ᶜeglâ*, 'young cow' (Judg 14:18; Hos 10:11). Other beasts of burden are not related by the OT to plowing.

To direct the animals, a goad, *malmēd* (Judg 3:31; also *dărbān*, 1 Sam 13:21; **dărbōnâ*, Eccl 12:11), was used. This implement had an iron tip set in a long wooden shaft. During the time of the Judges, the Philistine artisans charged "a third of a shekel" to fix and set the goad (Bewer 1942: 45–46). Goad-tips were found during excavations at Tell Beit Mirsim (Albright 1943b: 33,pl. 62:2), Tell el-Farᶜah (south; Petrie 1930: pls. 21:92, 26:98), Megiddo (Lamon and Shipton 1939: pl. 83:21), Tell Jemmeh (Petrie 1928: pls. 23:14, 32:25), and Tell en-Nasbeh (McCown 1947: pl. 96:6). In Mishnaic and Talmudic times the butt of the goad had a shovel-like implement, *ḥarḥûr*, affixed to it (Felix 1960: 147–48). It was used for removing the mud from the plow-tip. A similar object dated to the end of the eighth century B.C.E. was found at Hazor (Yadin et al. 1958: pls. 70:30, 153:19).[9]

[6] For the antiquity of the yoke see Dimbleby 1967: 69.

[7] For a detailed discussion of the yoke in Mishnaic times see Felix 1960.

[8] For another possibility of oxen, *ʾălāpîm*, and donkeys, *ᶜăyārîm*, used in tilling the land see Isa 30:24.

[9] There are many other implements found at Hazor which may be goads (Yadin et al. 1960: pls.58:14, 20; 165:9–10; etc.).

Fig. 5. Sowing and plowing, Tomb of Nakht, 18th Dynasty

Sowing

In biblical times there were two methods of sowing (*zera*ᶜ): (1) broadcasting the seeds by hand, and (2) using a seed-drill (Akkadian *abu, ittû*; Salonen 1968: 74, 81–82, fig. 4).

Broadcasting (*hpṣ, zrh, zr*ᶜ*, zrq*)

After the first rain the farmer went out to the fields to sow.[10] During Mishnaic times the farmer used to plow his fields first before broadcasting the seeds (Felix 1960: 156). It is possible that the same sequence was followed in biblical times.[11] In order to cover the whole field with seeds, the farmer first plowed at constant intervals single marking-furrows, *ma*ᶜ*ănâ* (1 Sam 14:14; also *ma*ᶜ*ănît*, Ps 129:3), to mark the distance he could cover throwing seeds. This is still practiced by Near Eastern farmers who do not use any drills (Dalman 1932: 2 figs. 23–25). The seeds, *zera*ᶜ (Num 20:5; Deut 14:22; 28:38; Isa 5:10;

[10] For the time of plowing see Dalman 1932: 2.174–79; and Avitsur 1972: 195.

[11] According to Avitsur (1972: 195), *pattiaḥ* refers to the first plowing. The second plowing, *śiddûd*, to cover the seeds, was performed at right angles to the *pattiaḥ*. Verb forms from these roots are used in this order in Isa 28:24 (*yĕpattaḥ wîśaddēd*). Galling (1937: 427) suggests that *śdd* is the poetic equivalent of *ḥrš*. Dalman (1932: 2.180) says only that *śdd* was some kind of activity related to plowing. According to BDB (1972: 961), *śdd* is 'to harrow', and it is compared to Akkadian *šadādu*, 'drag, draw'; see von Soden 1981: 3.1121. It seems that the last interpretation is the closest to the true meaning of *śdd*. It could be that the farmer used a certain implement which was dragged for leveling the ground, as suggested by Isa 28:25. It is also possible that this instrument was the **magrēpâ* mentioned in Joel 1:17, "the seeds are rotten under their *magrēpôt*."

Hag 2:18), were held in a bag, *mešek hazzera*ᶜ (Ps 126:6), and the farmer marched along the marking-furrows at a constant pace pulling handfuls of seeds from the bag and broadcasting them on the field (Gressmann 1927: pl. 165). The person engaged in this activity was called a *zôrēa*ᶜ (Isa 32:20; 55:10; Jer 50:16; Ps 126:6; Job 4:8) or was referred to by the poetic term *môšēk hazzera*ᶜ (Amos 9:13). The dependence on rain for watering the plants, the uncertainty of the quantity and timing of the rains, and the possibility of crop failure due to pests and diseases appear to have kept the farmer in a gloomy mood during sowing: "May those who sow in tears reap with shouts of joy! He that goes forth weeping bearing the seed bag shall come home with shouts of joy bringing his sheaves with him" (Ps 126:5–6). To secure the right amount and the correct timing of the rain (*gešem*, 'rain', *yôreh*, 'first, early rain', *malqôš*, 'last, late rain'; see Jer 5:24), the Israelite farmer was obligated to observe the covenant with YHWH (Deut 11:14).[12]

After spreading the seeds, the farmer hastened to plow the field to cover the seeds and protect them from birds and animals. Covering the seed is referred to, most likely, by the term *ḥārîš*, 'plowing', in Gen 45:6 and Exod 34:21, where it appears in parallelism with *qāṣîr*, 'harvest'. Another method used today by Near Eastern farmers to cover the seeds is to let a herd of animals on the field. The animals trample the seeds into the ground—provided, of course, that the field was first plowed. It is possible that the same method was also used in biblical times: "Happy are you who sow beside all waters, who let the feet of the ox and the ass range free" (Isa 32:20). In mountainous regions, where the topography did not allow the use of a plow, a hand tool, such as a hoe, *ma*ᶜ*dēr*, was used, as described in Isa 7:25 (Gressmann 1927: pl. 165).

There is an explicit prohibition against sowing or planting two different kinds of seeds or plants in the same field or orchard (*kil*ᵓ*ayim*; Lev 19:19; Deut 22:9). Although this prohibition appears as a religious taboo, there may be an agricultural basis for it.[13]

Using a Seed-Drill

In Mesopotamia the seed-drill was very popular, as known from artistic representations and from written documents (Salonen 1968: 74,

[12] The numerous Astarte figurines found in excavations at Israelite sites show that the Israelite farmer did not depend only on the covenant with YHWH for harnessing the natural forces and assuring the fertility of his fields. The Astarte figurines are another sign of Canaanite influence on Israelite agriculture.

[13] For details see the section Crop Rotation in chap. 11.

Fig. 6. Plow with a seed drill operated by three people (Cassite period)

81–82). In Mishnaic times the seed-drill was well known in Eretz-Israel (Felix 1960: 154–55), and its invention was attributed by the book of *Jubilees* to Abraham (11:23).[14] There is no direct evidence, documentary or archaelogical, for the use of the seed-drill in Eretz-Israel in biblical times. However, Isaiah (28:25) in his allegorical description of a farmer sowing seeds uses the verb *wĕśām*, 'and he puts', rather than a verb denoting throwing or scattering. Several kinds of crops are mentioned, including 'emmer in its proper place [*gĕbūlātô*]'. This suggests that special care was taken to avoid mixing different kinds of

[14] "And in the first year of the fifth week Abram taught those who made implements for oxen, the artificers in wood, and they made a vessel above the ground, facing the frame of the plough, in order to put the seed thereon, and the seed fell down therefrom upon the share of the plough, and was hidden in the earth, and they no longer feared the ravens" (Charles 1917: 87).

Fig. 7. Plow with seed drill, stela of Esarhaddon

seeds; the use of a seed-drill would have alleviated this problem. The seed-drill may have appeared in Eretz-Israel as a result of Assyrian influence.

Artistic representations (Salonen 1968: pl. 6:1) show how this implement was used. The team involved could include as many as three people: one directing the plow and pushing the handle down to facilitate soil penetration; the second person directing the animals; and the third person holding the seed bag on his shoulder and dropping the seeds into the drill. The drill consisted of a funnel, into which the seeds were dropped, and a pipe attached to the bottom of the funnel, through which the seeds fell, emerging behind the plow-point. This arrangement enabled the seeds to be covered immediately, by the loose soil falling behind the plow and the process of sowing required only one plowing. The drill was made of leather and wood, which might be the reason for the lack of archaelogical evidence. This type of implement is still used today in the Near East, especially with summer crops (Gressmann 1927: pl. 164; Dalman 1932: 2. pl. 26). Sowing with a seed drill is very efficient, and one man is able to perform all the tasks involved.

6
Harvesting Field Crops

Harvesting cereals, *dāgān*, was one of the most important activities of the agricultural year because it involved the ingathering of the main food staple of the ancient Israelite. Ingathering field produce included three separate activities: reaping, threshing, and winnowing. The end result of these activities was clean grain ready for milling.

Reaping (qāṣîr)

The fifth season in the Gezer Manual is *yrḥ qṣr śᶜrm*, 'a month of harvesting barley', and the sixth season is *yrḥ qṣr wkl*, 'a month of harvesting (wheat) and measuring (grain)'.[1] The OT refers to the former as *qĕṣîr śĕᶜōrîm* (2 Kgs 21:9; Ruth 2:23) and to the latter as *qĕṣîr ḥiṭṭîm* (Gen 30:14; Exod 34:22; Judg 15:1; 1 Sam 6:13; Ruth 2:23).

There are some variations in the actual time of cereal harvesting in the different parts of the country, depending on differences in climate. Where the climate is warmer, as in the Shephelah and the Jordan Valley, crops mature earlier than in regions where the climate is cool, as in the Judean hill-country and the Galilee (Dalman 1932: 2.216–17; 3.1–6). But the order of cereal ripening is maintained throughout Eretz-Israel; i.e., barley always ripens earlier than wheat. This is evident not only from the Gezer Manual, but also from the instructions for the festivals of *pessaḥ* and *šābūᶜôt*. *Pessaḥ* celebrates the beginning of barley harvesting, and *šābūᶜôt* celebrates the completion of wheat harvesting.[2]

Harvesting cereals started when the crops were ripe, *bāšal qāṣîr* (Joel 4:13), and ready for reaping. This stage in the development of cereal plants is called *qāmâ*, 'standing grain' (Exod 22:5).[3] The ear of the stalk, *šibbōlet* (Job 24:24), is dry enough to separate the grain from

[1] See chap. 4.
[2] See chap. 4.
[3] Also, Deut 16:9; 23:26; Judg 15:5; 2 Kgs 19:26; Isa 17:5; 37:27; Hos 8:7.

Fig. 8. Field work; upper register, harvesting of cereals; bottom register, plowing and ground preparation in the hill country (Tomb of Nakht, 18th Dynasty)

the spikelets by hand; at this point the ear of grain is called **mĕlilâ* (pl. *mĕlîlôt*, Deut 23:26).[4]

When a small area had to be harvested, it could be done by hand without any tools. The farmer would pull out the whole plant, uprooting it. Pulling out the whole plant rather than just the ear of grain kept the grain from spilling.[5] When a large area had to be harvested, the operation became complex, involving many people in many activities. The complexity of harvesting can be observed in Egyptian art, where people are shown cutting the crops, tying the stalks into sheaves, and transporting the harvested crops to the

[4] The origin of this term might be *mll* II, 'rub, scrape', or *mll* III, 'languish, wither, fade'; see BDB 1972: 576.

[5] The name of this activity was probably a form of the root *ntš*; see, e.g., Jer 31:28; 42:10; 45:4. For the use of this method in Mishnaic and modern times, see Avitsur 1976: 23.

Fig. 9. Harvesting of cereals and transportation to the threshing floor (19th Dynasty)

threshing area (Pritchard 1954: pl. 91; Gressmann 1927: pl. 166; Encyclopaedia Biblica 1962: 1015–16).

There is sufficient information in the OT to enable the reconstruction and description of harvesting in that period. Unlike the time of sowing, harvesting was a time of rejoicing as Isaiah observes, "they rejoice before thee as with joy at the harvest" (9:3[2]); and the Psalmist compares the mood during sowing and harvesting saying, "May those who sow in tears reap with shouts of joy" (126:5). The best description of a harvest is in Ruth 2, where one can see a large operation in progress. The reapers, *qōṣēr* (Amos 9:13; Jer 9:21; Ps 129:7; pl. *qōṣĕrîm*, 2 Kgs 4:18; Ruth 2:3),[6] were led by a foreman, *hanniṣṣāb ᶜal haqqôṣĕrîm* (Ruth 2:5–6). A similar picture emerges from the letter from Meṣad Ḥashavyahu (ca. 625 B.C.E.), where a worker who belongs to a group of reapers, *ᵓḥy . . . hqṣrm ᵓty*, implores a high official, *hśr*, to return to him his garment confiscated by the foreman named *ḥšbyhw bn šby*. Behind the reapers came other people who were engaged in the harvest, the maidens, *naᶜărôt*, and the young men, *nĕᶜārîm*.

Reaping was done with a sickle, *ḥermēš* (Deut 16:9; 23:26) or *maggāl* (Jer 50:16; Joel 4:13), held in one hand while a bunch of stalks, **ṣebet* (pl. *ṣĕbātîm*, Ruth 2:16), was seized with the other (Isa 17:5; Ps 129:7). In some cases only the top of the stalk was cut (Gressmann 1927: pl. 166; Pritchard 1954: pl. 91; Encyclopaedia Biblica 1962: 1015–16) leaving the rest of the plant standing in the field for grazing

[6] Also called *tōpēś maggāl*, 'seizer of sickle' in poetry (Jer 50:16).

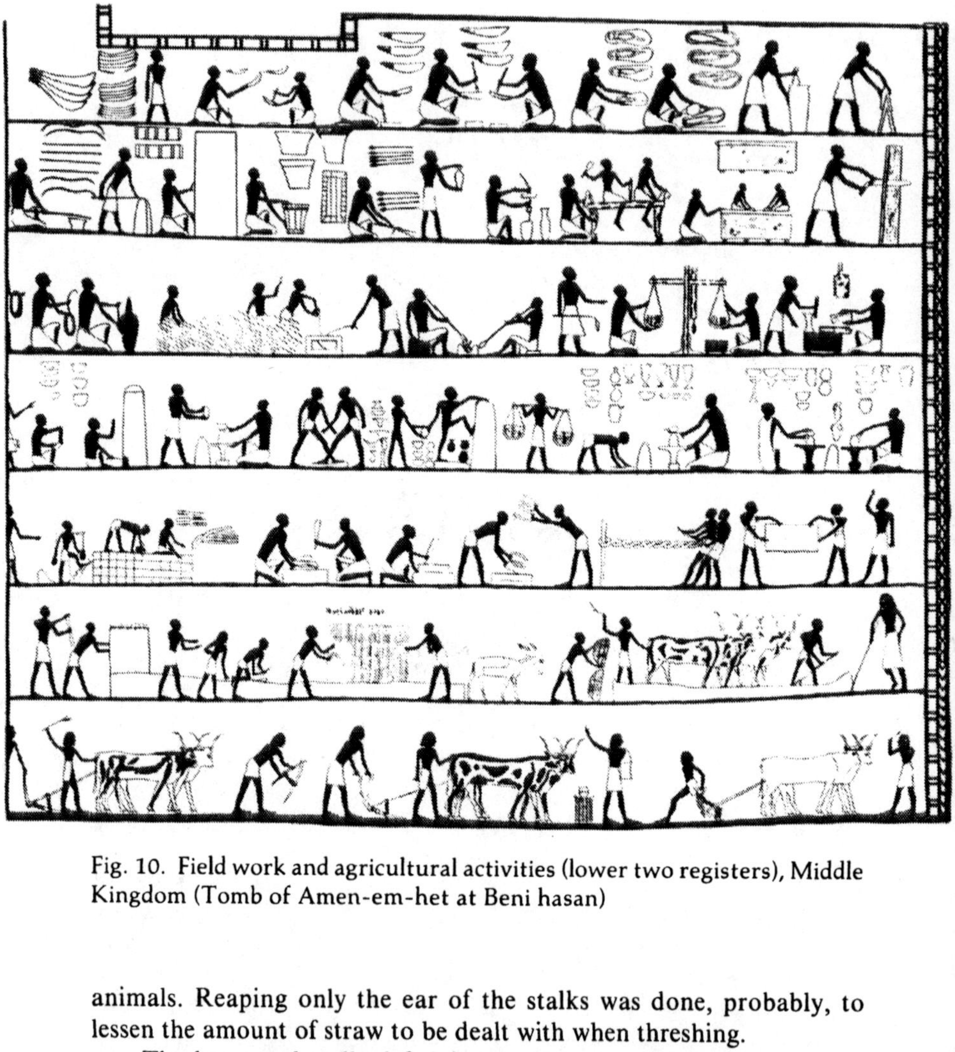

Fig. 10. Field work and agricultural activities (lower two registers), Middle Kingdom (Tomb of Amen-em-het at Beni hasan)

animals. Reaping only the ear of the stalks was done, probably, to lessen the amount of straw to be dealt with when threshing.

The harvested stalks left lying on the ground by the reaper are termed *ᶜāmîr* (Jer 9:21). They were collected by the *mĕᶜammēr* (Ps 129:7) into the bosom of his garment, **ḥēṣen* (Ps 129:7), and are referred to as *ᶜōmer* (Deut 24:19), a harvested bunch of stalks not yet bound into sheaves.[7] Behind the *mĕᶜammēr* came those who bound the *ᶜămārîm* into sheaves, *ᵓălummâ* (pl. *ᵓălummîm* or *ᵓălummôt*, Gen 37:7; Ps 126:6). The *mĕᶜammēr* could have also been the one to bind

[7] *ᶜōmer* is also a measure, equaling one-tenth of an *ᵓêpâ* (Exod 16:36). The terms *ᶜōmer* and *ᶜāmîr* are sometimes used interchangeably.

the sheaves. All the sheaves were put in a pile, *gādîš* (Exod 22:5; Judg 15:5), and were ready for transportation to the threshing floor.

Closing the list were those who were not directly connected with the operation but were present in the field as gleaners. They were the poor, who were allowed by religious law to perform *leqeṭ*, 'gleaning' (Lev 19:9; 23:22). The gleaners usually gleaned only the *šibbōlet* (Isa 17:5; Ruth 2:2). In the story of Ruth, where she was allowed to glean among the *ʿămārîm* before they were bound into sheaves, she managed to collect more (about an *ʾêpâ*) than was usually collected by a gleaner. Besides *leqeṭ*, religious law specified also that a corner of the field, *pēʾâ* (Lev 19:9; 23:22), would be left for the poor and not harvested by the landowner.

Harvesting was done in the summer, when the temperature is very high (Isa 18:4; Prov 25:13; 26:1), and water was provided for the workers and kept cool in jars (Encyclopaedia Biblica 1962: 1015–16). In the case of Ruth, who was not part of the working force, a special dispensation was made, and she was allowed to drink from the jars provided by the landowner, Boaz (Ruth 2:9). As for food, the workers ate bread, *pat*, dipped in vinegar, *ḥōmeṣ*, and parched grain, *qālî*, which probably was freshly prepared in the field (Ruth 2:14).

As mentioned above, the principal tool for harvesting was the sickle. There are two terms for this implement in the OT: *ḥermēš* (Deut 16:9; 23:26) and *maggāl* (Jer 50:16). The use of the former term in religious laws suggests that here we have an older term preserved in the law code. Some scholars suggest that the term *ḥermēš* is the result of an *l*/*r* interchange and is derived from the original material used in sickle making, *ḥallāmiš*, 'flint' (Deut 8:15; Avitsur 1976: 23). Since prehistoric times, pieces of worked flint were placed in wood or bone handles, and the resultant implements used for harvesting grass and cereals. Flint blades used in harvesting cereals can be distinguished from blades used for other purposes by the shining patina created by dirt on the stalks or by the silicon in the stalks. Flint sickles continued to be used in the Iron Age even after metal sickles made their appearance (Amiran 1958: 297–300).

Flint sickle-blades in Iron I strata were found at Tell Qasîleh (Mazar 1950–51: 195), Megiddo (Loud et al. 1948: 141–44), Tell el-Fûl (Sinclair 1960: pl. 19C:9, 11), Tell Deir ʾAlla (Franken 1975: 323), Bethel (Kelso 1968: 84, 85, 90, 91), Beth-shemesh (Grant and Wright 1939: 165–66), and other sites. Flint sickles were still in use in the Iron II period as can be seen from finds at Bethel (Kelso 1968: 84), Tell Jemmeh (Petrie 1928: pl. 16), Tell Qiri (Ben Tor 1977), and other sites. Bronze was used for making sickles to a limited extent during the Late Bronze Age. Bronze sickles were found at Gezer and Ugarit (Amiran

1958: 300).[8] When iron was introduced into Eretz-Israel, it began to be used for making sickles, and the quality of flint tools deteriorated. Although iron sickles were not immediately available to the Israelite farmer, as suggested by their absence from the list of agricultural implements in 1 Sam 13:19–22, they became part of the agricultural tool inventory at the beginning of the monarchy. It is also possible that at this time the term *maggāl* was introduced.

Iron sickle-blades have been found at many sites: Beth-shemesh (Grant and Wright 1939: 153, pl. 53), Tell Jemmeh (Petrie 1928: pl. 27:8–20), Tell Abu Hawam (Hamilton 1934–35: 26, 132), Gezer (Macalister 1912: 3.pl. 128:10–13), Megiddo (Lamon and Shipton 1939: pl. 82), Tell en-Nasbeh (McCown 1947: pl. 96:12–16), Tell Qasîleh (Mazar 1950–51: 195, no. 5565), and Tell Beit Mirsim (Albright 1943b: pl. 61:8, 9, 13). A very good collection of iron sickles was found at Hazor in several strata dated to the different phases of the Iron Age (Yadin et al. 1958: pls. 82:5; 149:21; 152:7; Yadin et al. 1960: pls. 59:30; 106:7, 20, 22, 34; 107:24; 165:3–6). Two iron sickles were found at Hazor near an Iron Age rectangular silo (Yadin et al. 1961: pls. 100:6, 258:19–21, 365:2–3). One of the sickles found at Tell en-Nasbeh (McCown 1947: pl. 96:12) illustrates well the structure of the sickle. The metal haft exhibits rivet holes, by means of which the blade was attached to a wooden handle (not preserved). Comparison of Iron Age sickles with sickles dated to the Persian period (Porath 1974: fig. 6:7–8, pl. 14:8) shows that there is no visible difference in the form and basic design of the tool between the earlier and the later periods.

Threshing (dayiš)

The separation of the grain from the stalk was done by threshing in the *gōren*, 'threshing floor' (2 Sam 24:16, 18, 21, 24; Ruth 3:2–3, 6,14; 1 Chr 21:15, 21–22, 28). Threshing had to be done immediately after the harvest to free the farmer for his next task—picking grapes. In a good year, when the yield was great, threshing and grape picking overlapped (Deut 26:5). The harvested crops were transported to the threshing floor (Mic 4:12) by different means, such as wagons, *ᶜăgālâ* (Amos 2:13), animals (Gressmann 1927: pl. 166), and people with large baskets (Pritchard 1954: pl. 91). If any unbound harvested stalk, *ᶜōmer*, was forgotten in the field, it was left for the poor (Deut 24:19).

The *gōren* was located outside the city where the prevalent west wind could be used for winnowing (Hos 13:3).[9] The exact location of

[8] An extraordinary find of bronze sickle-blades dated to the Persian period was made at Hazor (Yadin 1958: 6).

[9] The prevalent winds in Israel are from the west and they determine the location of the threshing floor. A threshing floor situated to make use of the west wind could not be

the threshing floor was determined by the local topography. Sometimes it was close to the city gate (Jer 15:7), and at times it was situated in an area somewhat lower than the city itself (Ruth 3:3). There is no direct statement in the OT concerning the ownership of the threshing floor, but the story of Ruth (chap. 3) implies the existence of private threshing floors. Because it was a large open space, the threshing floor was used for public functions (1 Kgs 22:10; 2 Chr 18:9); this suggests that at least some of the threshing floors were publicly owned. The use of these threshing floors was most likely directed by the village authorities.

Being outside the city, the site of the threshing floor could not be defended in case of attack, and thus we find Gideon threshing wheat in the *gat*, 'winepress' (Judg 6:11), inside the city,[10] as a precaution against the Midianites. The same problem is illustrated by the attack of the Philistines on the threshing floors of Qe^cilâ (1 Sam 23:1).

There were four methods of threshing: with a stick, with animals, with a threshing sledge, and with a wheel-thresher.

Threshing with a Stick

Under certain circumstances a stick, *šebeṭ* or *maṭṭeh* (Isa 28:27), was used to beat, *ḥbṭ*, the grain out of the *šibbōlet*. The OT describes some of these circumstances:

1. When a small amount of grain had to be threshed, as in the case of Ruth, who gleaned after the reapers (Ruth 2:17). This method was probably used by the harvesters in the field to provide grain for *qālî*.
2. When the threshing floor could not be used for security reasons, as in the case mentioned above (Judg 6:11).
3. When a crop had small seeds which could be harmed by the use of heavy equipment or which could not be collected after threshing at the *gōren* because of their size, as observed by Isaiah: "For with a rod black cumin should be threshed and cumin with a stick" (28:27).

Threshing with a stick was still being practiced in the Near East at the beginning of this century (Dalman 1932: 3.91–92, pl. 25).

Threshing with Animals

The separation of grain from the stalks can be done by having a group of animals tread over the stalks, *mĕdūšâ* (Isa 21:10). The animals

used during an east wind (which is sometimes present in the summer) since winnowing with the east wind would carry chaff and dust into the settlement. This is probably the background of Jer 4:11. For 'winnowing' used figuratively see Isa 41:16; Jer 49:32, 36; Ezra 5:2.

[10] See chap. 9; the *gat* was a winepress built inside the town, while the *yeqeb* was the term used for a winepress hewn in the rock outside of town.

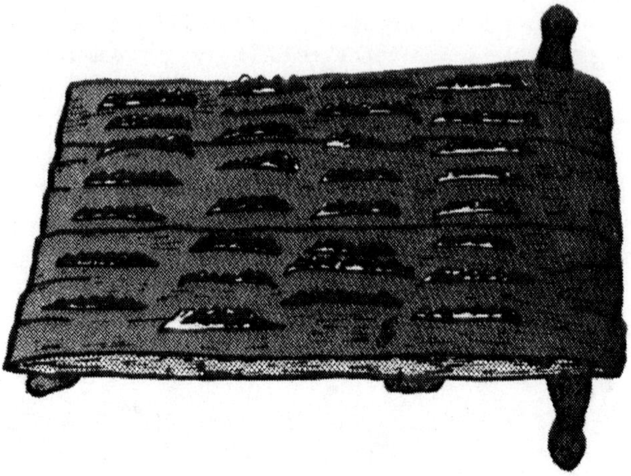

Fig. 11. A modern *morāg* (threshing sledge) made of wood with iron teeth

are tied together next to each other to form a row, *ribqâ*,[11] and are marched over the *mědūšâ*. In Egypt donkeys (Pritchard 1954: pl. 80) and oxen (Encyclopaedia Biblica 1962: 1015–16) were used for this purpose. The OT does not describe this method specifically, but it is possible that the prohibition against muzzling the ox while it threshes (Deut 25:4) and Hosea's description of Ephraim as "a trained heifer that loves to thresh" (10:11) are references to this method. It is, of course, possible that both references are to animals pulling a threshing sledge.

Micah's call "Arise and thresh, O Daughter of Zion, for I shall make your horn iron and your hoofs bronze" (4:12) makes a strong case for the use of animals in threshing during OT times. Among farmers who still use this method, the custom of attaching special metal shoes to the animals' feet is common (Dalman 1932: 3.107–8, pls. 13–15; Avitsur 1976: 213). There is no doubt that Micah spoke in reference to this practice.

Threshing with a Sledge

The most common and effective method of threshing which produces the best results for a large quantity of crops is by sledge, *môrāg*. As still can be observed in the Near East, the sledge is a

[11] From *rbq*, 'tie fast' (BDB 1972: 918).

platform made of two or three wooden boards. The front is upturned to prevent it from jamming into the floor when pulled by animals (Dalman 1932: 3.pl. 17; Gressmann 1927: pl. 168). The bottom of the sledge has hard stones (flint, basalt) embedded in it in order to break the grain away from the stalks and get it out of the spikelets.

With the introduction of iron into Eretz-Israel, some farmers chose to replace the stones in the underside of the sledge with pieces of metal. Such a sledge is called by Isaiah *môrāg ḥārûṣ ḥādāš baᶜal pîpiyyôt* (41:15). The adjective *ḥārûṣ*, 'sharp', is used substantively in Isaiah 28:27 and is there to be translated 'threshing sledge'; compare Amos 1:3: *ḥărūṣôt* (*ḥărîṣê* in 1 Chr 20:3) *habbarzel*, 'iron teeth'. *Ḥādāš* in Isaiah 41:15 does not mean 'new' but 'made of iron' (Leibel 1958). Threshing sledges with stones and with iron teeth are still in use, side by side, in the Near East (Dalman 1932: 3. pls. 17–18; Avitsur 1976: figs. 72–74).

Threshing with a Wheel-Thresher

A very common method of threshing in the Near East is with a wheel-thresher, *ᵓôpan ᶜăgālâ* (Isa 28:27–28). This method was very popular at the beginning of the twentieth century (Dalman 1932: 3. pls. 21–23). Instead of a sledge with stone or metal teeth, two or more rows of wheels are attached to a frame, and the structure thus formed is drawn by animals.

The only possible archaelogical find pointing to the use of this method in OT times is from Tell el-Farᶜah (south), where an object resembling a portion of a threshing-wheel was found (Petrie 1928: pl. 27:1). The suggestion made by Galling (1937: 137–38) that the objects depicted on pl. 39:15–18 in Petrie 1928 are threshing-wheels is unacceptable because they are made of clay. However, their form (round with sprockets) suggests that they are *models* of threshing-wheels (and not of chariots, as reported by Petrie [1928: 18]).

Winnowing (lizrôt or lĕhābēr)

After threshing, the grain had to be separated from the straw and chaff. First, the threshed material was thrown into the air with a fork, *mizreh* (Isa 30:24; Jer 15:7).[12] This tool is usually made of wood and has five or seven tines. The winnower throws the threshed material into the air and the wind separates the mixture according to the weight of

[12] For modern examples see Dalman 1932: 3.116–19, pls. 27–28; and Avitsur 1972: 214.

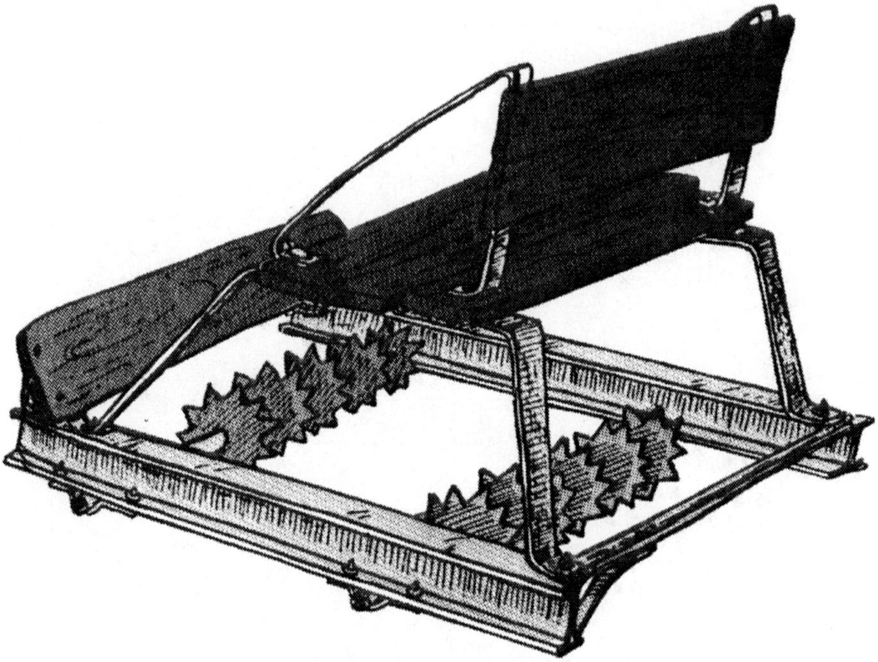

Fig. 12. A modern wheel-thresher

its different components.[13] The grain, which is the heaviest, falls down first, then the straw (*qaš*), the small pieces of straw (*teben*), and finally the chaff (*mōṣ*). The result is that each of the components of the mixture falls in a different place. This activity is called in the OT *lizrôt*, 'to winnow' (Jer 4:11). Sometimes, if there was a proper wind, winnowing took place at night (Ruth 3:2).

The next activity in the process of grain cleaning is *lĕhābēr*, 'to cleanse' (Jer 4:11), also done with the help of the wind and with a wooden shovel, *raḥat* (Isa 30:24; Dalman 1932: 3. 121–23). Using this tool enables the worker not only to continue the process of cleaning-by-throwing but also to collect the grain into a heap, *ᶜărēmâ* (Hag 2:16; Neh 13:15; Ruth 3:7; Cant 7:3).

The final cleaning of the grain was done with sieves. Two kinds of sieves are mentioned in the OT, *kĕbārâ* (Amos 9:9) and *nāpâ* (Isa 30:28). The first sieve has large holes and is used by moving it sideways and in a circular manner, which distributes the heavy

[13] For illustrations of ancient practices see Gressmann 1927: pl. 167; for modern practices see Dalman 1932: 3. pl. 30.

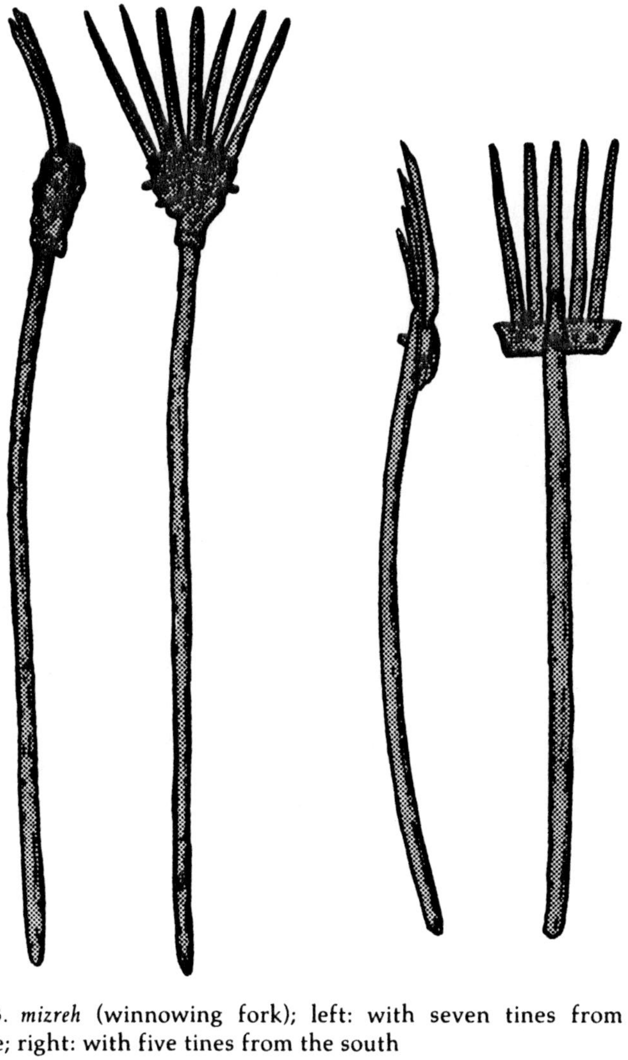

Fig. 13. *mizreh* (winnowing fork); left: with seven tines from Upper Galilee; right: with five tines from the south

particles, such as small stones, to the sides while the grain falls through the middle (Amos 9:9; Broshi 1962: 11).[14] The second type of sieve has small holes and is used by moving it up and down. This motion lets the small particles fall through the holes while the grain is left inside the sieve (Encyclopaedia Biblica 1962: 1017; Avitsur 1972: 214). The final product, the clean grain, is termed in the OT *bār* (Jer 23:28; Joel 2:24).

[14] For different types of sieves used in cleansing grain see Avitsur 1976: fig. 82.

Fig. 14. Winnowing (Tomb of Nakht, 18th Dynasty)

Observations made at the threshing floor at the end of the nineteenth and the beginning of the twentieth century show that the amount of *bār* produced there was 50–60 kg wheat per dunam, 50–70 kg barley, 35–40 kg legumes, and about 20 kg sesame (Avitsur 1972: 214). In comparison to the yield of the same crops today, it is very low, but it is probably similar to the yield of field crops in OT times, before new hybrid species were introduced. Out of the *bār* at the threshing floor the farmer was supposed to pay taxes and make donations to the Levites and the cult centers (Num 15:20; 18:27, 30; Deut 15:14). Measuring the grain is reflected in two inscriptions dated to the Iron Age. Line 5 in the Gezer Manual reads *yrḥ qṣr wkl*, which is interpreted 'a month of harvesting (wheat) and measuring (grain)'. The second inscription, the letter from Meṣad Ḥashavyahu, states, *wyqṣr ᶜbdk wykl*, 'and your servant harvested and took measure' (lines 4–5), and *kʾšr kl* [ᶜ] *bdk ʾt qṣr*, 'when your servant measured his harvest' (line 6).[15]

[15] For a discussion and bibliography see chap. 4.

After the completion of winnowing and sieving, the farmer had several products: *bār*, *qaš*, *teben*, and *mōṣ*. Each of them was saved for a different purpose. The use of *bār*, 'clean grain', is self-evident.[16] The use of the other products is described below.

Qaš, 'straw'. This category includes the larger parts of the stalk, which are lighter than the grain but heavier than the other particles created by threshing. In the OT, *qaš* is used symbolically to describe the insignificance of people or things (Isa 40:24; 41:2; Ps 83:14; Job 41:20–21). The daily use of *qaš* (or *ḥăšaš*, Isa 5:24; 33:11) was for kindling (Isa 5:24; 33:11; 47:14; Nah 1:10; Obad 18), and when cut into smaller pieces, *teben*, as described in Exod 5:12, it was used as binder in brick making.

Teben, 'small pieces of straw'. This product of the *gōren* was a direct result of threshing or was produced later intentionally by cutting *qaš* into small pieces (Exod 5:12). *Teben* was used as binder in mud-brick making (Exod 5:7, 12) as can be seen from finds at many sites in Eretz-Israel.[17] *Teben* was also the main component of fodder, *mispôʾ* (Gen 42:27; 43:24; especially Gen 24:25, 32; Judg 19:19). Animals were served it plain (Isa 11:7; 65:25) or mixed, *bĕlîl* (Job 6:5), with barley (1 Kgs 5:8). *Teben* was kept in heaps, *matbēn* (Isa 25:10). In the OT *teben* was sometimes used figuratively to depict the ineffectuality of worthlessness of people and things (Job 21:18; 41:19; Jer 23:28).

Mōṣ, 'chaff'. This term describes the smallest and lightest particles of the *mĕdūšâ*, 'threshed material'. It includes glumes, awns, and little pieces of leaves. One of the uses of chaff was for cushioning around grain-filled storage jars.[18] In the OT the term was also used figuratively (Isa 17:13; 29:5; 41:15–16; Hos 13:13; Ps 1:4; 35:5; Job 21:18).

After the completion of all *gōren*-related activities, the *bār* had to be transported to storage facilities, where it was kept for daily use until the grain of the next harvest was available.

[16] See the section Cereals in chap. 8.

[17] For an example see Stager 1975: 54, where he points out that some of the finds were "remnants of medium to well-fired mudbrick material made from calcic field clay and bonded together with much dung and chaff binder. The latter was produced from either wheat or barley straw."

[18] As I observed during the Gezer excavations in 1972, Field IV; Late Bronze Age.

7

Grain & Food Storage

Ingathering field crops and fruit was followed by storing the produce and products for future use in facilities which had to protect the foodstuffs from spoilage and wastage by humidity and dampness or by insects and rodents. To this end, a variety of methods were employed both by private individuals and by social organizations (such as the state and cult centers). Grain could be stored in bulk or in jars, and to protect it from spoilage the ancient farmer, after putting aside next year's seed, heated it "to a high enough temperature to kill the germ and so prevent germination during storage" (Dimbleby 1967: 83–84).[1] Other agricultural produce was stored in sealed jars.

Storage facilities used in antiquity can be categorized by (*a*) method of construction, (*b*) method of storage, and (*c*) inferred ownership. This results in the following divisions: (*a*) subterranean versus above-ground installations, (*b*) storage in bulk versus storage in containers, and (*c*) private, i.e., owned by an individual or a family, versus public, i.e., owned by a social organization such as the state or temple.

The study of storage facilities is seriously hampered by the confusion of terms used to describe these structures. Excavators use terms such as grain-pit, silo, granary, etc., to describe the same type of structure.[2] The situation is further complicated by excavation reports that give only a name to an installation and do not provide a description. In an effort to organize the available material and facilitate better understanding of the subject in the future, I propose the following terminology to be used in identifying the different types of storage facilities in antiquity.

[1] See also Helbaek 1963: 181. Heating the grain before threshing made the removal of hulls easier, and grain heated before storage was easier to grind into flour. (Dimbleby 1967: 83–84).

[2] See, for example, Ben-Dor 1955, where different types of storage facilities are presented under one term, *ʾăsām*.

A. Subterranean Facilities
   1. Grain-pit: a small stone-lined or plastered pit, for storage of grain in bulk, located in close relationship to a domestic area or dwelling
   2. Silo: a large stone-lined or plastered pit where grain was stored in bulk, located in close relationship to a public area or structure
   3. Cellar: a subterranean room used for storage, usually in containers, of grain and other foodstuffs

B. Above-ground Facilities
   1. Granary: a structure (sometimes semisubterranean) where grain was stored mostly in bulk, located in or near a public area
   2. Storehouse: a freestanding building, in a public area, where grain and other foodstuffs were stored in containers
   3. Public storeroom: a room in a public building where grain and other foodstuffs were stored in containers
   4. Private storeroom: either an exterior or an interior room of a private dwelling in which grain and other foodstuffs were stored in containers

To clarify these definitions examples of each group are presented below to illustrate each category.

Subterranean Facilities

Grain-pits

The most ubiquitous storage facility is the grain-pit. This type of structure has been discovered at both southern and northern sites. One southern site is Tell Beit Mirsim, where grain-pits were used during most of its history, from the Middle Bronze Age through the Iron Age. Stratum B (Iron I) yielded a large number of grain-pits, some of which were rectangular (Albright 1943b: pls. 2, 47:a–c). Pottery recovered from the Stratum B pits shows that they were used during three phases: B1, pre-Philistine; B2, contemporary with Philistine pottery; B3, post-Philistine (Albright 1932: 53–70). Albright concluded that the large number of grain-pits inside the settlement indicated that this border town was not very secure from outside threats (Albright 1943b: 1–4). A smaller number of grain-pits were dated to Stratum A (Iron II; Albright 1943b: pl. 3). The smaller number of grain-pits is attributed by Albright to the fact that at this period the town was well fortified and heavily populated, and the more secure conditions may have allowed grain to be stored outside the town or in aboveground facilities (Albright 1943b: 39–41).

Other southern sites also yielded large numbers of grain-pits that were constructed and used throughout the Iron Age. Some of these sites are Beth-shemesh (Grant 1934: 5, 61; Grant and Wright 1939: 55), Tell en-Nasbeh (McCown 1947: 136, 210–11, 215, figs. 52A–52B), Tell Nagila (Amiran and Eitan 1964: 202), Arad (Aharoni and Amiran 1963: 223), Beth-zur (Sellers et al. 1968: 8, 27, pl. 13b), and Tell Halif (Seger and Borowski 1977: fig. on p. 162).

Grain-pits were discovered in many northern sites. At Shechem an Iron II house was found where "the main living room of the house was Room 7 with its silo. A short corridor, Room 8, led to the kitchen area of the building, Room 11, where a smaller and typical saddle quern and grinding stone for flour were found in place together with a small silo" (Toombs and Wright 1963: 39). Similar storage facilities were found in Dothan in a domestic area adjacent to the administrative building in Area L. The domestic area included several houses dated to the eighth to seventh century B.C.E. "In connection with these houses a number of underground stone-lined storage chambers were uncovered as well as a plaster lined one, cylindrical in shape, with vertical sides and a flat base, five feet in diameter and over three feet deep" (1.55 m × 1 m; Free 1959: 24).

The close proximity of these installations to dwelling areas, where domestic activities like cooking took place, indicates that they were constructed to allow ready access to a family's store of grain for their daily needs. This is demonstrated most clearly by the evidence from Shechem, Tell en-Nasbeh, Dothan, Tell Beit Mirsim (Stratum B), and Tell Halif, where grain-pits are closely associated with dwellings.[3]

Silos

Structures identified here by the term *silo* are grain-pits which are usually larger than the ones associated with dwellings and which are in close proximity to public areas and structures. They are either stone-lined or plastered and were used to store large quantities of grain in bulk.

[3] Although the existence of grain-pits is recorded in many excavation reports, the relationship of these structures to dwellings is, in most cases, not specified; see, for example, Ben Tor 1977a: 26, where the excavator reports the uncovering of dwellings and grain-pits, but does not specify the relationship between the two. The accompanying plan (p. 24) is not very helpful. Recent excavations at Izbet Ṣarṭah (near Aphek) further clarify the relationship between grain-pits and private dwellings; see Kochavi 1977: 11, fig. 2; *BAR* 1978: plan on p. 26, photograph on p. 27.

The earliest Iron Age silo was discovered at Beth-shemesh. The total depth of this silo from the capstone to bedrock is 5.7 m, and its diameter is 7.5 m along the north-south axis and ca. 6.5 m east-west (Grant and Wright 1939: 69–71, pls. 14:4–5, 15:1). It is not clear whether the silo was built during the time of Stratum IIa (beginning of the tenth century B.C.E.) or IIb (the latter part of the tenth century B.C.E.), but it was used through the eighth century B.C.E. The silo was constructed next to the "residency," a large building resembling a palace. In the interpretation of the finds Grant and Wright say that "Beth-shemesh was a center of one of the districts of Solomon's fiscal system (1 Kgs 4:9) and, since the silo was built about the time of his reign, there is a possibility that it is to be connected with the fiscal system. In that case, the 'residency' might be that of the district governor. But for such supposition there is no proof" (Grant and Wright 1939: 71).

Another silo was discovered at Hazor in Area G Stratum VII (ninth century B.C.E., House of Omri). The silo was not completely cleared, but from the excavated portion it appears to be rectangular and 5 m deep. Its walls are lined with fieldstones. The part excavated was covered with a thick layer of ash, probably caused by the Assyrian destruction in 732 B.C.E. (Yadin 1958: 7; Yadin et al. 1961: pl. 85:1–2). The silo was constructed next to the city wall where a small gate facing the northern fields was found. The excavators theorize that grain harvested in these fields and threshed outside the city was brought directly to this silo (Yadin 1958: 7).

The largest example of a silo from the monarchic period was excavated at Megiddo, Stratum III (ca. 733/2–630 B.C.E.). Silo 1414 was at least 7 m deep. Its capacity was no less than 450 cubic meters, about 12,800 bushels (Lamon and Shipton 1939: 66–68, figs. 72, 77). "Its pair of winding stairs, presumably one for entrance and the other for exit, is unique. The entire construction, including the floor, was of uncoursed rubble, and the existence of chaff and some grain in the chinks between the stones indicates that the rough surface had not been plastered" (Lamon and Shipton 1939: 66).[4]

The large size of the silos described above suggests that they were not owned by an individual but by a large social organization, such as the state. Although the context of the silo at Megiddo is not clear, its

[4] Recently, four silos were discovered at Kadesh-barnea. The largest is approximately 5 m in diameter and 2.3 m in depth. The smallest is approximately 1.8 m in diameter. All are built of rough-hewn stones and small pebbles. They are dated to the eighth to seventh century B.C.E. (Cohen 1982: 71). Their location within the site and their size suggest very strongly that they were public structures.

size indicates that it did not belong to an individual. It might have belonged to the state and have been used to store grain produced in the royal estates or paid as taxes. The silo at Hazor is located in what seems to have been, during Stratum VII, a public area (Yadin 1958: 7), and it seems to have had a public function and ownership. A similar picture appears at Beth-shemesh, where the silo was built next to the "residency" (Grant and Wright 1939: 71). This area was, at least partially, public. Therefore, on the basis of size and location I suggest that these structures were the property of institutions and should be distinguished from grain-pits by the term *silos*.

Cellars

Cellars are not well attested in archaeological excavations. One of the reasons that archaelogists have not been able to identify more structures as cellars is the difficulty in excavating them properly and determining the relationship between the cellar and the building to which it belongs. This difficulty is exemplified by results from the excavations at Tell Beit Mirsim, where a structure identified as a "cellar" was uncovered in Area SE23B-8. Although Albright called the structure a cellar, he could not determine any relationship between it and any other building (Albright 1943b: 5). Because of the detached situation of the "cellar," Albright could not date it properly and oscillated between A1 (ninth century B.C.E.) and B3 (tenth century B.C.E.).

A cellar dated to the late Iron Age was discovered at Beer-sheba (Stratum II) and was designated a "basement house." According to Aharoni, the structure probably belonged to the local cult center which was dismantled during Hezekiah's reforms (Aharoni 1975: 158–63; Herzog 1977: 169–70).

A clearly identified cellar was excavated at Tell Jemmeh, where it forms a part of the Assyrian Building dated to the seventh century B.C.E. A preliminary report concludes that "it now appears certain that rooms A–F were partially subterranean. Fragments of large storage jars continue to predominate in the filling of the rooms, suggesting that they served as basement storerooms" (Van Beek 1974: 139). As for the building to which the cellar belongs, the excavators conclude that "the combination of barrel vaulting and imported Palace Ware establishes this structure as built and occupied by the Assyrians. It seems to have served as the residence of an important official, perhaps an Assyrian military governor" (Van Beek 1972: 245).

It is impossible to draw far-reaching conclusions on the basis of one clearly identified cellar, but the evidence from Tell Jemmeh suggests that this type of storage facility was used in a large building probably housing a state representative, such as a governor. The lack of further evidence for cellars can be atttributed, as I mentioned earlier, to the difficulty in excavating such structures; it may also, of course, be due to the fact that cellars were not common in Eretz-Israel. If the "basement house" at Beer-sheba is indeed a cellar, it is very possible that this type of storage facility was used in Eretz-Israel only in arid or semi-arid regions.

Above-ground Facilities

Granaries

Granaries, some of which are semisubterranean, were used in Egypt as early as the Old Kingdom. A wall painting dated to the Sixth Dynasty (2350–2200 B.C.E.) from Sakkarah shows a row of tall structures with rounded tops and with doors at the bottom for removing the grain (Pritchard 1954: 260, fig. 90). Another painting, found in a tomb dated to the Twelfth Dynasty (ca. 1991–1786 B.C.E.) at Beni Hasan in Egypt, shows a building without a door, with only a row of windows below the roof. Workers are seen climbing exterior steps leading to a flat roof, where they empty the grain. Similar granaries were used during the New Kingdom (Ben-Dor 1955: 478–80, fig. 1). One such example is an artistic representation from Thebes dated to ca. 1460 B.C.E. It shows a tall building with a domed roof. The roof has a window for the reception of grain. Workers carrying the grain in bags climb exterior ladders. Each granary has a door at the bottom for removing the grain (Gressmann 1927: pl. 177). Recently, a granary made of four cylindrical chambers was discovered at Bir el-ᶜAbd in northern Sinai. Each chamber is 3.8 m in diameter, and the brick walls are preserved to a height of ca. 1.8 m. Some walls still have bricks projecting out which "probably served as sills for doors to the top of the silos" (Oren 1973: 112).[5] The granary was part of an Egyptian fort built during the fourteenth century B.C.E. and used during the reign of Seti I (Oren 1973: 113).

The earliest archaelogical remains in Eretz-Israel possibly belonging to a granary were found at Beth-yeraḥ, where a large building (40 m × 30 m) dated to EB III was discovered at the northern edge of the tell. Within the building along the walls, in a cobbled floor 10 m wide, were found the foundations of ten stone circular structures, each

[5] Although the excavator uses the term *silo*, I present the structure here under the heading Granaries following the definition above. The structure was partially subterranean and in three chambers grain was stored in jars.

Fig. 15. Storing grain in granaries (Time of Thutmoses III, ca. 1460)

divided by walls into four quarters. It has been suggested that these are the foundations of a large granary similar to a stone model found on the Island of Melos (Negev 1972: 49; Hestrin 1975: 256–58). The size of the Beth-yeraḥ structure eliminates the possibility of its being owned by an individual.

A partially subterranean granary dated to MB IIA (Stratum XXI, ca. 1800 B.C.E.) was discovered at Gezer. The structure has a substantial stone foundation supporting a mud-brick superstructure, the walls of which are sealed with a coat of plaster up to 15 cm thick for protection against moisture and rodents (Dever 1972: 160; Dever 1975: 438). Another granary found at Gezer is dated to the Philistine period (mid-twelfth century B.C.E.), but no details are available yet (Dever 1975: 439). This structure is the only presently known granary dated to the Iron Age in Eretz-Israel.

Several granaries dated to the Persian period were found by Petrie at Tell Jemmeh (1928: 8–9, pl. 13). On the western edge of this site Petrie uncovered seven large circular mud-brick granaries which succeeded the AB building of the Iron Age. Three additional granaries were found along the southern edge of the tell. The recent Smithsonian expedition recovered another such structure. It is 2.2 m deep and has a diameter of 6.2 m. Two doorways, on the southeast and the northwest, lead into the granary. Steps led inside and down from the doorways to a high platform projecting out from the wall. Near the doorways, a portion of a conical dome may be preserved (Van Beek 1972: 245; Amiran and Van Beek 1975: 548). Petrie also found steps leading into the granaries located on the western ridge and remains of a conical superstructure. From representations of Assyrian buildings he reconstructed the shape of the granary (Petrie 1928: pl. 14) and its capacity (5,900 cubic feet), and suggested that the amount of grain stored in all the granaries found by him could supply 35,000 men for two months (Petrie 1928: 9).

The date of the recently discovered granary has not been fixed yet. Preliminary reports indicate that stratigraphically the structure is later than the sixth century B.C.E. and probably belongs to the fourth or even the early third century. The latest pottery shows that the granary was in use in the late third or early second century B.C.E. (Van Beek 1972: 245). In light of this evidence, Petrie's dating of the other granaries has to be reexamined.

Looking at the evidence pertaining to installations presented here as granaries, one notes their absence during the time of the monarchy. Although it is possible that continued archaeological work will uncover such structures, it seems more plausible that during the time of the monarchy other types of storage facilities were more popular. It should be pointed out, however, that the size, location, and construction methods of the granaries mentioned above suggest that granaries did not belong to individuals but to a large social organization, such as the state.

Storehouses

Several major sites in Eretz-Israel have yielded large structures dated to the monarchic period which are identified here as *storehouses*. These structures consist of a series of long and narrow rooms with thick walls and deep foundations. Such buildings were uncovered at Jericho (tenth century B.C.E.), Lachish (tenth century), Megiddo (tenth century), Beth-shemesh (first half of the tenth century), Tell Jemmeh (end of tenth/beginning of ninth century), Tell en-Nasbeh (ninth century), and Tell Beit Mirsim ("scarcely later than the ninth century"; Albright 1943b: 22–24). The appearance of these buildings in Eretz-Israel coincides with Solomon's reign, and their construction can be attributed in part to his economic reforms (1 Kgs 4:7–19). The form of the building "is related to their function as storehouses: thick double walls and deep foundations were necessary to insulate as far as possible against moisture, and the long narrow design, like that of modern American farm granaries, helped to keep grain from mouldering" (Albright 1943b: 24). Albright identifies these buildings with the OT *miskěnôt*, from the Akkadian *maškanâti*, 'threshing floors, granaries'; the Hebrew term appears in 1 Kgs 9:19, where Solomon's building activity is described.

The efficiency of this type of building for storage was recognized in later historical periods; e.g., similar storage facilities are found at Herodian Masada (Yadin 1966: pls. 90, 92, 99, 106).

Another type of Iron Age storehouse, this one unique to Eretz-Israel, can be called the *pillared storehouse* because of the characteristic monoliths used in its construction. Structures belonging to this group were found at Tell el-Ḥesi (Bliss 1894: 90–98), Tell Qasîleh (Mazar 1964: 11, fig. 6), Tell Abu Hawam (Hamilton 1934–35: 8–10, pls. 4, 7:1–2), Megiddo (Guy 1931: 37; Lamon and Shipton 1939: 32–47), Hazor (Yadin et al. 1958: 11–14, pls. 8–9, 172; Yadin et al. 1960: 6–9, pls. 200–201), Beer-sheba (Herzog 1973: 23–30), and other sites. Each of these buildings is an elongated rectangular structure with thick exterior walls. The interior is divided by two rows of stone pillars into three long rooms (Herzog 1973: fig. 1; pls. 10: 1–2; 11:1, 3; 91–92). Excavators have assigned various functions to these buildings, ranging from the cultic to stabling horses. Recent studies of the three structures uncovered at Beer-sheba reveal that they served as storage facilities for various foodstuffs. A variety of provisions—e.g., flour, oil, wine—were stored in different kinds of vessels in the side rooms (Herzog 1973: pls. 11:2; 12). The central room served as a passageway for the carrying in and out of the goods (Herzog 1973: 29). The Beer-sheba storehouses were adjacent to the city gate and in the city wall. Their location suggests that they served "the needs of the administrative unit (civilian or military) for which they were intended" (Herzog 1973: 29, pl. 84). These structures should also be identified with the *miskěnôt* mentioned in the OT in connection with the building activities of Solomon and Hezekiah. Their function is described well in 2 Chr 32:27–29; "And Hezekiah had very great riches and honor; and he made for himself . . . storehouses [*miskěnôt*] . . . for the yield of grain, wine, and oil."

At the conclusion of his study of pillared storehouses, Herzog states that they were unique to ancient Israel. "Their original design should definitely be linked with the system of tax collection and distribution for which evidence is found in the Samaria, Arad and Beer-sheba ostraca" (1973: 30).

The commodities in storehouses were kept in jars and other vessels, as is evident from the remains found in several of these buildings. Remains from Dothan show that, at least in some of the storehouses, the jars were stacked one on top of the other. At this site a large storehouse (Area L) was excavated yielding large quantities of broken jars of the same type ("Dothan jars No. 7"; Free 1958: 12, fig. 1) strewn in the destruction layer dated to the time of the siege of Samaria in 724–721 B.C.E. In one room four whole jars were discovered, and "we found that the base of one jar would fit into the mouth of another jar . . . , which would explain how they were stacked and why there was such a concentration of them in relatively small areas" (Free 1958: 12). According to Free it seems that the storehouse had more than one story, a feature which is not unique to Dothan. The remains from Dothan show that not only grain was stored in this storehouse but also olives. The same was true at Beer-sheba, judging from the different types of vessels used there for storage (Aharoni 1973: pl. 12).

In the discussion of the Dothan jars, Free says that "the presence of these standard measures suggests that this was a center for collecting taxes in wheat, oil, and other commodities" (Free 1960: 7). Although this assumption might be true, it seems to me that the use of standard-sized containers was to facilitate the distribution of stored commodities rather than the collection of taxes. The use of standard-sized containers would enable quick dispatching of commodities to the military and other administrative functionaries. It is very possible that tax collecting and distributing supplies were carried out not only in the same city but under the same roof.

Storehouses found in Hazor, Beer-sheba, and Arad were located near the city gate in the public domain. This location suggests the public nature of these structures, which is reenforced by their large size. The storehouse at Dothan, although architecturally different, exhibits the same characteristics of location and size which identify it as a public structure.

Public Storerooms

Storage of foodstuffs in storerooms is similar to storage in storehouses with two exceptions. Storerooms are smaller and are not freestanding but attached to other, large structures. In most cases storerooms were attached to structures identified as having a civic or religious function, e.g., palaces and cult centers, and that is why these facilities should be considered to have been owned by royalty or institutions.

Storerooms dating to Iron I were discovered at Beth-shan. Here, a large house surrounded on all sides by storerooms (House 1500; Level

VI) was excavated (James 1966: 6). The excavators postulate that the house was that of the Egyptian commander of Rameses III's "northern command" and that the structure served as his headquarters (James 1966: 13).

Another example of storerooms (referred to by the excavator as "bins") attached to a large building, probably having a civic function, was uncovered at Dothan in Area L. The building and the storerooms are briefly described in preliminary reports (Free 1958: 12; Free 1959: 122–23; Free 1960: 7; Ussishkin 1975: 339). The size and shape of the rooms cannot be discerned from these reports. A tenth century date was assigned to the construction of the rooms. They were in use until the destruction of the city in 724–721 B.C.E.

From Ta^{c}annek comes an example of a storeroom attached to a cultic structure where "jars of grain and a variety of complete vessels tend to indicate that Room 1 is associated with the cultic structure the destruction of which is dated to the 10th century B.C.E., probably caused by Shishak in 918" (Lapp 1964: 28, 73). No details of the size and shape of the room are given.

Storerooms attached to a cultic building were discovered at Tell Dan adjacent to the Israelite *bāmâh*, the construction of which is dated by the excavator to the tenth century B.C.E. This complex, probably built by Jeroboam I, with several later modifications, was used during the Iron Age until the final destruction of the city (Biran 1974: 40–43). Here, a series of rooms constructed of undressed basalt stones was attached to the northern side of the complex. These rooms served the cult precinct. Unfortunately, no additional information concerning these storerooms is available.

A storehouse with attached storerooms was found at Samaria. This structure consists of two elongated rooms and several smaller square rooms. It was attached to the palace of the kings of Israel in the upper city, which was built by Omri. Sixty-three ostraca were found in the building (Crowfoot, Kenyon, and Sukenik 1942: 5–7). It has been suggested that the ostraca are records of commodities brought in as taxes.[6] If this suggestion is correct, it is possible that the building served as a center for tax collection. The commodities mentioned in the ostraca are wine and oil, both of which were stored in jars in storehouses and storerooms. The presence of records of oil and wine in a storeroom is not unexpected, since such a structure was a repository for these commodities.

[6] See the section Private Land in chap. 3. It seems that some of the ostraca from Arad and Beer-sheba are also receipts for taxes (Aharoni 1966a: 1–7; 1966b: 14–16, fig 1; 1968: 2–32; 1970: 16–42; 1973: 15).

Table 4. Storage facilities used in antiquity

PUBLIC		PRIVATE	
Subterranean	Above-ground	Subterranean	Above-ground
Silo	Granary	Grain-pit (*ʾāsām*)	
Cellar	Store-house (*miskĕnôt*)		Storage-room
	Store-room		

Private Storerooms

The facility identified here as *private storeroom* is one which is a part of a dwelling unit, as opposed to a *public storeroom*, which is attached to a public building. During the Iron Age the most common dwelling structure was the "four-room house," used extensively in the north and in the south (Shiloh 1970, 1973, 1978). Although Shiloh does not specify in his studies which part of the house was used for storage, excavations at several sites revealed that certain rooms in the Israelite house were indeed used for storage of agricultural produce (Dothan 1955: 32; Beit Arieh 1973: 34–35; Aharoni, Fritz, and Kempinski 1975: 107–8). Sometimes, part of the private storeroom was used for other activities, such as grinding flour and cooking (Seger and Borowski 1977: 163).

Food was stored in jars in private storerooms. I assume that the agricultural produce kept in these rooms was for the daily use of the families residing in these houses.

From a cultural perspective, the two important defining characteristics of storage facilities are (1) size (large or small) and (2) location (in a public or a domestic area). When storage facilities are classified on the basis of these two categories, a dichotomy is formed. The large facilities are located in areas exhibiting a public character, and I assume that these were owned and operated by organizations such as the state or a cult center. The smaller facilities are located near or within structures identified as private dwellings; these storage areas were privately owned. Table 4 summarizes these observations.

There are several terms in the OT interpreted as signifying storage facilities: *mĕgûrâ* (Hag 2:19); *mammĕgūrôt* (Joel 1:17); *ʾăsuppîm* (Neh 12:25; 1 Chr 26:15, 17); *ʾăsāmîm* (Deut 28:8; Prov 3:10); *ʾôṣārôt* (Joel 1:17; Neh 12:44; 1 Chr 27:25, 28; 2 Chr 11:11); *miskĕnôt* (1 Kgs 9:19; 2 Chr 8:4, 6; 16:4; 17:12; 32:28). The last word has been identified as 'storehouses'. From context it seems that *ʾăsāmîm* refers to 'grain-pits'.[7] The other terms may designate public facilities; the evidence does not allow specific definitions.

[7] The use of the 2d. m. sg. possessive suffix with this noun suggests that it is a storage facility belonging to an individual, the most common of which are the grain-pits.

Part III
Cultigens & Cultivars

8
Field Crops

The domestication of field crops took place long before the Iron Age. The biblical farmer had a large variety of domesticated crops to choose from. This chapter attempts to identify those crops cultivated in Eretz-Israel during the Iron Age. This study is based on terminology used in the OT and organic remains recovered in archaeological excavations. It should be pointed out that only recently have archaeologists dealing with historical periods started actively searching for and retrieving plant remains. Since the interest in plant remains dated to historical periods is fairly recent, the information available regarding the Iron Age is meager.

Field crops cultivated during the Iron Age in Eretz-Israel are presented here in four groups: (*a*) cereals, (*b*) legumes, (*c*) spices,[1] and (*d*) other crops. In each group, where applicable, crops are presented in the following order: first, crops mentioned in the OT and represented in Iron Age archaeological samples; second, crops not mentioned in the OT but represented in Iron Age archaeological samples; third, crops mentioned in the OT but not represented in Iron Age archaeological samples; fourth, crops not mentioned in the OT and not represented in Iron Age archaeological samples but which were probably cultivated during the Iron Age.

Cereals

The domestication of cereals, *dāgān*, took place sometime before 7000 B.C.E. in the Near East and was an important factor in the establishment of permanent villages over a wide arc from Khuzistan in southwest Iran through the Zagros and Taurus mountains, Iraq, Turkey, and southward into Eretz-Israel. Wheat and barley became the major nutritional source, enabling man to make the transition from hunting and gathering to farming. The first domesticated cereals were

[1] I have not included plants for making incense and perfumes since they are beyond the scope of the present study for several reasons: (*a*) most of the finished products were imported; (*b*) production of perfumes was on only a limited scale; (*c*) there are no plant remains.

two-rowed barley, emmer wheat, an einkorn wheat (Harlan and Zohary 1966: 1074–80; Jarman 1972: 16, 25; Dimbleby 1967: 76, 78; Butzer 1971: 211, 235; Flannery 1973: 276). Cereals discovered in excavations of sites in the Near East and Europe dated to periods earlier than the Iron Age belong to the following genera: *Triticum* (wheat), *Hordeum* (barley), *Avena* (oats), *Secale* (rye), *Panicum* (Broom corn millet), *Setaria* (Italian millet), *Echinochloa* (barnyard millet) (Renfrew 1973: 30). Not all of these genera have been discovered in Iron Age contexts in Eretz-Israel, nor are they all mentioned in the OT, suggesting selection on the part of the biblical farmer based on growing conditions and utilization.

There are three stages in cereal ripening, in each of which the grain can be utilized. The first stage is termed in the OT *ʾābîb*. At this stage the plant is still green but the grain has already thickened, and it is possible to separate it from the ear, *šibbōlet*, and eat it raw or parched (Lev 2:14). The second stage is termed *karmel*, when the grain is somewhat harder than *ʾābîb* but is still damp and can grow larger. It is possible to eat *karmel* either raw, parched, or crushed, *gereś karmel* (Lev 2:14). When parched, *karmel* can be preserved for future use (Avitsur 1976: 2–4). The third stage is when the grain is dry and cannot grow larger. It is too hard to be eaten raw and has to be parched, *qālî* (Lev 23:14; Ruth 2:14), or ground to flour. There is no word in the OT for this stage, although it has been suggested that *qālî* is applied to describe this stage (Avitsur 1976: 4). This suggestion should be discarded because biblical references to *qālî* clearly describe parched grain.

The following three sections discuss cereals cultivated during the Iron Age as they are known from OT references and archaeological samples.

Wheat (*Triticum*)

Wheat, *ḥiṭṭâ*/*ḥiṭṭîm*, is one of the seven crops and fruit trees with which Eretz-Israel was blessed (Deut 8:8). It is a winter crop sown, according to the Gezer Manual, during *yrḥw zrᶜ* (end of October to mid-December). Wheat ripens later than barley and, according to the Gezer Manual, was harvested during the sixth agricultural season, *yrḥ qṣr wkl* (end of April to end of May). The time of wheat harvesting is designated in the OT as *qĕṣîr ḥiṭṭîm* (Gen 30:14; Judg 15:1; 1 Sam 6:3; 12:17; Ruth 2:23). The end of wheat harvesting was celebrated at *šābūᶜôt*. The OT regards wheat together with *kussemet* (emmer) as late crops, *ʾăpîlōt* (Exod 9:32).

The genus *Triticum* can be divided into three groups based on the number of chromosomes: (*a*) diploid group (14 chromosomes), (*b*) tetraploid group (28 chromosomes), and (*c*) hexaploid group (42 chromosomes). The diploid group has two hulled species; the tetraploid group has three hulled species, one of which is emmer, and five naked species, one of which is hard wheat (*T. durum* Desf.); the hexaploid group has three hulled species, one of which is spelt, and three naked species, one of which is common (or bread) wheat (*T. aestivum* L. = T. *vulgare* [Vill.] Host.; Renfrew 1973: 40).

It has been suggested by Zgorodsky that *ḥiṭṭâ* / *ḥiṭṭîm* in biblical contexts means *T. vulgare* and that *bār* means *T. durum* (1930: 373–76). As I explained earlier,[2] *bār* is the term used in the OT for the final product of winnowing, the clean grain. Recently, Kislev (1973: 244) has shown on the basis of linguistic, botanical, and archaeological evidence that in biblical times when wheat was mentioned in connection with Eretz-Israel, it meant hard wheat, and when mentioned in a Mesopotamian context, it meant soft (or bread) wheat.

Although the best conditions for a high yield of wheat are a comparatively high mean winter temperature and an annual rainfall of 500–700 mm (Renfrew 1973: 65), it can be cultivated in regions where the annual rainfall is above 225 mm and the growing season is longer than 90 days (Liphschitz and Waisel 1973: 36). The distribution of rainfall is of great importance, and "moderately heavy rain in early summer when the shoots are in full growth and ears developing is most beneficial, but heavy autumn and winter rains greatly retard the development of the plant and result in small grain yield" (Renfrew 1973: 65). Therefore we understand why a timely rainfall (Deut 11:14; 28:12) was important enough to be one of the rewards given in return for observing the covenant.

Wheat depletes the soil more than any other crop. It grows best in stiff clay loams which are well drained, hold and conserve water, and provide favorable conditions for the formation of nitrate, which is essential for the production of protein in the wheat grain (Renfrew 1973: 66). The amount and distribution of rainfall together with soil conditions limit the area in Eretz-Israel where wheat is cultivated to the coastal valleys, the Valley of Jezreel, the Upper Jordan Valley, and the Beth-shan Valley. In the northern Negev, wheat does well only in rainy years, which are not frequent (Zohary 1958a).

Wheat was used for bread and other baked goods (Exod 29:2), for porridge (Ezek 4:9),[3] and was eaten parched (Lev 23:14) and raw (2 Kgs 4:42), depending on its state of ripeness. Grinding the grain for flour was done with a mortar, *mĕdōkâ* (Num 11:8), and pestle or with

[2] Chap. 6, under Winnowing.

[3] Although Ezekiel is commanded to take different types of grains and legumes, put them in a vessel, and make *leḥem*, 'bread', it is very likely that the prophet made

grinding-stones, *rēḥayim.*[4] Many grinding-stones have been found in domestic and public areas dated to the Iron Age.[5] Good-quality flour is referred to in the OT as *qemaḥ sōlet* (Gen 18:6) or *sōlet* (Exod 20:2; Lev 24:5). Another type of flour, *hqmḥ hrʾšn*, 'the first flour', is mentioned in a sixth century B.C.E. ostracon from Arad. This phrase could mean flour either of "superior quality, or of an earlier harvest or consignment" (Aharoni 1966a: 3). A by-product of grinding and sifting flour is semolina (Arabic *smeed*), a jar of which was found in Beth-shemesh in an early Iron Age context (Grant 1931: 36). This might have been used in making *ripôt* (2 Sam 17:19; Prov 27:22), which is according to Avitsur (1976: 4) the Arabic *burghul* (bulgur).

Several sites have yielded samples of wheat in Iron Age contexts:

1. Carbonized wheat was found at Afula in strata dated to Iron I (twelfth to eleventh century B.C.E.; Zaitschek 1955: 71).

2. One grain of wheat, probably of a naked variety, was found at Khirbet Abū Ṭabaq in an Iron II context (Stager 1975: 75).

3. At Lachish in Iron Age contexts, more wheat was found than any other cereal. In Specimen B from a room destroyed ca. 700 B.C.E., a large quantity of *Triticum compactum* Host. (= *T. vulgare* Vill.) was discovered (Helbaek 1958: 309, 314–15). This is a very unusual find since it has been claimed that bread wheat was not cultivated in Iron Age Eretz-Israel (Kislev 1973: 244), but it can be explained as a newly introduced crop or as an imported commodity. There is, of course, the possibility that the sample was misidentified.

4. At Tell Qiri wheat was found in grain-pits dated to Iron II (Ben Tor 1977b).

5. Wheat was found in sixteen samples from Israelite Beer-sheba and in four samples from Israelite Arad (Liphschitz and Waisel 1973: 33–35).

6. A large quantity of charred wheat was found recently in grain-pits in Shiloh (Finkelstein, Bunimowitz and Lederman 1984: 22).

A special place should be devoted in the discussion of wheat to emmer, *Triticum dicoccum* (Schrank) Schuebl., because of the problem concerning its identification and because of its importance in ancient agriculture.

---

porridge, since the term *leḥem* in the OT applies also to food in general; see BDB 1972: 536–37. In addition, a mixture of legumes and cereals would not produce good dough, but would be perfect for porridge.

[4] Grinding-stones and saddle querns were used from the Neolithic period through the Iron Age; turning-stones for grinding were introduced in the Persian or Hellenistic period; for dates and details see Amiran 1956.

[5] Domestic: e.g., Dothan (Free 1960: 8, 10); Shechem (Toombs and Wright 1963: 39); Tell Halif (Seger and Borowski 1977: 163). Public: e.g., Taʿannek (Lapp 1964: 28).

Most scholars have identified biblical *kussemet/kussĕmîm* with *T. spelta* (Zgorodsky 1930: 376; Fohrer 1973: 125; BDB 1972: 493). However, through careful studies of linguistic sources and botanical and paleobotanical evidence, Kislev has demonstrated that the biblical *kussemet* is *T. dicoccum* (1973: 244). Like spelt, emmer is a hulled-grain wheat with two grains in each spikelet (Renfrew 1973: 51). The origin of emmer can be traced to the Israel-Jordan-Lebanon region. Its wild variety, *T. dicoccoides*, can yield up to 500–800 kg of grain per hectare (450–700 pounds per acre; Flannery 1973: 277–78).

Kussemet ripens late, at the same time as *ḥiṭṭâ* (Exod 9:32). The only mention in the OT of how emmer was used is in Ezek 4:9, where the prophet is commanded to use it in porridge. In order to use emmer the glumes have to be separated from the grain. One method of separation after threshing is by soaking the grain in water and then placing it in the sun to dry. When the grain is dry, the glumes can be separated easily (Kislev 1973: 94).

Emmer was cultivated extensively in Eretz-Israel before the Iron Age. Large quantities of emmer were found at the Chalcolithic site of Ḥorvat Beter (Zaitschek 1959: 49–50), in Early Bronze Age samples from Lachish (Helbaek 1958: 310, 313), in a mixed context (Chalcolithic or Roman) at Naḥal Mishmar (Zaitschek 1961: 71), and at other sites. In an Iron Age context, a small quantity of emmer and one einkorn seed (*T. monococcum*) were found in Specimen B at Lachish (ca. 700 B.C.E.; Helbaek 1958: 310, 313–14).

Barley (*Hordeum*)

Barley, *śĕᶜōrâ/śĕᶜōrîm*, is mentioned in Deut 8:8 as one of the crops with which Eretz-Israel was blessed. It is a winter cereal sown at the same time as wheat, but it ripens and is harvested earlier than wheat. Harvesting barley starts around the time of *pessaḥ* (Deut 16:9) and is called in the OT *qĕṣîr śĕᶜōrîm* (2 Sam 21:9; Ruth 1:22; 2:23). In the Gezer Manual, harvesting barley takes place during the fifth period, *yrḥ qṣr śᶜrm* (end of March to end of April).

Cultivated barley can be divided into three species: (*a*) six-row barley, *H. vulgare* L. emend., which has four subgroups; (*b*) two-row barley, *H. distichon* L., which has five subgroups; (*c*) irregular barley, *H. irregulare* Åberg and Weibe, which does not have any recognized subgroups (Renfrew 1973: 68). There are two wild species—two-row *H. spontaneum* C. Koch and six-row *H. agricrithon* Åberg—which can be crossed with the cultivated species (Renfrew 1973: 68; Harlan and Zohary 1966: 1075).

Barley does not tolerate sandy soil and grows best in well-drained, fertile, deep loam soils. It tolerates saline and alkaline conditions, but is sensitive to soil acidity like other cereals. Because of its tolerance of alkalinity, barley can be grown on soils derived from chalk or limestone. This enables barley cultivation in areas where other cereals would not thrive (Renfrew 1973: 80–81). Its tolerance of soil salinity was responsible for the shift to barley monoculture in southern Mesopotamia and extended the life of several city-states in this region for several centuries in the second half of the third millennium (Harlan 1972: 239).

Barley is a short-season crop. Its early maturity allows it to be cultivated in places where the growing season is short because of high altitude, high latitude, or low rainfall (Harlan 1972: 239). Barley seems to have been the main crop wherever rainfall agriculture was pushed to its absolute limit (Flannery 1973: 61).

Barley grain was eaten parched (2 Sam 17:28) and raw (2 Kgs 4:42). It was ground for flour, *qemaḥ śĕᶜōrîm* (Num 5:15), and used in bread, *leḥem śĕᶜōrîm* (Judg 7:13; 2 Kgs 4:42), and in other baked goods, *ᶜūgat śĕᶜōrîm* (Ezek 4:12). In antiquity, as in modern times, barley was used for the production of beer, referred to in the OT as *šēkār* (Isa 29:9), an intoxicating drink mentioned apart from wine. Barley was used in porridge, as suggested by Ezek 4:9 and reported by Pliny in *Natural History* 18.14.74.

Samples of barley were found at several sites:

1. Carbonized barley was found in an Iron I (twelfth to eleventh century B.C.E.) stratum at Afula (Zaitschek 1955: 71).

2. Parts of barley kernels (Stager 1975: 88, 144) and a fragment of barley grain (Stager 1975: 64) were found at Khirbet Abū Ṭabaq, dated to Iron II.

3. Barley remains were found in seven samples from Beer-sheba and four samples from Arad, dated to the Israelite (tenth to eighth century B.C.E.) period (Liphschitz and Waisel 1973: 33, 35).

It should be pointed out that no barley was found in Iron Age strata at Lachish, where it was very prominent—along with emmer—during the Early Bronze Age (Helbaek 1958: 310, 313).[6]

Millet

Millet is a collective term for a group of small-grained cereals belonging to several genera. The three most frequently found types in Europe and Asia in prehistoric contexts are *Panicum miliaceum* L. (broomcorn millet), *Setaria italica* (L.) Beauv. (Italian millet), and *Echinochloa crus-galli* (barnyard millet) (Renfrew 1973: 99–103).

[6] The only type of wheat found in the Early Bronze samples from Lachish was emmer.

According to Zohary (1954b: 649) the most suitable type of millet to be identified with biblical *dōḥan* is *Panicum miliaceum* although recently he suggested the identification of biblical millet with sorghum (Zohary 1982: 77). It is a spring-sown, annual crop with small round seeds. Its growing season is only 60–65 days and must be warm and frost-free. It usually requires only a small amount of water and can be grown in most soils except for coarse sand (Renfrew 1973: 100).

The term *dōḥan* is mentioned only once in the OT (Ezek 4:9), where a symbolic act of food preparation is described. Ezekiel is commanded to prepare food symbolizing the hard times coming to Jerusalem during siege. Having to use *dōḥan* suggests that this crop was locally grown rather than imported.

Rabin (1971: 509) proposes that *pannag* (Ezek 27:17) is a type of millet which originated in India. Rabin asserts an etymological connection between biblical *pannag* and Late Babylonian *pannigu, pennigu,* 'a baked food' (von Soden 1972: 2. 818) and perhaps with Hittite *punniki*, 'a baked food', and Latin *panicum, panicium*, 'millet'.[7]

There are no archaeological remains of millet dated to the Iron Age in Eretz-Israel, but the references to *dōḥan* and *pannag*, if their linguistic identification with millet is correct, suggest the cultivation of millet in Eretz-Israel, at least, at the end of the Iron Age.

Legumes

Several genera and species of legumes have probably been cultivated in the Near East for as long as cereals. Legumes have not been studied as extensively as cereals, but there is sufficient information to determine that they were part of early Neolithic farming. Carbonized remains of legumes have been found in Neolithic and Bronze Age sites in the Near East and Europe (Zohary and Hopf 1973: 887–94). There are two species about which more is known than the others: *Lens culinaris* Medik. (lentils; Zohary and Hopf 1973: 890–92; Renfrew 1973: 113–15) and *Pisum sativum* L. (peas; Zohary and Hopf 1973: 887–90; Renfrew 1973: 110–12). Other species cultivated by prehistoric and Iron Age farmers include *Vicia faba* (broad bean; Zohary and Hopf 1973: 892–93; Renfrew 1973: 107–9); *Vicia ervilia* (bitter vetch; Zohary and Hopf 1973: 893; Renfrew 1973: 116–17); *Cicer arietinum* (chick-peas; Zohary and Hopf 1973: 893; Renfrew 1973: 118–19); and *Lathyrus sativus* L. (grass peas; Renfrew 1973: 117–18).[8]

[7] Paul (1968: 886–87) has suggested that the term *nismān* (Isa 28:25) is a reference to millet, but this is hard to substantiate.

[8] Legumes found in Iron Age Arad have not been specifically identified yet (Liphschitz and Waisel 1973: 33). Several species of legumes were found at Tell Halif and identified, but they have not been published yet.

Legumes have been cultivated for two main reasons: (*a*) as a source of vegetable protein, obtained from the seeds;[9] (*b*) for enrichment of the soil with nitrogen, which is produced by the bacterium *Rhizobium radicicola* present in the root nodules.[10]

The following discussion includes legumes cultivated during the Iron Age in Eretz-Israel as known from OT references and archaeological samples.

Broad Bean (*Vicia faba*)

Broad bean, *pôl*, is a winter crop, although there is a spring-sown variety which tends to be smaller and more spherical in form (Renfrew 1973: 108). Beans do not tolerate low temperature. They flourish best in well-drained, stiff, strong clays (Renfrew 1973: 108–9; Zohary 1967: 151).

Broad beans are mentioned only twice in the OT; in one instance they are mentioned as one of many kinds of food given to David upon his arrival at Maḥanayim during his escape from Absalom: "and wheat and barley and flour and *qālî*, and *pôl* and lentils and *qālî*" (2 Sam 17:27). The fact that *qālî*, 'parched grain', is mentioned with broad beans and lentils suggests that legumes were also eaten parched, like cereals. The second time the crop is mentioned is in Ezek 4:9, a passage discussed above.

It is not yet known when exactly *Vicia faba* was domesticated, but during the Bronze Age the crop was already cultivated over the entire Mediterranean basin (Zohary and Hopf 1973: 892). In Eretz-Israel it has been found in Bronze Age strata at Jericho, Arad, and Beth-shan (Zohary and Hopf 1973: 892). It appears also in a sample from mixed context (Chalcolithic or Roman) at Naḥal Mishmar (Zaitschek 1961: 70–72). Two samples of broad beans were recovered from Iron Age contexts:

1. Carbonized seeds were found in storage jars at Afula (Iron I, twelfth to eleventh century B.C.E.; Zaitschek 1955: 71, 73).
2. One damaged cotyledon of *Vicia faba* L. was found at Lachish in Specimen B from ca. 700 B.C.E. (Helbaek 1958: 312).

Lentil (*Lens culinaris* Medic. = *L. esculenta* Moench)

In the Near East lentils, *ᶜădāšîm*, are usually a winter crop, but they can also be sown in the spring (Renfrew 1973: 114). Only two

[9] For example, *Vicia faba* contains 25.4% protein; *Pisum sativum* contains 22.5% (Renfrew 1973: 193–94).

[10] See the section Crop Rotation in chap. 11.

subspecies are cultivated: ssp. *microsperma* (Baumg.) Bar. and ssp. *macrosperma* (Baumg.) Bar. The former has small to medium-sized pods with small seeds, 3–6 mm in diameter; most prehistoric finds belong to this group. The latter has large flat pods with large seeds, 6–9 mm in diameter; each pod usually contains only one or two seeds (Renfrew 1973: 113–14; Zohary 1967: 153; Zohary 1971a: 96; Zohary 1976: 163).

ᶜădāšîm are mentioned in the OT four times and always in the plural form. According to 2 Sam 23:11–12, lentils were cultivated in fields rather than in gardens, "and the Philistines gathered at *Ḥayyâ* [?] where there was a tract of land [*ḥelqat haśśādeh*] full of lentils." In biblical times lentils were used for making pottage, *nāzîd* (Gen 25:29, 34; Ezek 4:9), and were eaten parched (2 Sam 17:28). From its mention in Gen 25:30 it seems that a red variety was cultivated in Eretz-Israel.

In pre-Iron Age strata, lentils were found in Neolithic Jericho (Hopf 1969: 355) and the Chalcolithic sites of Ḥorvat Beter and Beer Matar (Zaitschek 1959: 71), and other sites.[11]

In Iron Age strata, lentils were found only at Beth-shemesh. Here, charred lentils were found in jars together with other foodstuffs (Grant 1932: 67; Grant and Wright 1939: 129–30).

Bitter Vetch (Kirsenne; *Vicia ervilia* Wild.)

In the Near East, bitter vetch is a winter-sown crop. Since at least Roman times, the seeds of this crop have been utilized mainly for animal food. "It is regarded as a relatively inferior pulse for human consumption, and is consumed only by the very poor or in times of famine" (Zohary and Hopf 1973: 893). Although nothing is known of the use of bitter vetch during the Neolithic and Bronze ages, it has been suggested that the crop was cultivated for human consumption (Renfrew 1973: 116).

There is no word in the OT which can be identified with this crop, but its cultivation during the Iron Age is attested at several sites:

1. *Vicia* sp. was found in two Early Bronze and one Iron Age sample at Lachish (Helbaek 1958: 312).
2. *Vicia ervilia* seeds were found in grain-pits dated to Iron II at Tell Qiri (Ben Tor 1977b).
3. In the Iron I (twelfth to eleventh century B.C.E.) stratum at Afula, many carbonized seeds of Leguminosae were found in storage jars, several thousand of which are bitter vetch (Zaitschek 1955: 71).

[11] Beth-shan (Zaitschek 1959: 52), Lachish (Helbaek 1958: 312), Gezer (personal experience 1972: Field IV), and in a mixed context (Chalcolithic or Roman) at Naḥal Mishmar (Zaitschek 1961: 71).

The finds from Tell Qiri and, especially, Afula indicate that bitter vetch was used for human consumption. At Afula, the bitter vetch seeds were mixed with chick-peas, broad beans, and cereals such as wheat and barley. Since this mixture contains seeds we know were used for human consumption, we can infer that bitter vetch was used similarly. It seems that the mixture must have been intended for pottage.

Chick-pea (*Cicer arientum* L.)

This winter-sown crop is found occasionally at prehistoric sites in the Near East and Europe. Its seeds are larger than those of other legumes, except for broad beans, and each pod contains one or two seeds (Zohary 1967: 153; Renfrew 1973: 119). The chick-pea "is best adapted to warm, semi-arid conditions. . . . It is very drought-resistant and requires cool, dry climate and light well-aerated soils. It cannot tolerate heavy rains, and grows best on heavy clay soils with rough seed bed" (Renfrew 1973: 119).

Chick-pea seeds can be ground, eaten roasted and salted, or used for porridge and soup (Renfrew 1973: 119; Ramanujam 1976: 158). I suggest that the biblical term for this crop is *ḥāmîṣ* (in Arabic *ḥummuṣ*, *ḥummus*), mentioned in Isa 30:24, where the prophet depicts abundance, when the beasts of burden will be fed with crops usually reserved for human consumption: "And the oxen and the young asses that till the soil will eat chick-pea fodder [*bĕlîl ḥāmîṣ*] which was winnowed with a wooden shovel [*raḥat*] and a fork [*mizreh*]."

In Eretz-Israel chick-peas were found in Prepottery Neolithic B Jericho and in Early Bronze Age Lachish, Jericho, and Arad. In Iron Age strata, chick-peas were found in Iron I Afula (Zaitschek 1955: 71–72) and in Iron II Lachish (Helbaek 1958: 311–12).

Pea (*Pisum sativum*)

Peas are cultivated in the Near East as a winter-sown crop. They do not tolerate very cold or high temperatures. They do best with fairly abundant rainfall in well-drained clay loams of limestone origin (Renfrew 1973: 111; Davis 1976: 172).

The cultivation of peas is as old as that of wheat and barley—dating to the Neolithic period (ca. 7000 B.C.E.; Zohary and Hopf 1973: 887). The earliest archaeological finds of this crop in Eretz-Israel are from Prepottery Neolithic B levels at Jericho (Renfrew 1973: 110). Peas were also found at Early Bronze Age Arad (Zohary and Hopf 1973: 889, fig. 1). There is no term in the OT which can be identified with this crop, and there are no indications of the way it was used for food. The assumption is that peas were used like other legumes. Their cultivation during the Iron Age is attested from finds at Khirbet Abū Ṭabaq (Stager 1975: 84–85, 88), Tell Qiri (Ben Tor 1977b), and Tell Halif (Laustrup 1982). All these finds are dated to the Iron II period.

Fenugreek (*Trigonela graecum* L.)

Fenugreek is an annual plant of the Leguminosae family, which includes all the other cultivated legumes. Fenugreek is cultivated in India, the Near East, and Egypt for food and fodder (Helbaek 1958: 311). Fenugreek seeds are highly aromatic and rich in protein, oil, and carbohydrates. In India "they are used as a constituent of curry powders and as a condiment" (Renfrew 1973: 188).

Seeds of this species have been found at Tell Halaf (ca. 4000 B.C.E.) and at Meadi in Egypt (ca. 3000 B.C.E.; Renfrew 1973: 188).

There is no term in the OT which can be identified with this crop. The only reported Iron Age sample from Eretz-Israel was found mixed with cereals in Specimen B from Lachish. "Their occurrence in the Iron Age food may be accidental, but the possibility of seeds having been used as spice cannot be rejected" (Helbaek 1958: 311).

Spices

Several spice plants were grown in Eretz-Israel in antiquity. Three of them are mentioned in the OT and are described below.

Black Cumin (*Nigella sativa* L.)

Black cumin, *qeṣaḥ*, is an annual crop of the Runuculaceae family. Its fruit is a capsule containing small black seeds. It was used by the Greeks and Romans as a condiment and for medical purposes (Zohary 1967: 72–73; Mazar, Dothan, and Dunayevsky 1963: 42, n. 68).

This crop is mentioned in Isa 28:25 and 27, in an allegorical speech describing the farmer and his work. According to Isaiah, *qeṣaḥ* and *kammōn* were sown by hand in a graded field. Both were threshed with a threshing stick rather than by threshing sledge or wheel-thresher.

A carbonized sample of *Nigella* sp. was found at Tell Goren (ᶜEngedi) in Stratum V (end of the Israelite period, 625–582/1 B.C.E.) in a trefoil-mouth jug (Mazar, Dothan, and Dunayevsky 1963: 42).

Cumin (*Cuminum cyminum* L.)

Cumin, *kammōn*, is an annual crop of the Umbelliferae family. It is cultivated for its seeds, which contain an oil with a strong odor, and is used in spicing bread and drinks and for medical purposes (Zohary 1967: 270, 272).

In the OT cumin is mentioned three times in Isa 28:25 and 27, in the allegorical speech describing the farmer and his work. It is evident from this speech that cumin was cultivated by biblical farmers, but there are no reported archaeological samples.

Coriander (*Coriandrum sativum* L.)

Coriander, *gad*, is another crop of the Umbelliferae family, the seeds of which are used as a condiment. Its fruit is dark and round; it is mentioned twice in the OT (Exod 16:31; Num 11:7), in descriptions of the shape of the Manna (Zohary 1954a: 429; Zohary 1967: 274). Today it is not cultivated in Eretz-Israel but grows wild (Zohary 1954a: 429).

There are no reported archaeological samples of coriander from Eretz-Israel.[12]

Other Crops

Flax (*Linum usitatissimum* L.)

Flax, *pištâ/pištîm*, is a winter crop of the Linaceae family. Seeds and seed impressions of flax have been found at Neolithic sites in Europe and the Near East (Renfrew 1973: 120, 122). Throughout its history of cultivation, flax was grown for its fiber and seeds. The seeds were used by prehistoric man for food and oil; flax seeds are 35%–40% oil and about 20% protein (Renfrew 1973: 124). Fibers were used for linen and other products (Zohary 1967: 174).

Biblical references mention flax as raw material in weaving (Deut 22:11; Hos 2:7; Prov 31:13) and making clothes (Lev 13:47–48; Ezek 44:17–18). It was used for belts, *ʾēzôr pištîm* (Jer 13:1), ropes, *pĕtîl pištîm* (Ezek 40:3), and wicks for oil lamps, *pištâ* (Isa 43:17). People engaged in flax processing were called *ʿōbĕdê pištîm* (Isa 19:9).

As a cultivated crop, flax is mentioned in the OT only once—in connection with the plague of hail in Egypt (Exod 9:31). Some scholars argue that flax was not cultivated in Eretz-Israel during biblical times, since the references to its cultivation and processing (Exod 9:31; Isa 19:9) are in connection with Egypt (Zohary 1971b: 636). Zohary does not see any reason to doubt the cultivation of flax in Eretz-Israel during biblical times, but he does not present any supporting evidence (Zohary 1967: 174). In support of Zohary's contention it should be mentioned that 'flax stalks', *pištê ʿēṣ* (Jos 2:6), appear in the story of the Israelite spies sent by Joshua to Jericho, where Rahab "brought

[12] Coriander was found in the tomb of Tut-ankh-Amon and at Late Assyrian Nimrud (Renfrew 1973: 171). It was grown in Eretz-Israel during Mishnaic times (Zohary 1954: 429).

them up to the roof and hid them with the stalks of flax which she had laid in order on the roof." The mention of flax stalks in Jericho supports Zohary's hypothesis, because it is very unlikely that flax was imported to Eretz-Israel in its raw state and not as finished products. Although there is still a question regarding the settlement at Jericho in the Late Bronze and the early Iron Age, the perpetuation of the tradition of having flax stalks in Jericho suggests very strongly that this crop was cultivated there during the Iron Age.

There are no reported archaeological samples of flax seeds and products from the Iron Age in Eretz-Israel. Flax seeds dated by carbon-14 to 2550 B.C.E. ± 250 were found at Tell el-ᶜAreini in Stratum IV (Early Bronze Age; Yeivin 1975: 95), and pieces of flax fabric and remains of a horizontal loom were found in the Chalcolithic stratum of the Cave of the Treasure at Naḥal Mishmar (Negev 1972: 202).

Sesame (*Sesamum indicum*)

Sesame is an annual crop of the Pedaliaceae family. Its seeds have a high oil content (45%–60%), and sesame meal contains more than 20% protein (Nayar 1976: 231). It has been suggested that sesame was cultivated in Syria and Palestine during the Chalcolithic period (Nayar and Mehra 1970: 48; Nayar 1976: 232), but this claim has to be reexamined and substantiated by additional information produced by modern archaeological methodology.

The OT does not have a term which can be clearly identified with this crop. Zgorodsky (1930: 376) proposes that *nismān* (Isa 28:25) is a reference to sesame, but he does not explain why this enigmatic term was replaced by Mishnaic *šumšumîm* and completely forgotten.

Sesame seeds were found in Eretz-Israel only at Beth-shemesh, where two samples were found in Iron Age jars. One sample was of carbonized seeds in a Philistine jar fragment, and the second was mixed with meal (Grant 1934: 59, 79). No additional information concerning these samples is available and their identification is questionable. Even if these samples were properly identified, they cannot be used as direct evidence for the cultivation of sesame in Eretz-Israel, although the possibility remains.

The archaeological and literary evidence relating to the Iron Age in Eretz-Israel shows that the most important field crops were cereals (wheat, barley) and pulses (broad beans, lentils). Other crops belonging to the same families were cultivated but not to the same extent. The cultivation of spices was probably limited to small plots. Evidence for the cultivation of flax and sesame is scant and questionable.

9
Orchards & Vineyards

Fruit trees were an important element of the agricultural economy of Eretz-Israel. The grapevine and several types of fruit trees are mentioned in YHWH's description of the fertility of the land that he is giving to the Israelites (Deut 8:8). When the spies sent by Moses to Canaan returned to the wilderness, they brought with them samples of native fruit, evidence of the richness of the country (Num 13:23). In another reference showing the important place of fruit trees in the economy of Canaan, they are called *zimrat hāʾāreṣ*, 'the strength, power of the land' (Gen 43:11; Tur-Sinai 1954). Here, choice fruit is sent by Jacob to Egypt in return for certain favors.

The Israelites were commanded to plant fruit trees for their own use (Lev 19:23). They were forbidden to fell fruit trees even when besieging a city (Deut 20:19), while other trees could be cut down and used for the siege (Deut 20:20). That law was specifically set aside by Elisha when he spoke to Jehoram and Jehoshaphat before their campaign against Moab (2 Kgs 3:19, 25).

Fruit trees were usually cultivated in orchards, *gan* (pl. *gannîm*), containing more than one variety of fruit tree, of which the Garden of Eden (Gen 2:8–3:24) was the prototype.[1] Another description of a *gan*, or *ginnâ*, is in Cant 5:1 and 6:2, 11. The prophets also mention the *gannâ* (pl. *gannôt*) as a mixed orchard (Jer 29:5, 28; Amos 9:14). A later term for a mixed orchard is *pardēs* (Cant 4:13; Eccl 2:5; Neh 2:8), which was borrowed from Persian, where it means 'an area enclosed by a fence or wall' (Zadok 1971). Another term for orchard or a place for tree planting is *maṭṭāʿ* (Ezek 17:7; 31:4; 34:29; Mic 1:6), which was distinguished from other types of orchards by being irrigated (Ezek 17:7; 31:4). Although some orchards were irrigated (Num 24:6), most of them were in mountainous areas (Jer 31:4) and could not be watered (Deut 11:10).

There are cases in the OT where *ʿēṣ haśśādeh* refers to cultivated fruit trees, probably indicating those that were not in enclosed areas

[1] See Ezek 36:35; Joel 2:3. It seems that only grapevines and olives were cultivated in separate groves.

(Exod 9:25; 10:5, 15; Lev 26:4; Deut 20:19; Jer 7:20; Ezek 34:27). The phrase *ᶜēṣ hayyaᶜar* (Ezek 15:2, 6; Cant 2:3) may have been used similarly.

Major Fruit-bearing Trees

The following is a catalog of the major fruit-bearing plants cultivated in Eretz-Israel during the Iron Age. The presentation is based on relevant passages in the OT and, whenever possible, on archaeological evidence. The order of presentation follows the order of plants mentioned in Deut 8:8. Plants not mentioned in this passage follow in order of their importance to the economy and the data available.

Grapevine (*Vitis vinifera L.*)

The biblical *gepen*, 'grapevine' has been identified with *Vitis vinifera* L. (Moldenke and Moldenke 1952: 242; Walker 1957: fig. 223), which is the domesticated variety of *Vitis*. A wild variety, *Vitis silvestris*, still prevalent in certain parts of Europe, the Balkans, North Africa, Turkey, and the south Caspian belt, is believed to be the progenitor of the domesticated *vinifera* (Zohary and Spiegel-Roy 1975: 321–23; Renfrew 1973: 125–27). No remains of *Vitis silvestris* have been found in Eretz-Israel, and it has been suggested that domestication of this important fruit plant took place in northern Syria and the Aegean belt (Zohary and Spiegel-Roy 1975: 321). The biblical tradition that Noah planted a vineyard after the flood (Gen 9:20) suggests that the biblical writers were aware of the antiquity of viticulture and the location of domestication of the vine.

The earliest remains of cultivated grapes in Eretz-Israel date to the beginning of the third millennium B.C.E. and were found in Early Bronze Jericho and Arad (Zohary and Spiegel-Roy 1975: 321). Other EB remains of *Vitis vinifera* were found in Lachish (Helbaek 1958: 310–11), Taᶜannek (Liphschitz and Waisel 1980), and recently at the cemetary of Bab edh-Dhraᶜ (Schaub and Rast 1978: 3) and at Numeira (Schaub and Rast 1978: 4; McCreery 1978: 2).

During the Late Bronze Age the vine was an important part of the economy of Canaan. Grapevines were among the plants brought by Thutmoses III from Canaan to Egypt, as depicted in the reliefs of the "Karnak Botanical Garden" (Paul and Dever 1974: fig. 77). It is possible that this was an attempt on the part of the Egyptian king to introduce new or better varieties into Egypt. Recently, dry grapes dated to the Late Bronze period were discovered at Aphek (Owen 1978a, 1978b), a site located on the Via Maris.

The importance of the grapevine in Eretz-Israel during biblical times is reflected in the OT. In the list of plants with which the land was blessed (Deut 8:8), after the main cereals, wheat and barley, the grapevine is the first of the fruit-bearing plants mentioned. The vine appears in Jotham's Parable as one of the trees asked to reign over the others (Judg 9:12–13); and it occupies a prominent place in the account of the spies sent to Canaan by Moses (Num 13:23). The grapevine is the only fruit-bearing plant mentioned in the OT having different names for the plant, *gepen*, and the fruit, *ᶜēnāb* (Deut 32:14; pl. *ᶜănābîm*, Gen 40:10). It is also the only one mentioned in the OT for which the different parts are enumerated.[2] Its place in religious ritual and the law codes and the large number of place-names connected with viticulture and wine production[3] testify to the importance of the vine in the economy of Eretz-Israel. The vine is used many times by the prophets as a symbol for the people of Israel, their destruction, and restoration (Jer 2:21; 6:9; Ezek 15:6; 17:6–8; Hos 10:1; 14:8; and others). The vine and its fruit are prominent in descriptions of the devastation of Eretz-Israel, as expressed by Joel: "It [the locust = the enemy] has laid waste my vines and splintered my fig trees, it has stripped off their bark and thrown it down; their branches are made white" (1:7; also 12). The vine, together with the fig, is a symbol of peace and prosperity (1 Kgs 4:25 [5:5]; Mic 4:4). Planting vineyards was a sign of stability and permanent settlement, as shown in the code of the sons of Rechab (Jer 35:7, 9) and in many speeches of the prophets.[4] Planting a vineyard and enjoying its fruit were so important that a law stipulated a man could not go to war before he enjoyed the fruit of his vineyard (Deut 20:6; 28:30).

Grapevines were planted either in a vineyard by themselves, *kerem* (pl. *kĕrāmîm*), or in a mixed grove with fruit trees (Cant 6:11). It appears that when vines and trees were grown together, the vines were trained to climb on the trees. However, most vines were cultivated in vineyards, as many OT references point out.

Sometimes the combined vineyard/orchard was located near a dwelling (Ps 128:3). A mixed orchard in close proximity to a dwelling was convenient; it was a source of fruit for daily use. Some vineyards were located at considerable distances from settlements. This is documented in the story of the Benjaminites and the young women of

[2] For example, *dālît*, *zāg*, *zĕmôrâ*, *nĕṭîšâ*, *salsillâ*, *śārîg*.

[3] *ᵓĀbēl kĕrāmîm*, Judg 11:33; *Bêt-hakkerem*, Jer 6:1; *ᶜĒnāb*, Jos 11:21; *Naḥal ᵓeškôl*, Num 13:23; *Naḥal śôrēq*, Judg 16:4; *Karmel*, 1 Sam 25:2; *Gat*, 2 Sam 1:20; and others.

[4] Isa 37:30 = 2 Kgs 19:29; 36:17; 65:21; Jer 31:5; 32:15; Ezek 28:26; Hos 2:17; Amos 9:14; Ps 107:37.

Shiloh (Judg 21:20–21) and in the story of Samson and the lion cub (Judg 14:5).

Planting a vineyard required thorough ground preparation. The best biblical documentation of preparatory work for a vineyard is found in Isaiah's "Song of the Vineyard" (5:1–8), where, while reprimanding Judah for its iniquities, the prophet compares Judah to a vineyard and describes the work involved. Before the vinedresser (*kôrēm*, pl. *kôrĕmîm*) could plant (*nṭ*ᶜ) the vines, he had to prepare the ground. The first activity of the vinedresser is expressed by the root ᶜ*zq* (v 2), the meaning of which is unclear. Several scholars have tried to explain it linguistically and contextually. They have suggested 'dig about' (BDB 1972: 740), 'hoe' (Fohrer 1973: 200), and 'the first plowing' (Dalman 1935: 4. 709). These suggestions cannot be accepted, because the next activity described by the prophet is *sql*, correctly translated 'free from stones' (BDB 1972: 709). The vinedresser could not dig or hoe before the stones were removed from the plot destined to become a vineyard.[5]

The most logical suggestion was made by Puchačevsky (1924: 43–44), on the basis of the Arabic name ᶜ*ajjaq* of the *Pistacia lentiscus*, a common bush in the Judean Mountains.[6] According to this interpretation the vinedresser's first activity is uprooting the ᶜ*ajjaq*-bush; this is followed by clearing away the stones. Only then can the vinedresser plant his vines.

In Isaiah's account the vineyard owner chose a good stock of vines called *śōrēq* (BDB 1972: 977). There is a strong possibility that *śōrēq* was not just the term for a choice vine, but was the name of a variety producing red grapes, derived from *śārōq*, 'sorrel' (BDB 1972: 977). The cultivation of a red grape variety in Eretz-Israel is suggested by the metaphors *dam* ᶜ*ănābîm*, 'blood of grapes' (Gen 49:11), and *dam* ᶜ*ēnāb* (Deut 32:14).

Different combinations with *gepen* suggest the existence of several varieties: *gepen bôqēq* (Hos 10:1), a variety probably named for its green appearance or for its large bunches (BDB 1972: 132); *gepen śibmâ* (Isa 16:8–9; Jer 48:32), named after the Moabite site *śibmâ*; *gepen* ᵓ*adderet* (Ezek 17:8), probably a climbing variety forming a dense (cloaklike) cover (BDB 1972: 12) over trees planted in the same grove. There is also the possibility that *sĕmādar*, mentioned only in Cant 2:13, 15 and 7:13, is a variety of grapes rather than 'grape blossom', as it has been translated (BDB 1972: 701; Aḥiṭuv 1968: 1052).

[5] Cf. Isa 62:10, *saqqĕlû mē*ᵓ*eben*, 'clear [the road] from stones'. Yeivin suggests that ᶜ*zq* is the removal of big rocks, but his suggestion is without documentation (1962: 35).

[6] See 'mastic-tree', in Moldenke and Moldenke 1952: 177–78 and fig 74.

This hypothesis is strengthened by the discovery of a Hebrew inscription at Hazor (Area B, Stratum V) which, according to Yadin (1960: 177; 1975b: 489), should be read *lpqḥ smdr*, 'belonging to Peqaḥ, *sĕmādar*'. Apparently, the inscribed jar contained wine made from the *smdr* variety.[7]

There were also wild plants looking like the *Vitis* that produced grapelike fruit (*gepen sĕdōm*, Deut 32:32), but they were bitter and in the case of *gepen śādeh* (2 Kgs 4:38) even poisonous.

The vinedresser, who prepared the ground and chose the variety of vine, "hoped for a yield of good grapes" (Isa 5:2). To protect the grapes from animals and people, the vineyard was surrounded with a fence, and a watchtower was built inside the grove. According to Isaiah there were two kinds of fences, *mĕśûkâ* and *gādēr* (5:5b). The *mĕśûkâ*, 'hedge' (BDB 1972: 962), was made of thorny bushes which were gathered and piled up to form a hedge. One such bush, the *ḥedeq*, is mentioned in Prov 15:19 as used for this purpose. On the basis of the Arabic names *khādak* and *hedek* for the Palestine nightshade, the biblical *ḥedeq* has been identified as *Solanum incanum* L., "a coarse stiff-branched shrubby plant, growing 1½ to 4 or 5 feet tall, . . . the branches and leaves armed with reddish recurved spines like a true brier" (Moldenke and Moldenke, 1952: 221–22, fig. 79). In addition to the *ḥedeq*, other bushes are mentioned as used for hedges, e.g., *sîrîm* (Hos 2:8). The cactus (*sābreh*, Arabic; *ṣabbār*, Hebrew), which is widely used today for hedges by Arab farmers, was imported in the nineteenth century from the New World. Another thorny bush used today for fencing, among other things, is the *Sarcopeteria spinosum*. This bush might have been used for making hedges around cultivated areas in ancient times.

A more massive and permanent protection was gained by erecting a stone wall, *gādēr ʾăbānîm* (Prov 24:31). By surrounding the vineyard with a stone wall, the vinedresser protected it from people and animals (Isa 5:5; Ps 62:4). The verb used to describe the building of the *gādēr* is *bnh* (Amos 9:11; Mic 7:11), which is also the verb used in the OT to describe the construction of larger building projects, such as city (Gen 4:17), temple (1 Kgs 6:1), and palace (1 Kgs 7:1–2). The use of *bnh* to describe *gādēr*-building shows that this activity was a hard task. Several references in the OT show that there were professionals engaged in this task called *gôdĕrîm* (2 Kgs 12:13; 22:6; Ezek 22:30). Many of the stones used in building this protective wall came,

[7] Y. Aharoni and R. Amiran read the inscription *lpqḥ smrh*. However, even if Yadin's reading is correct, the whole thing could be a personal name, *lpqḥ* [*bn*, 'son of'] *smdr*. See Aḥiṭuv 1968: 1052.

undoubtedly, from the area designated to become a *kerem*. Building a wall was not only a protective measure but also a way to recycle the stones removed from the vineyard and avoid wasting ground with a stone dump. Employing professional *gādēr*-builders suggests that the wall, in many cases, was an integral part of an agricultural terrace, the construction of which required experience.

In regions where many vineyards were under cultivation next to each other, the walls around them created narrow paths, *miš*ᶜ*ôl hakkĕrāmîm*, as described in the incident of Balaam and his ass: "Then the angel of YHWH stood in the narrow path between the vineyards; with a wall on either side" (Num 22:24). It is possible that the same situation existed in Edom and Moab, where the Israelites under Moses' leadership were refused permission to pass through (Num 20:17; 21:22), and around the town of Timna, where Samson met a lion between the vineyards and slew it bare-handed (Judg 14:5).

Although the law code states: "When you go into your neighbor's vineyard, you may eat your fill of grapes, as many as you wish, but you shall not put any in your vessel" (Deut 23:25), vinedressers did not trust human nature, and in order to protect their fruit they built certain structures which afforded them shelter while they were guarding their vineyards during the seasons of grape ripening and harvesting. Some of these structures, *sukkâ* and *mĕlûnâ*, were temporary (Isa 1:8). The function of the *sukkâ* is described by Isaiah: "The *sukkâ* will be for shade in the daytime from heat, and for shelter and refuge from torrent and rain" (4:6).[8] The flimsy nature of the *mĕlûnâ*, 'an overnight hut', is also described by Isaiah: "The earth staggers like a drunken man, it sways like a *mĕlûnâ*" (24:20). Those who could afford to do so built a stone watchtower, *migdāl*, which besides offering better shelter for the vinedresser and his family showed serious intentions regarding the groves (Isa 5:2).

When watchtowers were built by the state, the building activity could be interpreted as a political statement, as in the case of Uzziah: "And he built towers (*migdālîm*) in the desert, and hewed out many cisterns, for he had large herds, both in the Shephelah and in the plain, and he had farmers and vinedressers in the hills and the Karmel, for he loved the soil" (2 Chr 26:10). The towers built by Uzziah were obviously for the protection of the agricultural workers and agricultural produce in newly acquired territories.[9] Those who guarded the

[8] See also Jonah 4:5; for illustrations of modern-day structures, see Dalman 1935: 4 pl. 93.

[9] For illustrations of modern watchtowers, see Avitsur 1976: figs. 93–94; and Dalman 1935: 4 pl. 94.

Fig. 16. *ma'dēr* (hoe) made of iron

vineyards were called *nôṭĕrîm*; the reference in Cant 8:11–12 indicates that some were paid guards. According to Cant 1:6, women also served as vineyard guards. A variant form for watchman is *nôṣĕrîm* (Jer 31:5), which is used in agricultural contexts in Isa 27:3, Prov 27:18, and Job 27:18.

There were two methods of cultivating the vines. Both methods were practiced side by side and are still used today. The first method allowed the vine to spread on the ground, *gepen sôraḥat* (Ezek 17:7).[10] In this case, only a hoe, *maʿdēr*, could be used between the rows, not a plow. This method was probably practiced in small plots where natural conditions did not permit the use of a plow, e.g., stony or hilly country, as described by Isaiah: "And as for the hills which used to be hoed with a hoe, you will not come there for fear of briers and thorns" (7:25). The hoe probably was also used for cultivation close to the vines and near the vineyard fence, where a team of oxen with a plow could not approach. Examples of Iron Age hoes were found at Tell Jemmeh[11] and Lachish.[12] A hoe found at a site dated to the Persian period (Porath 1974: pl. 14:10), when compared with the rectangular ones

[10] Artistic representations of the *gepen sôraḥat* method as practiced in the region of Lachish can be seen in the siege reliefs from Nineveh (Goor 1966a: fig. 2; Albenda 1974: figs. 13–15).

[11] A rectangular hoe is shown in Petrie 1928: pl. 66:5. A triangular hoe which was found at the same site is shown in Avitsur 1976: fig. 32. Other triangular and rectangular hoes are shown in figs. 30 and 31 of Avitsur 1976.

[12] See Avitsur 1976: fig. 33; the objects from Lachish are two metal frames for hoelike tools, indicating that at times only a part of the digging tool was made of metal.

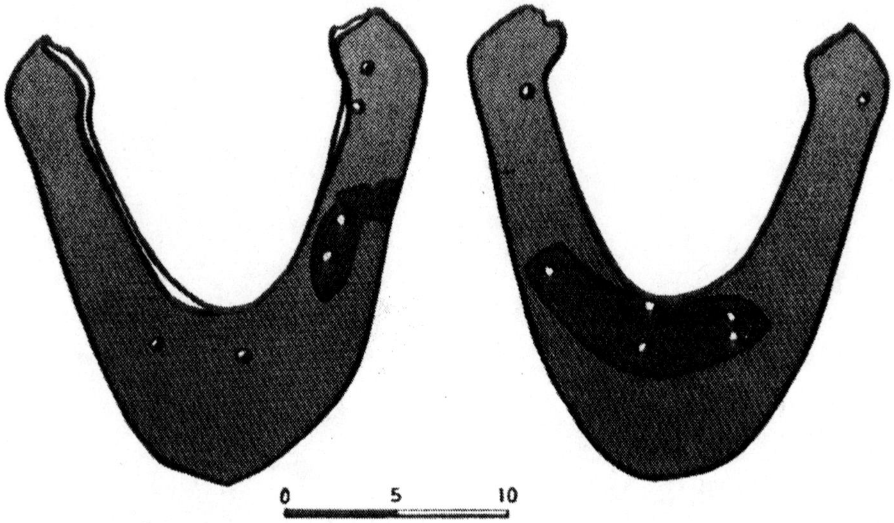

Fig. 17. An iron frame for an agricultural tool (hoe) from Lachish

from Iron Age Tell Jemmeh, shows that the design of the tool remained the same for hundreds of years.

Another tool used for digging was the *ʾēt*, erroneously translated 'plowshare' (BDB 1972: 88). The *ʾēt* is mentioned together with the plow in 1 Sam 13:20–21. In this passage the plow is mentioned twice specifically; therefore the term *ʾēt* (pl. *ʾētîm*, 1 Sam 13:21; *ʾittîm*, Isa 2:4; Mic 4:3; Joel 4:10) must indicate another tool close in function to the *maʿdēr* (Cohen 1965).

The second method of viticulture consisted of training the vines on trellises or poles, which provided a canopy-like form, or on trees (for the last, see Albenda 1974: figs. 8, 10; Gressmann 1909: figs. 273–74). The biblical term for this type of vine is apparently *gepen ʾadderet* (Ezek 17:8). Whether poles or trees were used, grapes grown this way were easier to harvest since the bunches hung down from the vine and hence were more accessible (Pritchard 1958a: fig. 19; Gressmann 1927: 58, fig. 183). This method was also more convenient for soil cultivation between the rows because it permitted the use of plows. Some vineyards covered so large an area that they required ten teams of oxen to plow for a whole day or ten days for one team (Isa 5:10). Use of the vine-training method produced pleasant shaded areas symbolic of security and prosperity: "Judah and Israel dwelt in

Fig. 18. Grape harvesting and wine making (18th Dynasty); notice the vine trained as *gepen ᵓadderet*

safety, from Dan even to Beer-sheba, every man under his vine and under his fig tree" (1 Kgs 5:5 [4:25]).

To train the vine for maximum yield the vinedresser had to prune, *zmr*, exessive branches, *zĕmôrâ* (Num 13:23). Pruning was done with a pruning knife, *mazmērâ* (pl. *mazmērôt*), a tool which is regarded in the OT as a symbol of peace: "And they shall beat their swords into *ᵓittîm* and their spears into pruning knives [*mazmērôt*] (Isa 2:4). The *mazmērâ* resembled a sickle, but its cutting edge was thicker and the curved knife was shorter than the sickle (Avitsur 1970: 325–33; Avitsur 1976: figs. 90, 405–7).

A description of pruning the vine is given by Isaiah: "He will cut off the tendrils [*zalzallîm*] with a pruning knife and the spreading branches [*nĕṭîšôt*] he will remove" (18:5). The pruned branches were used for fuel (Ezek 15:2–4). Pruning may have been called *zāmîr*, but *ᶜēt hazzāmîr*, 'time of the *zāmîr*' (Cant 2:12), must be referring to grape harvesting since the passage clearly describes the period after the winter is over (Cant 2:11). Pruning is an activity performed mostly during the fall before the vines become dormant. The period *yrḥw zmr* in the Gezer Manual, which is regarded by some scholars as two months for "the pruning and cleaning of the grapevines which took place in the unoccupied time after the harvest" (Wright 1955: 3, 54), is more likely the grape harvest time. Since the *mazmērâ* was in all likelihood used also for cutting off grape bunches, the Gezer Manual uses the term *zmr* for grape harvesting rather than *bāṣîr*, which is the word for grape harvest in the OT.

During the Sabbatical Year pruning the vine was forbidden (Lev 25:4) and grapes produced by an unpruned vine, *ᶜinnĕbê nāzîr* (Lev 25:5, 11), were forbidden for consumption. The same rule was applied during the Jubilee.

The time of grape harvesting varied from region to region, but generally it came between the period for grain harvesting and threshing and the period for plowing and planting field crops (Lev 26:5; Amos 9:13). It was time for rejoicing, *hillûlîm* (Judg 9:27), and merry-making (Isa 16:9–10). The harvesters, *bôṣĕrîm* (Jer 49:9; Obad 5; sg. *bôṣēr*, Jer 6:9), went out to the vineyard when the grapes ripened[13] and cut off the grape clusters (*ᵓaškōlôt*, Cant 7:8; sg. *ᵓeškôl*, Num 13:23) with a knife, probably the same one used for pruning.

Grapes could be harvested only from vines which were four years old or more. Those produced by a vine less than four years old were called *ᶜărēlîm*, 'uncircumcised' (Lev 19:23); the fourth year's yield had to be brought to YHWH. Only the fifth year's grapes could be consumed by the farmer (Lev 19:24–25). The shift in status of the vineyard from forbidden (or holy) to permitted (or profane) was so important that a man who had planted a vineyard but was called to military service before he had a chance to enjoy its fruit was released from duty so that he could be present at the critical time: "And whoever planted a vineyard and did not enjoy its fruit [*ḥillĕlô*][14] let him go back to his home, lest he die in the war and another man enjoy its fruit [*yeḥallĕlennû*]" (Deut 20:6). Participating in this conversion is regarded by Jeremiah as a sign of hope and restoration (31:4). Deprivation of this natural right and reward is one of the curses for breaking the covenant (Deut 28:15, 30).

Other stipulations related to grape harvesting are the prohibitions against (1) gleaning or going over a second time, *ᶜll* (Lev 19:10; Deut 24:21), to collect the *ᶜōlēlôt* (Judg 8:2; Isa 24:13; Jer 6:9; 49:9); and (2) collecting the *pereṭ* (Lev 19:10), 'a cluster made of two or three grapes'.[15] Both *ᶜōlēlôt* and **pĕrāṭîm* were left in the vineyard for the poor. Similar provisions were made in reference to the cereal harvest.

The high point of the *bāṣîr* was wine making, an activity which was carried out by the vinedresser and his family. The installation used for wine making, the press, was a simple one. It was made of a hard,

[13] Unripe grapes are called *bōser* (Jer 31:28–29; Ezek 18:2). The hiphil of *bšl* is used for the ripening of grapes in Gen 40:10; the qal is used for the ripening of cereals in Joel 4:13.

[14] Literally, 'pollute, defile, profane' (BDB 1972: 320).

[15] According to BDB 1972: 827, *pereṭ* is "the broken off, i.e. fallen grapes"; the meaning of *pereṭ* presented here is based on a common phenomenon known only to those who have had the chance to harvest grapes.

flat surface for treading the grapes and a receptacle for the juice, with a channel connecting the two. During the Roman and Byzantine periods presses were constructed with more than one receptacle in order to refine the juice.

Archaeological finds show that there were at least three types of winepresses: (1) a press hewn in the rock within or next to the vineyard; (2) a press built of stones and mortar within the confines of a city; (3) a portable stone press. Biblical passages use three terms for winepresses, *yeqeb*, *gat*, and *pûrâ*, all of which have been regarded as synonyms. I suggest that these three terms should be equated with the three types of presses. *Yeqeb* is the term used for a wine-pressing installation hewn in the rock near or in the vineyard, as described by Isaiah: "He built a watchtower in the midst of it [the vineyard] and hewn out a *yeqeb* in it" (5:2). The *yeqeb* was used not only for pressing grapes, but also for olive-oil making, as described by Joel: "The threshing floors shall be full of grain, and the *yĕqābîm* shall overflow with wine and oil" (2:24). The *yeqeb* is mentioned seven times with *gōren*, 'threshing floor', which is another installation connected with food processing, located outside the protective walls of the city of town. *Gōren* is never used in parallelism with *gat*, which is most likely the term used for a winepress built of stones and mortar within the city. The reference to "Gideon . . . beating out wheat in the *gat*, to hide it from the Midianites" (Judg 6:11) is a clear indication for the location of this installation inside the city.[16]

The third type, the portable winepress, is not known to me from Iron Age contexts, unless "a portable olive press" reported by Free to have been found at Dothan is really a winepress (1959: 28). The term *pûrâ* in Isa 63:2–3 may refer to the portable press. Another occurrence of this term in Hag 2:16 suggests that *pûrâ* was a unit of measure. It is barely possible that portable installations had a standard or close to standard size which could have been used for measurement.

Examples of the first type, *yeqeb*, have been found near several sites in Eretz-Israel. Unfortunately these installations are isolated and out of archaeological context, and dating their original construction is very difficult, especially since they were used for long periods of time. The second type, *gat*, is very common in Iron Age strata throughout Eretz-Israel; the best examples of this installation were found at Tell Qasîleh (Mazar 1950–51: 137), Gezer (Negev 1972: fig. on p. 110), and Beth-shemesh. In one section of the Iron II city of Beth-shemesh, many winepresses of this type were uncovered, a situation suggesting a

[16] Walker (1957: 222) is mistaken in his statement that these winepresses were "sometimes as large as a room and constructed underground. . . ."

wine-making center (Grant and Wright 1939: 75–76, pls. 18:2–4, 19:1–2, 20:1–2). More recently two winepresses of the *gat* type were found in the Iron II stratum of Tell Qiri (Ben Tor 1977a: 26; Ben Tor 1977b: Ben Tor 1977c).

Another wine-making center was discovered by Pritchard in el-Jib, biblical Gibeon. According to the excavator's report, Gibeon was a center of wine making and exporting. Jars discovered in the Gibeon pool were inscribed with names of winemakers, an indication that these jars were returnable. The inscribed labels were in different styles to enable easy identification of the owner. Jars of this type had not previously been found at any other site (Pritchard 1958b: 16). Supporting the theory of a wine-making center are a funnel and stoppers which were found with the jars (Pritchard 1958b: 17). Another important point is the fact that 75 of the 80 *lmlk* jars discovered at Gibeon were found with the local type in the pool (Pritchard 1958b: 18). Without entering into the controversy over the *lmlk* jars and their function, it should be pointed out that at the same time that the *lmlk* jars were in use, a special type of jar was developed locally at Gibeon for use by private wine makers.

Treading the grapes, *drk*,[17] was accompanied by much singing and noise, *hêdād*: "And joy and gladness are taken away from the *karmel* and in the vineyards no songs are sung, no shouts are raised; no treader treads out wine in the presses, the *hêdād* is hushed" (Isa 6:10).[18] Egyptian art depicts grape treading as an activity accompanied by music (Pritchard 1954: fig. 90), which may have been the custom of the Israelites as well.

The fresh juice was collected into large jars with a capacity of 9¾ gallons (ca. 37 liters). The mouths of the jars were sealed with clay, leaving only a small hole in the neck to permit the escape of the gases produced through fermentation (Negev 1972: 110; Avitsur 1976: 96). These jars were placed in rock-cut cellars; sixty-three cellars were found in the course of excavations at Gibeon. The cellars provided a constant temperature of 18° C (65° F), which was needed for the fermentation process. When fermentation ended, the large jars were completely sealed. For transportation of the final product (wine, *yayin*) smaller jars were used (Pritchard 1958b: 12–13; Pritchard 1975: 449). Other wine cellars were found at Tell Qasîleh (Mazar 1950–51: 62, 130), Khirbet Jemaᶜin (Dar 1980: 99, photo on p. 100), and other sites.

[17] As in *dôrēk ᶜănābîm* (Amos 9:13) and *dôrēk baggat* (Isa 63:2).

[18] See also Jer 25:30; 48:32–33. Tur-Sinai (1954: 807) sees a close relationship between *hêdād* and thunder, called in Ugaritic *hd*, and the god Hadad (in Aramaic; Adad, Addu, in Akkadian). According to him the *hêdād*-shouts were imitations of the thundering sound made by the god treading the heavenly press.

The term *tîrôš* (also spelled *tîrōš*), which is synonymous with *yayin*, is used in the OT in ritualistic, religious, and poetic contexts, such as blessings (Gen 27:28, 37), laws (Deut 12:17; 14:23), parables (Judg 9:13), and prophecies (Isa 24:7; Jer 31:11; Hos 2:10–11; and others). In most cases its appearance with *dāgān* and *yiṣhār* ('grain' and 'oil') creates a formula for prosperity later adopted in formal language (Neh 5:11; 10:38, 40; 13:5, 12; 2 Chr 31:5; 32:28). This formula was closely connected with Yahwistic cultic language, and it is interesting to note that it was also used by the Assyrian Rabshakeh when he tried to convince the Judahites under Hezekiah to surrender to Sennacherib (2 Kgs 18:32 = Isa 36:17). Some scholars, on the basis of Mic 6:15, suggest that *tîrôš* is fresh grape juice, but its occurrences with other final products, *dāgān* and *yiṣhār*, demonstrates that the term is synonymous with *yayin*.

Different kinds of wine are designated in the OT with the following words, usually used with *yyn*: *lĕbānôn* (Hos 14:8), *ḥelbôn* (a place in Lebanon; Ezek 27:18), *mezeg* (Cant 7:2), *reqaḥ* (Cant 8:2), *ᶜāsîs* (Joel 1:5), and *ḥemer* (Deut 32:14) or *ḥāmar* (Ps 75:9). The last two terms could mean either 'red wine' or 'fermenting or sparkling wine'. Other wine names have been found in inscriptions and include *tmd* (Negev 1972: 110), *smdr* (Yadin 1975b: 489), *yšn* (Diringer 1934: 24–26, 31), *hᵓgnt* (Aharoni 1966a: 3), *ᶜšn* (Demsky 1979: 163), *kḥl* (Avigad 1972; Demsky 1972), and *mz.ṣmqm.šḥrt* (Lemaire 1980).

Certain regions in Eretz-Israel were known for their vineyards, such as ᶜEn-gedi (Tell Goren), Samaria, Shechem, Timnah, Shiloh, and Baᶜal-hamon; and in Moab and Edom, the towns of Heshbon, Yaᶜazer, and Śibmah.

Besides fresh grapes (*ᶜănābîm lāḥîm*, Num 6:13) and wine, there were several other products of the vine which were appreciated, such as vinegar, *ḥōmeṣ*, used as a condiment (Ruth 2:14), and raisins, *ṣimmûqîm* (or *ṣimmūqîm*; 1 Sam 25:18, 30:12; and others), which were mostly used for provisions on a long march or journey. Raisins were pressed into cakes, sometimes called *ᵓăšîšâ* (2 Sam 6:19 = 1 Chr 16:3; pl. *ᵓăšîšê ᶜănābîm*, Hos 3:1; *ᵓăšîšôt*, Cant 2:5). One place famous for its raisin cakes was Qir-ḥaroshet (Isa 16:7). Another grape product very common today among Arabs is *dibs*, which is grape juice boiled down to syrup (Moldenke and Moldenke 1952: 224; Avitsur 1972: 202). It may be the *mišrat ᶜănābîm* of the OT (Num 6:3), one of the grape products forbidden for a *nāzîr*.

Because of the nature of grapes, very few whole grapes have been discovered in archaeological excavations. Grape pips in Iron Age strata were found at Lachish (Helbaek 1958: 310) and Khirbet Abū Ṭabaq (Stager 1975: 54). More recently some grape pips were found in oms at Tell Qiri (Ben Tor 1977b) and Tell Halif (Laustrup 1982), finds suggesting the consumption of fresh grapes or raisins in these loci. More recently charred raisins were found at Shiloh (Finkelstein, Burnimowitz, and Lederman 1984: 22 and photograph on p. 22).

Fig (*Ficus carica* L.)

The common fig, *tĕʾēnâ* (pl. *tĕʾēnîm*), which is mentioned numerous times in the OT, is identified as *Ficus carica* L. (Moldenke and Moldenke 1952: 103–6; Walker 1957: 76, fig. 77). It is a tree indigenous to the Near East (Goor 1965: 124; Zohary and Spiegel-Roy 1975: 324). The OT writers were aware of this fact when mentioning the fig in Deut 8:8. The earliest fig remains in Eretz-Israel come from Neolithic, Chalcolithic, and Bronze Age Jericho (Goor 1965: 124). Cultivation of the fig in Canaan before the Israelite conquest is well documented in Egyptian sources, so it is no surprise that the spies sent to Canaan by Moses brought back figs upon their return to the wilderness (Num 13:23).

The domesticated fig is vegetatively propagated, while the propagation of the wild fig, *Ficus carica* var. *silvestris* Nees, depends entirely on seeds disseminated by birds and bats which eat the ripe fruit. Pollination is highly specialized and is carried out by a small symbiotic wasp, *Blastophaga psenes* L., which enters the syconia (fruit) and carries the pollen from the male flowers to the female flowers (Zohary and Spiegel-Roy 1975: 324). Cross-pollination between the wild and cultivated varieties is done by suspending branches of wild fig over the flowers of cultivted figs (Moldenke and Moldenke 1952: 106). This practice is called caprification and was learned by the Palestinian farmer from the Greeks, but it was not practiced during the Iron Age in Eretz-Israel (Goor 1965: 129). Both varieties do well on stony ground with thin soil cover where the rainfall is as little as 300 mm and in semi-arid regions.

The importance of the fig tree as one of the mainstays of biblical economy cannot be overemphasized. The fig tree is depicted in Jotham's Parable (Judg 9:10–11) as one of the trees asked to reign over the others. Whenever an economic calamity is predicted, the destruction of the fig tree serves as an illustration (Jer 5:17). The destruction of the fig tree is predicted as punishment for breaking the covenant; the punishment can be carried out by an invading enemy or by locusts and other natural disasters (Isa 34:4; Jer 8:13; Amos 4:9; Joel 1:7, 12; Hab 3:17; Hag 2:19). The restoration of the economic system after its destruction is also described in terms of reviving the fig tree (Joel 2:22).

The fig tree, because of its prominence in the economic system, served as a symbol of peace and prosperity in the days of Solomon

(1 Kgs 5:5). The prophets also used the fig tree as a symbol of the prosperous situation to come when the people of Israel are restored (Mic 4:4; Zech 3:10). The Assyrian Rabshakeh promises the Judahites that by making peace with Sennacherib they could prosper and "every one of you [the Judahites] will eat of his own vine, and every one of his own fig tree" (2 Kgs 18:31 = Isa 36:16).

The fig tree would not disappoint those who took care of it and dressed it: "He who tends a fig tree will eat its fruit" (Prov 27:18). The fig has two crops, the first, or winter crop, ripens in June; and the second, or summer crop, ripens in August and September (Moldenke and Moldenke 1952: 105). The first crop when ripe, *bakkūrôt* (Jer 24:3; also *bikkûrîm*, Nah 3:12; sg. *bikkûrâ*, Hos 9:10), was eaten fresh and was always considered a delicacy. The second crop, *qayiṣ* (Isa 16:9; Jer 48:32; Mic 7:1), was dried and used as food during the winter time or as provisions on long marches (2 Sam 16:1–2; Jer 40:10, 12; Amos 8:1–2). Ripe figs were easily removed from the tree, a circumstance which is used symbolically by Nahum to describe the imminent destruction of Nineveh (3:12).

The unripe fig is called *pag* or *paggâ*, and the verb used to describe its ripening is *ḥnṭ* (Cant 2:13), 'spice, make spicy, embalm' (BDB 1972: 334). Bad-tasting figs are called *tĕʾēnîm rāʿôt* (Jer 24:2–3) or *tĕʾēnîm šōʿārîm* (Jer 29:17).

As mentioned before, figs were dried for long-term storage and use. There are three ways to prepare dried figs: (*a*) dry individually, (*b*) dry on strings, (*c*) mash into cakes (Goor 1965: 130; Avitsur 1972: 203). In the OT a cake of dried figs is called *dĕbēlâ* (1 Sam 30:12; also *dĕbelet tĕʾēnîm*, 2 Kgs 20:7 = Isa 38:21; pl. *dĕbēlîm*, 1 Sam 25:18; 1 Chr 12:40), which in addition to its nutritional use could be used medicinally to heal skin infections, *šĕḥîn* (2 Kgs 20:7 = Isa 38:21). Although there is no clear reference in the OT to dried figs on a string, it seems that *qayiṣ* as used in 2 Sam 16:1–2 might refer to it: "two hundred bread loaves [*leḥem*], and a hundred cakes of dried grapes [*ṣimmûqîm*] and a hundred *qayiṣ* and a skin-bottle of wine [*nēbel yāyin*]." This list of provisions should be compared with another list which clearly mentions fig cakes: "two hundred bread loaves [*leḥem*], and two skin-bottles of wine, and five prepared sheep and five *sĕʾîm* [measures] of parched grain [*qālî*], and a hundred cakes of dried grapes [*ṣimmūqîm*] and two hundred *dĕbēlîm*" (1 Sam 25:18). Since both lists are very explicit, it seems that the term *qayiṣ* refers to something other than the *dĕbēlâ* and could very well refer to figs dried on a string. Another product of the fig is wine, which is mentioned only once in the OT (Neh 13:15).

Fig remains are rarely found in paleoethnobotanical material (Renfrew 1973: 134) because the seeds are so small, but it is possible to retrieve them through flotation. Only a few samples were recovered from early periods (Renfrew 1973: 134). The only sample of figs dated to the Iron Age in Eretz-Israel was found at Beth-shemesh. Here, several jars containing lentils and "pressed figs" were found in a storeroom (Grant and Wright 1939: 129–30). No other details are available concerning this find. It is very surprising that no figs were recovered from any of the caves in the Judean Desert, where remains of many types of fruit from the Chalcolithic and Roman periods were found.

Fig trees appear in the reliefs at the palace of Nineveh describing the siege of Lachish by Sennacherib (Pritchard 1954: pl. 374). The depiction of fig trees in these reliefs serves as evidence for their cultivation in the region of Lachish during the Iron Age.

Pomegranate (*Punica granatum* L.)

The biblical *rimmôn* is identified with *Punica granatum* L. (Moldenke and Moldenke 1952: 189, fig. 76; Goor 1967: 215; Walker 1957: 166, fig. 167), which is usually a small and bushlike tree with thorny branches. Occasionally it may become a large tree reaching a height of six to ten meters (Moldenke and Moldenke 1952: 190). One of these large trees appears in the story of Jonathan's victory over the Philistines at Michmash (1 Sam 14:2).

The pomegranate tree can still be found in the wild state in the Near East; on the basis of this some scholars suggest that the domestication of the pomegranate took place in this region (Goor 1967: 215). Others maintain that it was domesticated somewhere around the southern coast of the Caspian Sea and northeastern Turkey (Zohary and Spiegel-Roy 1978: 21). The OT writers regard the pomegranate as one of the native fruit trees of Eretz-Israel (Num 13:23; Deut 8:8). Remains of domesticated pomegranate fruit were found in Early Bronze sites, such as Gezer, Jericho, and Arad (Zohary and Spiegel-Roy 1975: 324). Documentary evidence from Egypt (Harris Papyrus, ca. 1150 B.C.E.) shows that the pomegranate was cultivated in pre-Israelite Canaan and its fruit was imported to Egypt. Although pomegranates were grown in Egypt (Num 20:5), it seems that the Palestinian varieties were preferred by the Egyptians in later periods, as reported by Zenon (ca. 200 B.C.E.). Although the pomegranate was not as economically important as the fig, the grapevine, or the olive, its destruction (Joel 1:12) and restoration (Hag 2:19) signify YHWH's wrath and Israel's salvation.

The pomegranate blooms at the same time as the grapevine (Cant 6:11; 7:13) and ripens in the summer. Its fruit contains several compartments filled with small juicy seeds. The seeds can be eaten fresh or can be dried and stored. The juice squeezed out of the seeds, *ᶜāsîs* (Cant 8:2), can be drunk fresh or fermented for wine or used for syrup. The hard rind was used by the Egyptians to guard against respiratory ailments, stomach trouble, and intestinal worms (Goor 1967: 218). It was also used for leather tanning (Moldenke and Moldenke 1952: 190).

The pomegranate was always considered a symbol of fertility, probably because of the large number of seeds in each fruit. The beautiful shapes of the flower and fruit inspired artists and served as models for the decorations of the High Priest's garments, Solomon's temple, and Solomon's crown. In daily life the pomegranate served as a model for the decoration of *kernoi*, ritual clay vessels used all through the Iron Age (Amiran 1963: fig. 358). A shallow bowl decorated in the middle with a raised molded pomegranate was discovered in an eighth century B.C.E. tomb at Tell Halif (Seger and Borowski 1977: fig. on p. 166), offering another example of Israelite art. The beauty and symmetry of this fruit invited its comparison with beautiful women: "Your *raqqâ* [cheek or temple] is like a slice of pomegranate [*pelaḥ hārimmôn*]" (Cant 4:3; 6:7).

Pomegranate remains dated to the Iron Age in Eretz-Israel were discovered in Iron II storage-pits at Tell Qiri (Ben Tor 1977b) and in a destruction layer (ca. 700 B.C.E.) at Tell Halif (Borowski 1981: 3).

Olive (*Olea europaea* L.)

The olive, *zayit* (pl. *zêtîm*), identified as *Olea europaea* L. (Moldenke and Moldenke 1952: 157; Walker 1957: 154, fig. 155),[19] was a very important fruit tree in the economy of Eretz-Israel. It is a native of the East Mediterranean basin; the domestication of its progenitor, *O. europaea* var. *Oleaster*, took place in this region some time during the Chalcolithic period (fourth millennium B.C.E.). The earliest stones (pits) of domesticated olives were found at Teleilat Ghassul in association with cereal grain, dates, and pulses. Other remains of olives from the Chalcolithic period were discovered in the Cave of the Treasure near ᶜEn-gedi and at Tell Mashosh near Beer-sheba (Zohary and Spiegel-Roy 1975: 319). Samples from the Early and Middle Bronze ages are more common and were found at Arad, Bene-beraq, Lachish, Megiddo, Gezer, Beth-shan, Beth-yeraḥ, Afula, Taᶜannek, Aphek, and Tell Halif (Zohary and Spiegel-Roy 1975: 319; Goor 1966: 223;

[19] The expression *ᶜēṣ šemen*, 'oil-tree' (1 Kgs 6:23, 31–33; Neh 8:15), has been explained by several scholars as a reference to the narrow-leaved oleaster, *Elaeagnus angustifolia* L., the wild variety of *O. europaea* (Moldenke and Moldenice 1952: 97–98, 159; Dalman 1935: 4. 163).

Renfrew 1973: 132; Laustrup 1982). During the Middle and Late Bronze ages olive cultivation became popular throughout the Mediterranean basin and reached Spain (Renfrew 1973: 132). Unlike other fruit trees native to Eretz-Israel, the olive never gained prominence in Egypt as a cultivated plant, and oil always had to be imported from Canaan (Goor 1966: 231–32). The same is true for Lower Mesopotamia, where the olive never played an important role in agriculture (Zohary and Speigel-Roy 1975: 320).

The importance of the olive for the Israelite farmer is shown by its mention as one of the seven species with which Eretz-Israel was blessed (Deut 8:8) and by the many references in the OT to this tree and its main product, oil (*šemen*). It is the first tree in Jotham's Parable to be asked to reign over the others (Judg 9:8–9); and fields, vineyards, and olive orchards are said to be the possessions which would be confiscated by the newly chosen king and given to his servants (1 Sam 8:14). During the time of the early monarchy its prominent place in the economy is shown by the reference to an overseer who was in charge of the royal olive groves: "And over the olives and the sycomores which are in the Shephelah, Baᶜal Ḥanan the Gederite" (1 Chr 27:28). The royal groves produced such a great quantity of oil that another overseer had to be appointed by David to take care of the stored oil (1 Chr 27:28). Like the destruction of the grapevine and the fig, the olive's destruction signified an economic disaster brought upon Israel for her transgressions by natural agents, such as disease and locust (Deut 28:40; Amos 4:9; Hab 3:17; Hag 2:19), or by enemy attack (Mic 6:15).

The olive tree was considered a symbol of beauty: "his beauty shall be like the olive tree" (Hos 14:7; also Jer 11:16; Ps 52:10). The silvery sheen of the olive's leaves might have been the source of its name. It has been proposed that the origin of the name is the noun *ziw*, 'brightness', or *zhh*, 'be bright, splendid' (BDB 1972: 264; Goor 1966: 223–24).

The olive, which is best adapted to the Mediterranean climate, is a large tree sometimes reaching a height of more than seven meters. It thrives best in well-drained sandy or rocky soils, where its extensive root system can develop (Renfrew 1973: 133–34; Moldenke and Moldenke 1952: 158). While wild olives are reproduced from seeds, "cultivated varieties are maintained by vegetative propagation . . . [which] depends primarily on utilization of knobs . . . that develop at the base of the trunk and root easily when cut off" (Zohary and Spiegel-Roy 1975: 320). This characteristic makes killing an olive tree by cutting it down a very difficult task since new sprouts are sent up from the roots around the old stump, forming a small grove of two to five trunks (Moldenke and Moldenke 1952: 159). This is the background for the Psalmist's simile "Your sons like olive suckers [*šĕtīlê zêtîm*] around your table" (Ps 128:3), symbolizing continuity; this is further emphasized in the final verse of the psalm: "And you shall see your sons' sons" (v 6). Undoubtedly, the tenaciousness of the olive tree is also the background for Isaiah's prophecy "There shall come forth a shoot [*ḥōṭer*] from the stump of Jesse, and a sprout [*nēṣer*] shall grow out of his roots" (11:1). Olives were planted in separate groves, as the numerous passages in the OT indicate; but it seems that they did not need the same kind of protection given to a vineyard, i.e., fencing. Only in one case where *kerem zayit* is mentioned (Judg 15:5) does it appear that the grove was fenced.

The olive tree has many branches, with leaves that are green on the upper surface and silvery on the bottom. The leaves are leathery and stay on the tree all year round. Its flowers, which appear at the beginning of the summer, are small and white and are arranged in bunches (Moldenke and Moldenke 1952: 158). Botanists claim that only one out of every hundred flowers become a fruit (Shewell-Cooper 1962: 34). By the end of the blooming period the petals fall, as Eliphaz the Temanite observed: "he shall cast off his *niṣṣâ* [petals] like an olive tree" (Job 15:33). The fruit ripens after five or six months, and harvest takes place during the period designated in the Gezer Manual *yrḥw ʾsp*, which is September–October.

When the fruit was ripe, it was harvested by beating the branches with sticks, *ḥbṭ* (Deut 24:20), an activity called *nōqep zayit* (Isa 17:6; 24:13). As with other domesticated plants the harvesters were not permitted to glean and had to leave the *ʿōlēlôt* (Isa 17:6; 24:13) for the poor, especially when the olives were at the top of the tree, *bĕrōʾš ʾāmîr* (Isa 17:6).[20] Gleaning of olives is called **paʾēr* (Deut 24:20), which means going over the branches.[21]

The fallen olives were collected into baskets and taken to the press for expressing the oil, contained in the fleshy body of the fruit. This activity is referred to only once in the OT: 'you will tread olives', *tidrōk zayit* (Mic 6:15). This should not be taken literally since this method is ineffective and the stones might cause harm to the feet of the treader. Besides, expressing oil requires long and constant pressure, so it should be understood that the locution is used only as a poetic expression of oil pressing.

Several methods of oil production were in use during the Iron Age, one of which produced for the eternal light *šemen zayit zāk kātît*

[20] In this verse the fruit of the olive tree is called *gargĕrîm*, a *hapax*.

[21] From the noun **pōʾrâ*, 'bough' (BDB 1972: 802); pl. *pōʾrōt* (Ezek 17:6).

lammāʾôr, 'pure oil of crushed olives for lighting' (Exod 27:20; Lev 24:2). *Šemen kātît* in small quantities was produced by pounding a few olives in a stone mortar, sometimes carved in the natural rock near the grove. Then the oil was scooped out, mostly for immediate use. But in the case of Solomon, who sent Hiram of Tyre 20,000 baths of oil (2 Chr 2:9),[22] a different method of production had to be employed. It is possible that Solomon's oil was produced in presses similar to the Late Bronze installations found at Tell Beit Mirsim (Albright 1943b: 20–21) and Bethel (Kelso 1968: 30, pls. 85:b, 89:c–d). The latter is described by the excavator briefly as follows:

> It consists of three installations. There was a large stone mortar used to crush the olives, with the major exterior dimension *c.* 1 m. and the major interior dimension *c.* two-thirds as much. Its interior depth was just over 50 cm. The crushed olives were removed from this mortar to a much larger plaster vat somewhat rectangular in shape. Here water was added so that the best olive oil could rise to the surface. The vat was approximately 2 m. × 1 m. with a roughly spherical basin 60 cm. deep except for a slightly lower small collection basin, which made possible easy removal of the last of the oil. Between the two vats stood a stone bench on which baskets of olives could be placed for sorting and small jars could be placed to be filled with oil. . . . *Zebâr*, the refuse left after the process was completed, was found in considerable quantity N of the factory (Kelso 1968: 30).

Oil production installations from the Iron II period were found at several sites, one of which is Beth-shemesh, where remains of a large oil industry were discovered. Besides the numerous oil presses described by the excavators (Grant and Wright 1939: 75–76, pls. 18:2–4, 19:1–2, 20:1–2), an installation termed "an olive oil refinery" was found which included

> two large stone vats and four huge clay jars. Two of the jars were in good condition and two were crushed. One vat was square and the other round. Each was served by two jars set in masonry, one on either side of a vat. The jar on the south side of a vat contained many olive pits, now charred. Each jar had four handles. On one was a scratched ט in the old form, a circle enclosing a cross (Grant 1931: 73, plan on p. 78; pl. 1).

Installations belonging to a different type of oil press were discovered in Iron Age strata at several sites. These installations have a

[22] Ca. 440,000 liters; calculations are based on measurements in Paul and Dever 1974: 175. The reference in 1 Kgs 5:25 should be emended from "twenty kor *kātît*-oil" (ca. 4,400 liters) to "twenty thousand baths of *kātît*-oil," unless the reference in 1 Kgs is to only a single year's payment. Dalman (1935: 4. 290) uses the figures 728,000 and 7,280 liters.

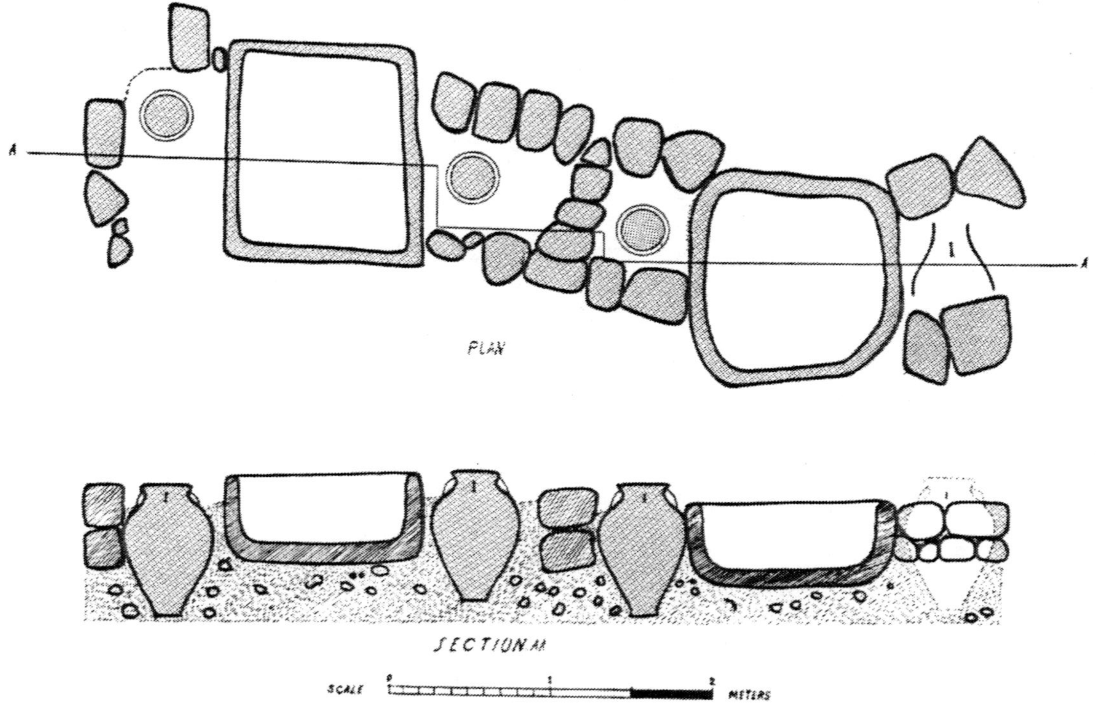

Fig. 19. Olive oil refinery from Beth Shemesh

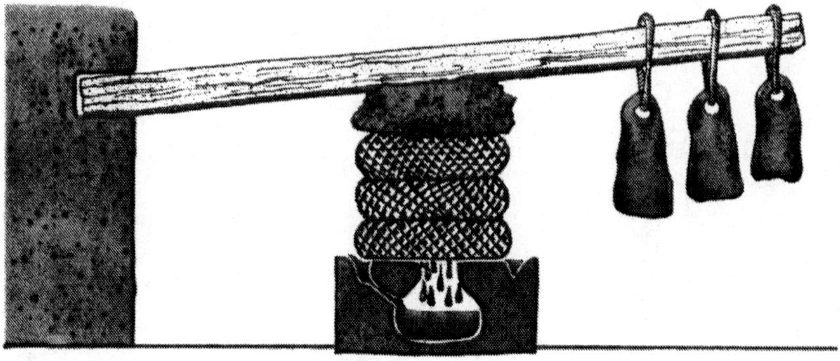

Fig. 20. A beam olive press

flat surface surrounded by a groove with a spout guiding the oil into a collection jar (Avitsur 1976: pls. 237–38). To extract the oil, baskets filled with crushed olives were placed on the flat surface; stone weights were laid on top of the baskets to press out the oil.

An improvement to this oil-pressing method was adopted during the Iron II period with the introduction of the beam-press.[23] This press uses a beam inserted either into a niche in a wall or into a large stone; stone weights are tied to the other end of the beam. The olive baskets are placed under the beam in a collection basin. Excavations at Beth-shemesh uncovered stone weights used with beam-presses (Grant 1931: 25, 27; Grant 1934: pls. 18:1, 5; 21:4). Each of these stones had a hole "for the purpose of tying them to the long end of the beam or lever to which the press was attached" (Grant and Wright 1939: 75). Beam-presses of many shapes and forms were used during the Iron II period, as evident from the discoveries at several sites. One such site is Gezer, where an oil press was discovered in Stratum 6A in Field VII and dated to the second half of the eighth century B.C.E. (probably destroyed by Tiglath Pileser III in 733 B.C.E.). Here, a large, circular stone basin was found sunk into the floor and covered by a thick layer of sediment composed of crushed olive pits and "impregnated with olive oil residue" (Gitin 1976). On the floor, a few centimeters away from the basin, was found a large stone weight with a hole cut into its narrow top. In another room, immediately to the west of the press, the surface was found to contain "carbonized, pulverized olive pits" (Gitin 1976).

[23] Several scholars assign this invention to the Hellenistic or the Roman period (Dalman 1935: 4. 221; Noth 1966: 164).

Other discoveries show that the beam-press gained popularity in the Iron II period. Recently, an installation termed by its excavator "a cultic installation for water libation" was uncovered at Tell Dan (Biran 1980: 91–98), but it appears from the information available that it is actually an olive beam-press which combines some of the features of the Beth-shemesh "refinery," i.e., basins and collection jars, with the flat pressing surfaces of the beam-press. Several stone weights found in close proximity to this installation clearly identify it as a beam-press (Borowski 1982a; Borowski 1982b; Stager and Wolff, 1981). A beam-press carved in bedrock near what seems to have been an olive grove was recently found at Khirbet Jema^{c}in (Dar 1980: 99, photo on p. 100). Both of these installations are dated to the Iron II period. Other beam presses were found at Tell Batash (Timna) (Kelm and Mazar 1983) and Tell Miqne (Ekron) (Gitin 1985: 2), both dated to the end of the seventh century B.C.E.

The claim that the beam-press was commonly used during the Iron II period has been strengthened by the proof provided by Eitam (1979) and Amit (1979) that the stone installations found at Tell Beit Mirsim and elsewhere which were identified by W. F. Albright as "dye vats" are really basins of beam-presses. While pressing techniques were improved during the Iron II period, the next significant improvement took place much later, probably in the Roman period, when the crushing installation using a large stone wheel was introduced and widely used in Eretz-Israel. An example of this type of installation is described by Hestrin and Yeivin (1977). Although olive presses were available during the Iron II period, one OT reference (Joel 2:24) shows that oil was sometimes produced in the *yeqeb*.[24]

It should be mentioned here that a "portable olive press" found by Free in Dothan (1959: 28) could be a *pûrâ*; only publication of the object and its immediate context will confirm this. An installation first excavated by Sellin in Ta^{c}annek and referred to as an oil press was reexcavated by Lapp (1964: 29, 32), who has suggested that the installation is cultic and had to do with libations.

The OT has absolutely no reference to raw olives being eaten, and since untreated olives are very bitter, it is hard to accept the undocumented claim made by several scholars (Moldenke and Moldenke 1952: 158; Renfrew 1973: 134; Goor 1966: 223) that raw olives were eaten before pickling or salting was introduced in the Hellenistic or Roman period (Dalman 1935: 4. 198–99; Haran 1962: 547). As a matter of fact, the reference in Deut 8:8 is very clear concerning the

[24] For beam-presses from different periods and other related installations see Dalman 1935: 4.: pls. 48–74.

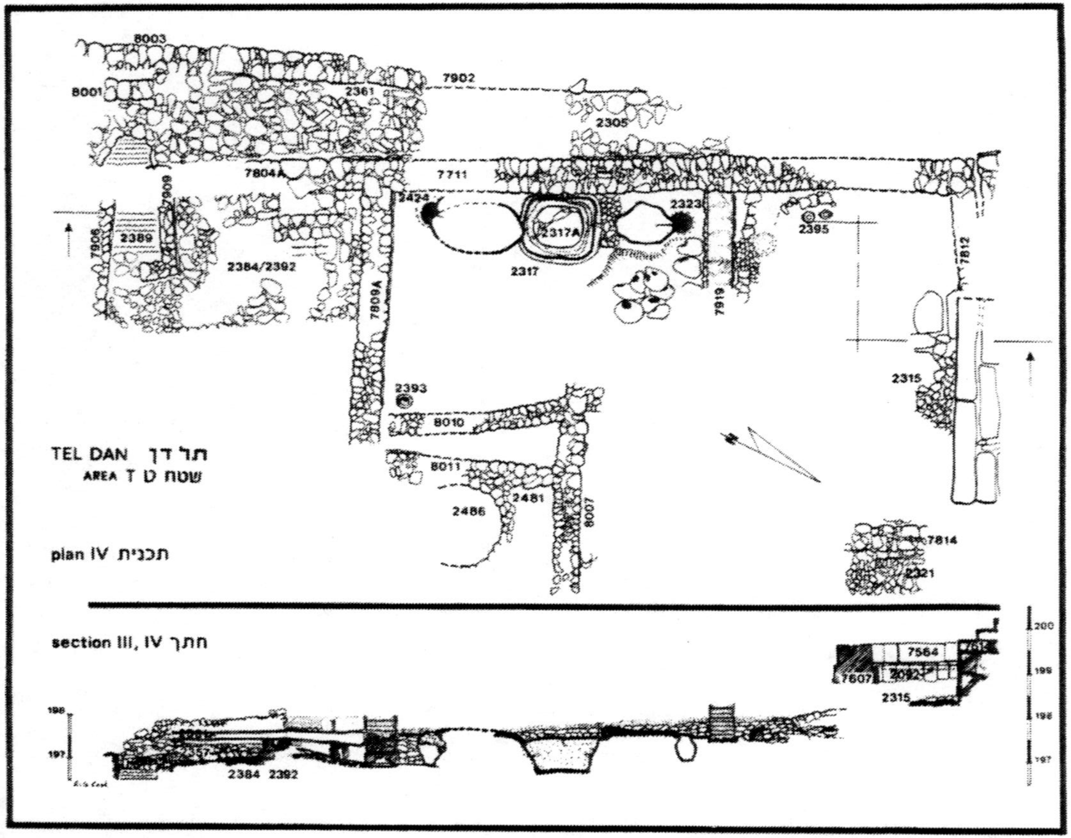

Fig. 21. A top plan and section of the olive press in the temenos at Tel Dan

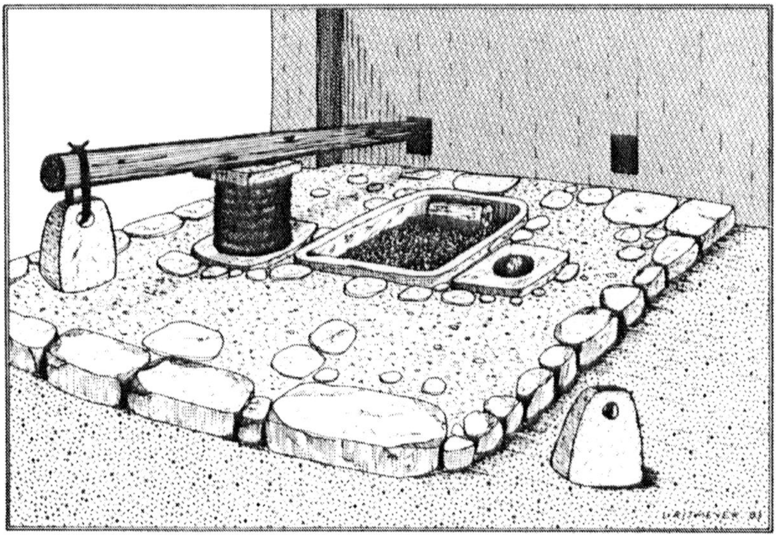

Fig. 22. Reconstructed olive press from Tel Batash (Timnah), Iron II

function of the olive: "a land of olive for oil."[25] In Jotham's Parable, the olive tree refuses the kingship over the other trees, saying, "Have I [the olive] stopped producing my fatness [reference to oil] with which gods and people are being honored? . . ." (Judg 9:8–9). The view that oil was the sole product of the olive tree is confirmed by passages foretelling the destruction of the economic system when oil will not be available for anointing the body (Deut 28:40; Mic 6:15). All of these passages mention the olive tree as a source of oil, but never as a source of raw fruit for consumption.

Olive oil was used for many purposes, secular and cultic. In daily life oil was a very important staple (Jer 40:10; 41:8; Ezek 16:13, 19; Hag 2:12) and was used in food preparation, such as frying. It was used for anointing the body (Deut 28:40; Mic 6:15) and in the treatment of open wounds (Isa 1:6). The royal olive-oil storehouses, *ʾōṣĕrôt haššemen*, were stocked with oil from the royal groves (1 Chr 27:28) and from private sources. The latter source is documented by an ostracon discovered in Tell Qasîleh, which reads *lmlk ʾlp šmn wmʾh ḥyhw*, 'to the king, one thousand and one hundred (measures of) oil,

[25] See also 2 Kgs 18:32, "a land of bread [grain] and vineyards, a land of olive for oil [*ʾereṣ zêt yiṣhār*]."

om) [A]ḥiyahu' (Mazar 1950–51: 208; Paul and Dever 1974: 175, fig. 6). The Samaria Ostraca also reveal that a certain kind of oil, *šmn rḥṣ*, came from private sources (Diringer 1934: 35–36; Aharoni 1967: 315–27). Although the OT does not mention the domestic use of oil for lighting, oil is mentioned in reference to the lighting of the Tabernacle and the Temple. However, the large number of oil lamps discovered in archaeological excavations testifies to the widespread use of oil for lighting in the home. One of the vessels in which oil was stored is called *ṣappaḥat haššemen* (1 Kgs 17:12, 14, 16), which was used also for carrying water (1 Sam 26:11–12, 16; 1 Kgs 19:6); this vessel may be the so-called pilgrim flask, a clay vessel common in Iron Age strata.

Besides being used for lighting (Exod 25:6; 35:14; 39:37; Num 4:16), oil had a prominent place in cultic life as an offering. In this context a different word is used, i.e., *yiṣhār*, which is probably derived from *zhr/ṣhr* (*ṣhl*), 'shine' (BDB 1972: 843–44). The term *yiṣhār*, together with *tîrôš* and *dāgān*, is used in cultic contexts when the blessings (Deut 7:13; 11:14) and curses (28:51) are recited, and when certain laws concerning the offerings to the Temple (Num 18:12; Deut 18:4) and the eating of the *maᶜăśēr* (Deut 12:17; 14:23) are presented. The same term is used in the poetic language of the prophets (Jer 31:12; Hos 2:10, 24; and others) and appears in late official language (Neh 5:11; and others).

Oil was used for anointing prophets (1 Kgs 19:16), kings (Judg 9:8), priests (Exod 28:41), and the Tabernacle and its vessels (Exod 29:36). In some cases the anointing was done with holy ointment made of oil, *šemen hammišḥâ* (Exod 25:6); hence the anointed was called *māšîaḥ*.

The by-products of oil production are not mentioned in the OT at all, but it can be assumed that the refuse and crushed stones were used for kindling and were not thrown away.[26]

In addition to the olive remains mentioned above, remains were found in Iron Age strata at Lachish (Helbaek 1958: 310, 313), Beer-sheba and Arad (Liphschitz and Waisel 1973: 30), Tell Qiri (Ben Tor 1977b), and Tell Halif (Borowski 1981: 3; Laustrup 1982).

Although the use of oil in later periods for making soap is documented (Dalman 1935: 4.277), there is no indication in the OT for such use.

Date (*Phoenix dactylifera* L.)

The date palm, *tāmār* or *tōmer* (Judg 4:5), has many varieties, mostly wild. The variety cultivated in the Near East in antiquity and

[26] For use of olive leftovers, *gepet*, in the Mishna as kindling for bread baking, see discussion in Dalman 1935: 4. 17–18.

today is *Phoenix dactylifera* L. (Moldenke and Moldenke 1952: 169, fig. 70; Walker 1957: 160, fig. 161). The date palm was probably domesticated first in Lower Mesopotamia, where it was cultivated as early as 4000 B.C.E. (Zohary and Spiegel-Roy 1975: 323). In Eretz-Israel its earliest occurrences are in the Chalcolithic site of Teleilat Ghassul (Kenyon 1970: 72) and in the Cave of the Treasure at Naḥal Mishmar (Zaitschek 1961: 71).

Date palms grew in Eretz-Israel along the northern seacoast (Phoenicia, 'Land of Palms'), south of Jaffa and around Gaza, and in the Jordan Valley. The OT mentions a few places known for their date palms, such as Jericho, *ᶜîr hattĕmārîm*, 'the city of date palms' (Deut 34:3; Judg 1:16; 3:13; 2 Chr 28:15). The oasis ᵓElim in the Sinai desert was famous for its dates (Exod 15:27; Num 33:9); one special date palm located between Ramah and Bethel was used by Deborah as a place for judgment (Judg 4:5). Date palms grew during the Iron Age around the city of Lachish, as depicted in bas-reliefs from Nineveh describing the siege of Lachish by Sennacherib (Pritchard 1954: pl. 374), and along the western coast of the Dead Sea (Stager 1976: 145). As a fruit-bearing tree the date palm is mentioned in the OT only once (Joel 1:12); in other passages the palm is used in similes to describe a person's stature and character (Cant 7:8; Ps 92:13). Palm branches were used ritualistically in the celebration of Sukkot, as commanded in Lev 23:40 and described in Neh 8:15.

The cultivated date palm is vegetatively propagated, mostly by suckers growing next to the mother plant. Dates are dioecious and the female clones are artificially pollinated by hanging male flowers near the female flowers (Zohary and Spiegel-Roy 1975: 323; Goor 1967: 330). This method was learned by the Israelites from the Egyptians and Babylonians (Goor 1967: 330).

The date palm has many uses. It is used in the construction of buildings and huts; its leaves can be woven into mats, baskets, etc.; its fibrous sheath is used for making ropes, pillows, and matresses; from its trunk, juice can be extracted to be drunk fresh or fermented (Hareᵓuveni 1974: 55; Landsberger 1967). This drink was a favorite of the Egyptians and the Babylonians (Goor 1967: 323; Moldenke and Moldenke 1952: 170). One product of the date, *dĕbāš*, 'honey', represents this tree in the list of Deut 8:8. There is a possibility that the honey mentioned in the phrase *ᵓereṣ zābat ḥālāb ûdĕbāš* (Exod 3:8; and others) is a reference to the product of the date tree.[27]

The use of palm trees in construction influenced the decoration of the Solomonic Temple (1 Kgs 6) and served as a model for a special

[27] Honey was one of the goods exported from Eretz-Israel (Gen 43:11; Ezek 27:17).

type of Israelite pillar capital, *timōrâ*, used in the construction of royal palaces and buildings (Shiloh 1977, 1981).

Remains of dates in Iron Age strata were found at Beer-sheba and Arad (Liphschitz and Waisel 1973: 30–36).

Sycamore (*Ficus sycomorus* L.)

The biblical *šiqmîm* (or *šiqmôt*) have been clearly identified as *Ficus sycomorus* L. and should not be confused with the sycamore of North America, *Platanus occidentalis* L., or with that of the Old World, *P. orientalis* L., or with the sycamine (mulberry), *Morus nigra* L. (Moldenke and Moldenke 1952: 106–8; Walker 1957: 199, fig. 200). The sycamore originated in eastern Central Africa and Yemen, and from there it was introduced to Egypt and the rest of the Near East. Its multiple functions in Egypt caused it to be held sacred to several deities, especially Hathor, the goddess of love (Galil 1968: 178). The Egyptians used the sycamore fig as food; the wood was used in house construction and in the making of furniture, coffins, and other objects. The importance of the sycamore tree to the Egyptians is expressed in Ps 78:47: "He destroyed their vines with hail, and their sycamores with *ḥănāmāl*."[28]

During the Iron Age the sycamore was well established in Eretz-Israel and grew mainly in the plain (1 Kgs 10:27 = 2 Chr 1:15; 9:27). Sycamores were also grown around Teqoᶜa, Amos's hometown (Amos 7:14), south of Bethlehem. In the time of the monarchy, sycamores were used in building (Isa 9:9). David appointed Baᶜal Ḥanan the Gederite as overseer "over the olive trees and the sycamore trees which [were] in the Shephelah" (1 Chr 27:28).

Sycamore trees produce up to six crops a year, mostly during the hot summer months and occasionally during the winter (Galil 1968: 188). Although sycamore figs were used as food, they were always considered inferior to the common fig, *Ficus carica* L., and were mainly consumed by the poor (Goor 1965: 124, n. 2). It seems that the royal sycamore groves in the time of David were maintained for timber rather than food. This source of timber was apparently disregarded by Solomon, who preferred to bring cedars from Lebanon (1 Kgs 5:20–26; 10:27 = 2 Chr 1:15; 9:27).

As known from archaeological remains in Egypt and from present practices in Cyprus, sycamore figs have to be gashed or pierced to permit ripening of the fruit. It was formerly believed that gashing was necessary to get rid of the wasps, *Sycophaga sycomori* and *Apocrypta longitarsus*, which pollinate the flowers and cause the fruit to ripen

[28] See chap. 12.

(Galil 1968: 188). Recent studies show that although the sycamore wasp is important in the process of pollination and ripening (Galil and Eisikowitch 1968), the cause of ripening is ethylene gas, the production of which is increased by gashing (Galil 1968: 189). Gashing, which was performed in ancient Egypt with a special knife (Galil 1968: fig. 1), is depicted in bas-reliefs found in Thebes (Galil 1968: fig. 2), and gashed sycamore figs have been found in Egyptian tombs (Galil 1968: 179). This raises the question of Amos's profession in his statement to Amaziah "I am not a prophet or a member of a prophetic group, but a herdsman and *bôlēs šiqmîm*" (Amos 7:14). The word *bôlēs* has been translated as "a dresser of sycamore trees" (RSV), "a tender of sycomores" (BDB 1972: 1054), and "a piercer of sycamore figs" (LXX). The last translation is probably the correct one. Galil (1968: 188) admits that there is a certain difficulty in accepting this view, since contemporary Israeli plants produce edible fruit without gashing. He explains that the translation of *bôlēs* as 'piercer' is logical, because the Israeli sycamores are descended from the Egyptian and in ancient times were of the same varieties as those in Egypt. He further explains that it is conceivable that in the time of Amos the old varieties were still in existence, but by the continuous selection under Mediterranean climatic conditions new varieties of sycamore evolved in Israel.

No remains of sycamore figs or wood are reported from Iron Age sites in Eretz-Israel.

Other Fruit Trees

Uncertainty still exists as to the identification of two of the fruit trees mentioned in the OT. Also, there are fruit remains in archaeological deposits which cannot be related to any of the fruit trees named in the OT. The following is a brief discussion of the unidentified terms and of the archaeological evidence.

Tappûaḥ

Tappûaḥ occurs in Joel 1:12 and Cant 2:3, 5; 7:9; 8:5. It is rendered by the different Bible versions and dictionaries as 'apple' (BDB 1972: 656; Fohrer 1973: 303). According to these biblical passages the *tappûaḥ* is a cultivated tree (Joel 1:12; Cant 2:3), known for its shade (Cant 8:5) and good fragrance (7:9). These characteristics are not quite specific enough to enable a sure identification of the tree. The 'apple' has been identified with the fruit of 'the tree of knowledge' in the Garden of Eden (Moldenke and Moldenke 1952: 186), a tree which has also been identified with the fig (Moldenke and Moldenke 1952: 105) and the date palm (Moldenke and Moldenke 1952: 172).

The phrase *tappûḥê zāhāb*, '*tappûḥîm* of gold' (Prov 25:11), has been taken to indicate that the *tappûaḥ* is some kind of citrus tree (Shewell-Cooper 1962: 23), but this is incorrect because, as Moldenke and Moldenke point out (1952: 185–87), this family of trees is not native to the Near East and was imported to this region only after the Iron Age.

Another possible identification for the *tappûaḥ* is quince, *Cydonia oblonga* Mill. (Moldenke and Moldenke 1952: 186), which is very common in Eretz-Israel and Syria. It is a native of northern Persia and Asia Minor, and is known for its fragrance. However, its fruit is not sweet, but very acrid (Moldenke and Moldenke 1952: 186) and therefore does not meet all the requirements for being a *tappûaḥ*.

One fruit tree which fulfills all the requirements for being a *tappûaḥ* is the apricot, *Prunus armeniaca* L., also known as *Armeniaca vulgaris* Lam. It is a common tree in Palestine and Syria, in both the wild and cultivated states. Its fruit is known for its fragrance and sweet taste, and its color is gold (Moldenke and Moldenke 1952: 187; Walker 1957: 22, fig. 23). Although the fruit of the apricot contains one large pit, there are no remains reported from archaeological excavations.[29]

Bākāʾ (pl. *bĕkāʾîm*)

Shewell-Cooper (1962: 29–30, 113–14) identifies the *bākāʾ*, mentioned in 2 Sam 5:23–24 = 1 Chr 14:14–15 and Ps 84:7, as the black mulberry, *Morus nigra* L.[30] Moldenke and Moldenke (1952: 141) identify the trees mentioned in 2 Sam 5:23–24 and 1 Chr 14:14–15 as aspens, *Populus euphratica* Oliv., because of the sound of the leaves referred to in these passages, but they maintain that *Morus nigra* was cultivated in Eretz-Israel during biblical times (see also Zohary 1982: 71).[31] A later reference in Luke 17:6 to the "sycamine" is, according to Walker (1957: 204, fig. 205), to the mulberry and not to the sycamore. Both Moldenke and Moldenke (1952: 140) and Shewell-Cooper (1962: 30) agree that the black mulberry was cultivated in Iron Age Israel for its fruit and not to feed silkworms, which eat the leaves of the white mulberry, *Morus alba* L. The term *mešî* in Ezek 16:10, 13, sometimes translated 'silk' (BDB 1972: 603; Fohrer 1973: 164), cannot serve as evidence for silk manufacturing in ancient Israel and for the cultivation of the white mulberry.

[29] An uncarbonized peach pit found in an EB I shaft tomb at Bab edh-Dhraᶜ raises the possibility that the *tappûaḥ* should be identified with this fruit tree. For the reported find see McCreery 1978: 2.

[30] BDB 1972: 113 translates *bākāʾ* as 'balsam-tree'.

[31] Remains of *Populus euphratica* were found in Iron Age levels at Arad (Liphschitz and Waisel 1973: 32, and Table 2).

Carob

Another tree native to Palestine is *Ceratonia siliqua* L., commonly known as carob, locust bean tree, or St.-John's-bread. It is not mentioned at all in the OT, which is very surprising. In the NT it is mentioned in Luke 15:16 (although translated as 'husks' or 'pods'), and some commentators suggest that the 'locust' in Matthew 3:4 and Mark 1:6 is really the carob tree (Moldenke and Moldenke 1952: 72–73; Walker 1957: 120, fig. 121; Shewell-Cooper 1962: 28–29). If this suggestion is correct, then the *ḥāgāb*, 'locust', in Eccl 12:5 could also be the carob.

Fragments of carob beans with seeds were found in the Roman level at the Cave of the Pool (Zaitschek 1962: 185, pl. 21:b). No Iron Age remains are reported.

Nuts

Nuts were a very important dietary component for ancient man, who recognized their nutritional value (Renfrew 1973: table on p. 194). Different kinds of nuts have been found in archaeological contexts, but it is impossible to determine whether they were cultivated or gathered in the wild. Today, some of these types of nuts are both cultivated and available in the wild. In some cases biblical passages suggest the cultivation of certain nuts. The following discussion includes only domesticated nuts and excludes nut trees known to grow only in the wild state, even when found in archaeological contexts, e.g., the oak, *Quercus ithburensis* (Decne.) Boiss., the biblical *ʾallôn*.

Almond (*Prunus amygdalus* Stokes)

The biblical *šāqēd* (pl. *šĕqēdîm*) is identified as *Prunus amygdalus* Stokes (Moldenke and Moldenke 1952: 35; Walker 1957: 12, fig. 13; Shewell-Cooper 1962: 96–98). The Hebrew name is derived from the root *šqd*, 'watch, wake', and the tree is "so called from its early *waking* out of winter sleep" (BDB 1972: 1052), usually as early as January when the flowers appear before the leaves (Walker 1957: 12). The flowers of the almond tree were regarded as being so beautiful that in the construction of the Tabernacle and the Menorah they served as models for decorations (Exod 25:33–36; 37:19–20). The blooming of the almond tree had a special significance since it is used in Num 17:16–24 as a sign of the selection of Aaron; when Jeremiah saw an almond tree (Jer 1:11), it must have been in bloom. The reference in Eccl 12:1 must also be comprehended in this light; i.e., the white flowers should be understood as a symbol, probably, for old age and maturity.

Another name for the almond in the OT is *lûz* (Gen 30:37; BDB 1972: 531; Fohrer 1973: 134). *Lûz* was the former name of Bethel (Gen 28:19; Jos 18:13; Judg 1:23; and others) and might indicate that almond trees were in abundance in this region during the pre-Israelite period.

Almonds are known to grow in the wild (Renfrew 1973: 157), but most of their nuts are bitter in this state. Therefore, it is very likely that the *šĕqēdîm* (Gen 43:11) sent to Egypt by Jacob were domesticated almonds. When Jacob sent to Joseph some "fruit of the land," including almonds, he sent only delicacies and could not risk sending bitter almonds.

In Iron Age deposits in Eretz-Israel almonds were found at Beth-shemesh (Grant 1934: 22).[32] During the Iron Age almond wood was used in construction at Tell el-Fûl. Here, almond beams used in the second story of Fortress III replaced the coniferous cypress and pine beams used in Fortress I. "It seems that the coniferous forests had already disappeared from the environs of Tell el-Fûl" (Sinclair 1960: 28) at the time of Fortress III (eighth to seventh century B.C.E.).

Pistachio (*Pistacia atlantica* Desf.)

One of the gifts carried by the sons of Jacob on their second journey to Egypt was *boṭnîm* (Gen 43:11), now identified by scholars as pistachio nuts. There is still an argument as to which of the several kinds of pistachio growing in Eretz-Israel the OT refers. The LXX translated the Hebrew term as τερέβινθος, and the Vulgate translated it as *terebinthus*, but Zohary (1954c) claims that the *Pistacia terebinthus* does not grow in Eretz-Israel and the reference is, probably, to the fruit of the *P. palaestina* or *P. atlantica*, both of which are common in Eretz-Israel. The latter is called in Arabic *buṭm*. Others maintain that biblical *boṭnîm* are the nuts of the *P. vera* (Moldenke and Moldenke 1952: 179–80; Walker 1957: 146, fig. 147). Zohary (1954c) agrees that the nuts of *P. vera* are better tasting than those of the *P. atlantica*, but he points out that the former was not cultivated in Eretz-Israel in biblical times, and that the name in Mishnaic Hebrew for *P. vera* nuts is *fistĕqîn* and in Arabic it is *fustuq*, a name borrowed from Persian.[33] On the basis of this evidence it seems that *boṭnîm* should be identified as *P. atlantica*.

The biblical place-names *bĕṭōnîm* (Jos 13:26) and *beṭen* (Jos 19:26) might be derivatives of the Hebrew name of the *P. atlantica*, similar to

[32] Almonds were also found in the Chalcolithic and Roman levels in the caves of Naḥal Mishmar (Zaitschek 1961: 72), in the Roman level in the Cave of the Pool (Zaitschek 1962: 12), and in the LB II level of Tell Batash (Mazar and Kelm 1980: 92).

[33] Recently, Zohary (1982: 65) identified the OT *boṭnîm* with *Pistacia vera*.

the present Arabic names of Wadi Buṭmî, Kh. el-Buṭm, and others which are derived from the Arabic name of this plant.

Remains of *P. atlantica* Desf. nuts were found in EB Lachish (Helbaek 1958: 310–11). In Iron Age strata remains of *P. atlantica* and *P. palaestina* were found at Beer-sheba and Arad (Liphschitz and Waisel 1973: 32, tables 1–2).

Walnut (*Juglans regia* L.)

The biblical *ʾĕgôz*, translated as 'nut' (Fohrer 1973: 3) and 'nuts' (BDB 1972: 8), is now identified as *Juglans regia* L., the Persian, or common, walnut (Moldenke and Moldenke 1952: 119–20; Zohary 1982: 65). Previously, the scientific term was applied to the *ʾalmuggîm* (1 Kgs 10:11–12) and *ʾalgûmîm* (2 Chr 9:10), now identified as *Pterocarpus santalinus* L. f., red sandalwood (Moldenke and Moldenke 1952: 188–89; Walker 1957: 14, fig. 15; Shewell-Cooper 1962: 98), or *Sabina excelsa* (Bieb.) Antoine, Grecian juniper (Moldenke and Moldenke 1952: 209).

The term *ʾĕgôz* appears only once in the OT in the phrase *ginnat ʾĕgôz*, 'walnut garden' (Cant 6:11), which suggests the cultivation of this tree.

Walnuts have been found in archaeological deposits in Europe (Renfrew 1973: 156). There are no remains of walnuts reported from Iron Age levels in Eretz-Israel.[34]

The importance of fruit in the diet of the inhabitants of Palestine and of fruit trees in the economy of this land cannot be overemphasized. While in the period of the tribal league and the monarchy it manifests itself in the numerous OT passages mentioning fruit and fruit trees, in later periods the importance of fruit found its expression on coins. Starting with Jewish coins from the period of the Second Commonwealth, different fruits, such as grapes and pomegranates, were adopted as symbols, and these motifs later found their way also into other modes of art, such as mosaics and oil lamp decorations.

[34] Reported walnut remains from Eretz-Israel come from the Chalcolithic and Roman levels at Naḥal Mishmar (Zaitschek 1961: 72) and from the Roman level in the Cave of the Pool (Zaitschek 1962: 185).

10
Vegetables

Vegetables are referred to in the OT by the collective terms *zērûaᶜ* (Lev 11:37)[1] and *yārāq* (Deut 11:10; 1 Kgs 21:2; Prov 15:17). Only once does the OT enumerate several vegetables. This occurs in the description of the incident at *Qibrôt-hattaʾăwâ*, 'Graves of Craving', where the Israelites, while in the desert, craved in addition to meat and fish "the cucumbers, the melons, the leeks[?], the onions, and the garlic" (Num 11:5) that they were familiar with in Egypt. The information contained in this passage relates to gardening in ancient Egypt, where horticulture was very well developed because of the availability of water for irrigation and suitable terrain (Wilkinson 1841: 49–63; MacKay 1950: 102). There are no such passages in the OT relating to Eretz-Israel. The lack of explicit references to gardening in Eretz-Israel can be attributed to the state of horticulture in this region during the Iron Age. This branch of agriculture was not well developed for two reasons: (1) the scarcity of convenient water sources for watering garden plots and (2) the hilly terrain dominating the countryside. Both conditions are well described in Deut 12:10–11:

> For the land which you are entering to take possession of it is not like the land of Egypt, from which you have come, where you sowed your seed and watered it with your feet, like a garden of vegetables. But the land which you are going over to possess is a land of hills and valleys, which drink water by the rain from heaven.

The underdeveloped state of horticulture could be behind the Israelite attitude that held vegetables in low regard, as exemplified by the proverb "Better is a meal of vegetables [*ʾărūḥat yārāq*] where love is than fatted ox and hatred with it" (Prov 15:17).[2] Nevertheless, gardening was practiced to a certain extent, especially where there were

[1] Pl. *zērûᶜîm*, Isa 61:11; *zērōᶜîm*, Dan 1:12; *zērᶜōnîm*, Dan 1:16 (see Bevan 1892: 62; Hammer 1976: 17).

[2] From the story of Daniel and the Israelite children it appears that vegetables were not considered as nutritious as other foodstuffs (Dan 1:11–16).

favorable conditions for establishing a garden near the house. One such situation is reflected in the conflict between Ahab and Naboth, described in 1 Kgs 21:2: "Ahab said to Naboth, 'Give me your vineyard, that I may have it for a vegetable garden [*gan yārāq*], because it is near my house." Another garden located close to a royal palace was *gan-ᶜuzzāᵓ*, "the garden of Uzza" (2 Kgs 21:18, 26), where Manasseh and Amon were buried. The garden is described as *gan bêtô*, 'the garden of his house'. Other references to a royal garden, *gan hammelek*, within the walls of Jerusalem are included in the story of the flight of Zedekiah from the besieged city (2 Kgs 25:5; Jer 39:4; 52:7) and in the description of the reconstruction of Jerusalem under Nehemiah (Neh 3:15). It is not clear from these passages whether the royal garden in Jerusalem was a mixed orchard, a vegetable garden, or both. One metaphorical vegetable garden is mentioned by Isaiah: "As a garden [*gannâ*] causes its vegetables [*zērûᶜeyhâ*] to spring up, so the Lord YHWH will cause righteousness and praise to spring forth before all the nations" (61:11).

There is one piece of evidence showing that not all gardens were near houses. When Isaiah (1:8) describes the fate of Jerusalem, he compares the city to "an overnight shelter [*mĕlûnâ*] in a cucumber field [*miqšâ*]." A *mĕlûnâ* would not have been constructed in a garden next to a house, and the implication is that there were gardens outside the settlement and they required protection from people and animals. These gardens were located so that they would be near water sources (Isa 1:30; 58:11; Jer 31:11; Cant 4:15; Neh 3:15). They were protected from birds by scarecrows, *tōmer miqšâ* (Jer 10:5; BDB 1972: 1071).

Not all vegetables and greens were grown in gardens. Sometimes they were gathered in the wild, as in the case of Elisha's helper who went out to the field to gather *ᵓōrōt*, but by mistake collected the poisonous fruit of the wild vine (2 Kgs 4:38–40). It is also possible that some of the weeds hoed during *yrḥ ᶜṣd pšt* were gathered for human consumption. The practice of gathering wild vegetables for part of the daily diet is attested by the remains of bulbs of wild plants discovered together with remains of cultivated plants in the caves of Naḥal Mishmar (Zaitschek 1961: 72).

Vegetable remains in archaeological contexts are very scarce because of the nature of vegetables; they tend to go bad soon after harvest and so must be eaten fairly quickly. Only under very dry conditions can vegetables be preserved. Hence, archaeology is not of much help when studying Iron Age horticulture.

The following is a catalog of vegetables probably cultivated in Eretz-Israel during the Iron Age. The order of presentation follows the order in Num 11:5, our major literary source for vegetables in the OT.

Qiššūʾîm

The word for cucumber appears only once in the OT, in the plural form, *qiššūʾîm* (Num 11:5).[3] The singular form has been suggested to be *qiššūʾâ* (BDB 1972: 903; Fohrer 1973: 252) or *qiššût* (Zohary 1955: 21–22; Yaffe 1943a: 42–44; Yaffe 1943b: 85–88; Cziżik 1943: 302–3; Ben-Hayim 1943: 89–92). Walker (1957: 64, fig. 65) identifies this plant as the cucumber *Cucumis sativus* L. Moldenke and Moldenke (1952: 88) offer two possibilities, *C. sativus* or its close relative *C. chate* L. Zohary (1955) maintains that only *C. chate*, known in Arabic as *faqûs*, was cultivated in ancient Egypt. *C. chate* "is usually considered the finest of all melon and melon-like fruits. . . . Its flesh is melon-like and more watery than that of the common cucumber. Hasselquist[4] calls it 'the Queen of the Cucumbers'" (Moldenke and Moldenke 1952: 88).

The cultivation of *qiššūʾîm* in Eretz-Israel is attested by the term *miqšâ*, 'a field of *qiššūʾîm*' (Isa 1:8; Jer 10:5). No remains of *C. sativus* or *C. chate* are reported from Eretz-Israel.

ʾĂbaṭṭîḥîm

According to Zohary (1955), only two out of the four species of the Cucurbitaceae family were cultivated in Egypt and Eretz-Israel in biblical times: *Citrullus vulgaris* and *Cucumis melo*. W. Smith (in Moldenke and Moldenke 1952: 81) reports that both are named in Arabic *batêkh*. G. E. Post says that muskmelon, *Cucumis melo*, is called in Arabic "*battîkh-asfar*" and watermelon, *Citrullus vulgaris*, is called "*battîkh-akhdar*" (in Moldenke and Moldenke 1952: 81). Zohary (1955) maintains that only the *Citrullus vulgaris* is called *baṭṭîḥ* in Arabic, and it should be identified with biblical *ʾăbaṭṭîḥîm* (sg. **ʾăbaṭṭîaḥ*).[5]

Watermelon seeds were found recently at the EB site of Bab edh-Dhraᶜ, near the Dead Sea (McCreery 1978: 2). In Iron Age strata from Eretz-Israel watermelon seeds were found at Arad (Liphschitz and Waisel 1973: 35, table 2, pls. 8, 9A, 9B). The absence of muskmelon seeds from Iron Age deposits in Eretz-Israel does not make the identification of *ʾăbaṭṭîḥîm* as watermelons conclusive.

[3] All vegetables in the following sections, except for *ḥāṣîr*, appear only in their plural form and are mentioned only in Num 11:5.

[4] F. Hasselquist traveled in the Levant in the 1800s.

[5] The latest identification of *ʾabaṭṭîḥîm* by Zohary (1982: 85) is with *Citrullus lanatus* (Thumb.) Mansf. (watermelon), and of *qiššūʾîm* is with *Cucumis Melo* L. var. chatae Nand. (Zohary 1982: 86).

Ḥāṣîr

Most scholars agree that *ḥāṣîr* when used in Num 11:5 refers to leeks, *Allium porrum* L. (Zohary 1958b; Moldenke and Moldenke 1952: 34–35; Walker 1957: 110, fig. 111), a plant which is related to the onion and which was cultivated in Egypt. Since the meaning of the Hebrew root *ḥṣr* is 'be green' (BDB 1972: 348), some commentators have identified *ḥāṣîr* with fenugreek, another plant commonly cultivated in Egypt. Its seeds are used as spice and its green leaves are eaten raw (Moldenke and Moldenke 1952: 34).

Those who favor identification as 'leeks' rely on the position this term occupies in the verse, i.e., before onions and garlic. This can hardly be a good reason since *ḥāṣîr* follows cucumbers and melons with no apparent division, and hence it might belong to this group of plants.

The use of the term *ḥāṣîr* in other OT passages (2 Kgs 19:26 = Isa 37:27; Ps 129:6) suggests that in these cases the underlying characteristics are the green color of the plant and its close relationship to other grasses. There is a possibility that *ḥāṣîr* was a plant with large green leaves similar to salad greens today. A definite identification based on the information available is impossible.

Bĕṣālîm

The biblical *bĕṣālîm* (sg. **bāṣāl* or **bāṣēl*) have been identified as *Allium cepa* L., the common onion (Zohary 1954d; Walker 1957: 157, fig. 157). Moldenke and Moldenke claim that the biblical plant should be identified with the variety known as the Egyptian onion; according to F. Hasselquist, "whoever has tasted onions in Egypt, must allow that none can be had better in any part of the universe" (in Moldenke and Moldenke 1952: 33). Egypt was always known for its onions, and the proximity of Egypt to Eretz-Israel might have influenced onion cultivation there (Zohary 1954d; Moldenke and Moldenke 1952: 33).

No remains of onions are reported from Iron Age Eretz-Israel. Remains of onions were found in EB and MB Jericho (Renfrew 1973: 201) and in the caves of Naḥal Mishmar (Zaitschek 1961: 72).

Šûmîm

Like most of the other vegetables mentioned above, *šûmîm* appears only once in the OT (Num 11:5), in its plural form; the singular form would be **šûm* (BDB 1972: 1002) or **šûmâ* (Freedman 1978). This plant is identified as the common garlic, *Allium sativum* L. (Walker 1957: 90, fig. 91). Some scholars identify *šûmîm* as *A.*

ascalonicum L. (Moldenke and Moldenke 1952: 32; BDB 1972: 1002), but the latter is only a variety of *A. cepa*, identified as *bĕṣālîm*. "The epithet Ascalonia applied by the Roman writers Columella and Pliny to a variety of onion merely indicates that it was cultivated about Escalon" (W. T. Stearn in Moldenke and Moldenke 1952: 32).

The bulb of *A. sativum* contains many cloves; they are used in cooking as a spice or eaten raw (Moldenke and Moldenke 1952: 32; Walker 1957: 90).

Remains of garlic were found in the caves of Naḥal Mishmar (Zaitschek 1961: 72) and in the Cave of the Pool (Zaitschek 1962: 185). No garlic remains are reported from Iron Age deposits.

The small number of vegetable samples from Iron Age deposits does not indicate that vegetables were a minor component of the daily diet during that period. However, as I pointed out above, the small number of references to vegetables and the low regard in which vegetables were held suggest very strongly that vegetables were not considered very nutritious and did not constitute an important part of the Iron Age diet in Eretz-Israel.

Part IV

Factors in Soil Fertility and Crop Yield

11

Restoration of Soil Fertility

Continuous use of the soil depletes the nutritional resources available to plants, which, in turn, lowers the yield. To maintain a high level of agricultural production, soil fertility has to be restored. Restoration of fertility can be accomplished in several ways, some of which were available to agriculturalists in biblical times.

Three methods for fertility restoration could have been used by farmers in antiquity: (*a*) fallowing, (*b*) organic fertilizing, and (*c*) crop rotation. Each one of these methods could have been employed by itself or in combination with others. Archaeologically, fertility restoration is a subject which is hard to study because it did not leave direct evidence in soil deposits. The lack of direct evidence and documentation for fertility restoration discouraged scholars from dealing with the subject and led others to conclusions such as: "Fertilization was well known in Roman times; but in the periods before and after, until the present day, the soil was spoilt" (Reifenberg 1955: 80).[1]

Recent studies of prehistoric agriculture by Dimbleby (1967) show that the decrease in soil fertility

> can be made good if he [the farmer] will after a time leave the land to restore itself by successional development. Studies of prehistoric agriculture and present-day land use in primitive societies show that this was learnt early. . . . The land is used until fertility falls off; then it is abandoned to natural regrowth and it may be many years before the same piece of ground is returned to (Dimbleby 1967: 24).

[1] See also Gvaryahu 1954: 510. For a detailed discussion of manuring in the Roman period see Fussell 1971: 13–29. MacKay (1950: 203–4) proposes that human remains were used to fertilize the soil in biblical times. He bases his theory on passages such as 2 Kgs 9:37; Jer 9:22; 16:4; 25:33; Ps 83:10. He explains the origin of this practice as the result of placing cereal grain in human burials. "In due course the enriched soil returned a bumper crop of barley and oats, and the spirit of the departed was doubly blessed." This theory has to be discarded for the following reasons: (1) in most cases the dead were buried too deeply for the seeds to sprout and produce a high yield; (2) he does not understand the metaphors in the passages he cites. For an explanation of these metaphors see below, Organic Fertilizing.

But when populations had increased, the demand for land forced shorter periods of fallow, and since fertility had not been built up again, other methods for restoring fertility had to be found.

> Even in prehistoric times it is likely that something was known about restoration of fertility by other means [than fallow] such as addition of wood ash or household refuse, and today the use of fertilizers of one sort and another has largely replaced the older practices of fallow and rotation of crops (Dimbleby 1967: 24–25).

The following is a discussion concerning each of the methods of fertility restoration available to the biblical farmer and the evidence for its employment.

Fallowing

With the increase of population and the scarcity of agricultural land, a cycle of sowing and fallowing had to be developed. The OT addressed itself to this problem, and in the law code it is determined that

> for six years you shall sow your land and gather its yield; but the seventh you shall leave it [*tišměṭennâ*] and forsake it [*něṭaštāh*], that the poor of your people may eat. . . . You shall do likewise with your vineyard and with your olive grove (Exod 23:10–11).

The reason given for the fallow year is not agricultural but rather social, i.e., concern for the poor. However, knowledge of the agricultural benefits resulting from fallowing can be inferred from the Sabbath law, which immediately follows the law of fallowing:

> Six days you shall do your work, but on the seventh you shall rest; that your ox and your ass may have rest, and the son of your bondmaid, and the alien may be refreshed (Exod 23:12).

The rest provided by the Sabbath law is the reason for its institution and serves also as a brief explanation for the fallowing year mentioned in the preceding law.

Several scholars believe that "letting the land lie fallow was clearly to provide permanent sustenance for the poor and wild animals" (Phillips 1973: 104; also, Carmichael 1974: 85), but it is obvious that the first year aftergrowth, *sāpîaḥ* (2 Kgs 19:29), could hardly sustain all the poor for six years. There were other provisions to take care of the poor (e.g., Lev 19:9; 23:22; Deut 14:28–29; 24:19–21). It seems more reasonable to believe that the law of fallowing was primarily meant to provide the land with rest. Leaving the aftergrowth for the poor was only a secondary consideration.

Phillips (1973: 104) maintains that "fallowing cannot have taken place simultaneously throughout Israel, but must have been staggered by a system of rotation." I suggest that each farmer left a seventh of his land fallow each year, thus providing rest for the land and food for the poor. During fallowing no plowing took place, as implied by the verb *nĕṭaštāh*, 'you will forsake it'.[2] The institution of a universal Sabbatical Year was ordained only in Leviticus 25, which is exilic or post-exilic.[3]

Organic Fertilizing

There are no direct references in the OT to organic fertilizing, but it is alluded to in several passages. Organic fertilizing can be achieved by application of manure, household refuse, and ashes to the soil.

In the case of manure, the OT makes a very careful distinction in the terms used to describe different types of dung and their sources. Human excrement, *ṣēʾâ* (Ezek 4:12) or *ṣōʾâ* (2 Kgs 18:27 = Isa 36:12), was prohibited from use, as stated by the Deuteronomic law which stipulates that it has to be buried with a special tool, *yātēd* (Deut 23:14). This prohibition is the reason for Ezekiel's dismay when he is ordered to use human excrement as fuel for baking the symbolic barley bread (Ezek 4:14). Human excrement, therefore, can be ruled out as organic fertilizer. On the other hand, animal dung was not prohibited from use. One primary use of animal dung in Eretz-Israel was for fuel, especially for bread baking. Dry dung, *gālāl* (1 Kgs 14:10; pl. *gĕlālîm*, Zeph 1:17; or the hapax *ṣpwᶜy* [Qere, *ṣpyᶜy*] *hbqr*, Ezek 4:15), was, most likely, collected in the animal sheds or wherever the cattle grazed.

Another term for animal dung used by the OT is *dōmen*. This term applied to manure left in the field as organic fertilizer. *Dōmen* is always used as a metaphor to describe corpses lying on the ground, *ᶜal pĕnê haśśādeh* (2 Kgs 9:37; Jer 9:21; also *ᶜal pĕnê hāʾădāmâ*, Jer 8:2; 16:4; 25:33). While the ultimate function of *dōmen* is not very clear from these references, it becomes clear from the following one, which states: "Do to them [the enemies] as thou didst to Midian . . . who became *dōmen* for the soil" (Ps 83:11).[4] In this verse there is a clear reference to dung and to its function as organic fertilizer. The agricultural use of *dōmen* is also alluded to by Jeremiah when he describes in agricultural terms the end of Jerusalem, saying: "The dead

[2] Modern practices in Israel employ two- or three-year cycles during which only part of the land is left fallow. When these cycles are practiced, fallow land is left plowed.

[3] The laws in Deut 15:1–2 and 9 related to *šĕmiṭṭâ* do not mention the land at all; they are concerned with release of debts. Therefore, they should be regarded as a different set of laws developed to remedy an existing condition.

[4] Here the word is *lāʾădāmâ*, 'for the soil', with the preposition *l* denoting 'for, for the benefit of'; see BDB 1972: 514–15.

bodies of men shall fall like *dōmen* upon the field, like ᶜ*āmîr* ['harvested stalks'] behind the reaper, and none shall gather them" (Jer 9:21[22]).

The gathering of *dōmen* mentioned by Jeremiah is evidence for another agricultural practice. *Dōmen* was collected into heaps and mixed with straw to produce compost, *madmēnâ* (Isa 25:10).[5] The cities Madmen (Jer 48:2), Madmenâ (Isa 10:31), Madmannâ (Jos 15:31), and probably also Dimnâ (Jos 21:35) could have specialized in compost making. MacKay (1950: 205) suggests that these "widely separated places may have specialized in compost making, selling the finished product to local farmers and vineyard owners." This also explains why these communities would allow themselves to be called 'dung heap' or 'compost heap', which otherwise would be a slur.

The use of household refuse as organic fertilizer is not attested in the OT, but Dimbleby (1967: 25) has suggested that this practice was already known to prehistoric man. If the farmer of biblical times used household refuse, he probably used it in small plots and gardens near the house or in the close vicinity of the settlement. This can be inferred from the fact that large quantities of household refuse cannot be stored for a long period before they decay completely and cannot be transported to the distant fields. Household refuse can be used as organic fertilizer when it is buried in the ground immediately, and then the most practical place is near the house. Household refuse can also be used when mixed with other organic matter in a compost pile.

Another substance that can be used in organic fertilizing is ash. There are several terms used by the OT to refer to ash, but with one exception, that of *dešen*, no distinction is made as to the source or the use of the ash. Two terms will be discussed here, ᵓ*ēper* and *dešen*, and an effort will be made to identify the source of each type of ash and to determine whether or not there is sufficient information in the OT to show that ash was used as organic fertilizer.

The first term, ᵓ*ēper*, is mentioned many times in the OT and is used to express worthlessness, ignominy, mourning, contrition, and distress.[6] Several times ᵓ*ēper* appears in poetic parallelism with ᶜ*āpār*, 'dry earth, dust' (Gen 18:27; Job 30:19; 42:6; Ezek 27:30; BDB 1972: 779), denoting worthlessness—but ᶜ*āpār* is not as worthless as it

[5] Mixing of straw with *dōmen* is an indication for *dōmen* being wet rather than dry dung, *gĕlālîm*. Dry dung, which is quite hard, cannot be mixed with straw or any other substance unless water is added. The Ketiv *bĕmê*, 'in the water of', is correct and not the Qere *bĕmô*, 'in'.

[6] Worthlessness: Gen 18:27; Isa 44:20; Job 13:12; 30:19. Ignominy: Ezek 28:18; Mal 3:21. Mourning: 2 Sam 13:19; Isa 61:3; Jer 6:26; and others. Contrition: Job 42:6; Dan 9:3. Distress: Lam 3:16.

appears in poetry and proverbial sayings, and neither is *ʾēper*. As a matter of fact, in Ps 147:16, "He gives snow like wool; he scatters hoarfrost like ashes," *ʾēper* appears in a description of the beneficial acts performed by God.

Except for the explicit reference in the case of the red heifer (Num 19:9–10),[7] *ʾēper* is probably the term used for ashes produced by domestic activities, such as baking (Mal 3:21). When ashes are mentioned in Ezek 28:18, the implication is that they are scattered on the ground. This is clearly stated in Ps 147:16, where the root *pzr*, 'scatter', is used. These two references imply that *ʾēper* was used as fertilizer. After a certain amount of ashes were collected in one place, the ashes would be taken outside the settlement to the gardens and the fields and scattered there as organic fertilizer.

While the source of *ʾēper* is not made explicit, the source of *dešen* is clearly stated to be animal sacrifices burnt on the altar (Num 4:13; 1 Kgs 13:3, 5). The term *dešen*, which also means 'fatness' and 'oil' (Jud 9:9), is applied to the altar ashes because of their high content of animal fat. A second reason might be the fact that altar ashes "fatten" the soil when used as fertilizer. The *dešen* which was cleared off the altar was placed outside the Israelite encampment (Lev 1:16; 4:12; 6:4) or outside the city wall (Jer 31:39) in a designated place, *mĕqôm haddešen* (Lev 1:16); this place was considered pure, *māqôm ṭāhôr* (Lev 6:4). There was a specific procedure to be followed when removing the *dešen* from the altar. First, the ashes were taken off the altar and placed beside it, and then after the High Priest changed his clothes, he transferred the ashes to the pure place outside the camp. It seems that once the ashes were outside the camp, they became available to the community for general use. I suggest that the *dešen* was commonly used for agricultural purposes. *Dešen* could have been produced in any of the temples and shrines scattered throughout the land and available for local use.

The use of animal remains as fertilizer can be inferred from several passages in the OT. Lev 3:17 and 7:23, 26–27 clearly state that the Israelites were prohibited from eating blood and animal fat. Yet, several references point out that blood and animal fat were sources of healthy growth, as depicted in Deut 32:14 and Ps 63:6. These metaphors can be understood only in the light of an agricultural practice that used animal remains as fertilizer. This practice must have served as the

[7] In Num 19:9–10 the *ʾēper* of the red heifer is mentioned in a context similar to that of *dešen* in Lev 4:12 and 6:3–4, the agricultural function of which is discussed below. The ashes of the red heifer were prohibited from any use except that of making the 'water of impurity' for washing away sins.

background for Isaiah's pronouncement (34:7) "Wild oxen shall fall with them, and young steers with the mighty bulls. Their land shall be soaked with blood, and their soil made rich with fat [*yědušsān*]." This passage gives a clear picture of the use of blood and animal fat as organic fertilizer.

The use of *dešen* as organic fertilizer to rejuvenate the soil and restore its fertility explains many OT passages employing *dešen* metaphorically, such as Isa 4:6; 55:2; Jer 31:14; Job 36:16. In Ps 92:13–15 the righteous are depicted as trees growing in the Temple courtyard: "They still bring forth fruit in old age; they are well fertilized with *dešen* and are luxuriantly green."[8] Ps 36:9 and 63:6 should also be understood to refer to this agricultural practice. The former should be translated "They are sated with *dešen* of your house [Temple]; you water them from the stream of your delicacies"; and the latter, "My soul is sated with fat [*ḥēleb*] and *dešen*." Both passages use *dešen*, the organic fertilizer from the Temple, as a metaphor to describe a source of strength.[9]

Crop Rotation

The continuous cultivation of a single crop in the same field depletes the soil of certain nutrients and encourages the proliferation of pests and diseases which attack that crop. The result is a low yield. This situation can be partially remedied by using crop rotation, the cultivation of different crops in the same field in successive seasons. Crop rotation can be practiced in a well-planned cycle resulting in optimum yield.[10] In addition, this method helps to control erosion (Thompson 1952: 282–84; Russell 1973: 783–84).

Different plants use different amounts and different proportions of nutrients from the so l. Cereals absorb fewer mineral nutrients than pulses (Russell 1973: 23), and pulses help replenish the soil with

[8] The righteous placed in the Temple courtyard were near the source of *dešen*; therefore I translate *děšēnîm* here as 'well fertilized with *dešen*'.

[9] Another example is Ps 65:12. The second half of this verse is translated by the RSV as "the tracks of thy chariot drip with fatness"; Dahood (1968: 109) translates "may your pastures drip fatness." Ps 65:10–14 is a hymn praising God for blessing the world with agricultural abundance. In addition to watering the land (vv 10–11), God blesses his people by giving them *dešen*, which enriches the soil, rather than just 'fatness' or 'oil', a blessing which is very limited.

[10] A well-planned cycle is based on factors such as topography, nature of the soil, and type of farm maintained. For modern practices and studies see Thompson 1952: 248–69.

nitrogen, which is essential for plant growth (Russell 1973: 31).[11] In the organic farming practiced in antiquity, the restoration of minerals to the soil could have been carried out by adding manure and ash, while the restoration of nitrogen could have been achieved by legume rotation.[12] The use of legumes as part of an agricultural cycle is documented in Theophrastus's book *Enquiry into Plants* (Hort 1916: 185) and is reported by several Roman writers.[13] In modern agriculture, crop rotation relies heavily on scientific research for best results. In antiquity, crop rotation was the result of observation and experience.

Although there is no direct evidence in the OT for the practice of crop rotation, three passages may have relevance. The first two passages deal with the taboo of *kilʾayim*, 'mixture of two kinds' or 'hybrids' (Lev 19:19; Deut 22:9); the third passage is known as the "Proverb of the Farmer" (Isa 28:24–29).

The taboo of *kilʾayim* is a puzzling one, especially since the Holiness code (Lev 19:19) does not supply a reason or explanation for it; the prohibition is just prefaced with the command "You shall keep my statutes." Neither is there a reason given by the Deuteronomic code (Deut 22:9), only a punishment for breaking the law. The Babylonian Talmud and the Tosefta, both of which treat the question of *kilʾayim* at length, deal with this subject as a practical matter, detailing its proper implementation, but they do not explain the reason behind the prohibition. However, as Singer (1928: 79) observes: "Taboos, like other social regulations, survive chiefly because they contain some value to man, or such value is ascribed to them." Smith (1894: 163–64) makes the same observation:

> Unreasonable taboos . . . are sure to be evaded in the long run because public opinion is against them, whereas taboos that make for the general good and check wrongdoing are supported and enforced by the community, and ultimately pass into laws with civil sanction. But no ancient society deemed it good order to be sufficiently secured by civil sanctions alone; there was always the last recourse to the curse, the ordeal, the oath of probation at the sanctuary—all of them means to stamp an

[11] The process by which pulses replenish the soil with nitrogen is carried out by the bacterium *Rhizobium*, which enters the roots of the legumes and causes the formation of nodules containing nitrogen (Meyer and Anderson 1952: 517–19; Thompson 1952: 140–46; Malherbe 1953: 25, 275).

[12] Russell 1973: 275–81. "Green-manuring" is the modern method and is accomplished by plowing whole legume plants back into the soil at a certain stage of their growth. The ancient method utilized only the roots and is termed "legume-rotation" by Gras (1925: 31–35).

[13] See Russell 1973: 13–29; Gras 1925: 31–35, and n. on pp. 47–50.

offender with the guilt of impiety and bring him under the direct judgment of the supernatural powers.

Thus, an understanding of the taboos concerning the mixing of certain things involves determining the underlying reasons for their creation.

Both the Levitical and Deuteronomic prohibtions mention three types of mixtures which are taboo:

Holiness Code	*Deuteronomic Code*
Cross breeding of animals	Powing with an ox and ass team
Wearing a *šaᶜaṭnēz* garment	Wearing a *šaᶜaṭnēz* of wool and flax
Sowing *kilᵓayim* in the field	Sowing *kilᵓayim* in a vineyard

It is obvious that in both codes these prohibitions were placed next to each other because all had to do with combinations of two things; however, the specific taboos do not necessarily stem from the same source or reason. Scholars explain that in the case of *šaᶜaṭnēz* "there is evidence that cloth mixtures had associations with magic" (Eiselen, Lewis, and Downey 1929: 291).[14] As for the matter of mixing seeds, "the underlying conception may be that of distinction of species (cf. Gen. 1:11, 12, 24f): each species has its distinct and divinely given characteristics which are not to be interfered with" (Eiselen, Lewis, and Downey 1929: 334–35). These explanations are ideological and do not reflect the practical background and reasons for instituting such prohibitions.[15]

To understand the reason for the *kilᵓayim* taboo one must understand the term and its application. The root of *kilᵓayim* is *klᵓ*, 'shut up, restrain, withhold, confine, imprison'. Agriculturally, *kilᵓayim* means 'one kind imprisoned, confined by the other', i.e., the effect which one plant exerts over the other when sown in close proximity or mixed together. Such effects have been observed in the field and reported by Russell (1973: 553)[16] and could have been noticed and interpreted by the biblical farmer as one plant exploiting the other. One kind exploiting the other could have been also the reason for the

[14] Carmichael (1974: 164) suggests that "wool and linen worn together specifically suggest the trade of the harlot."

[15] The prohibition against cross-breeding animals is puzzling since mules were known in Israel (2 Sam 13:29; 1 Kgs 10:25; and others). The prohibition against plowing with a mixed team can be explained as a humane approach to the treatment of animals.

[16] Russell (1973: 553) states that: "excretions from the roots of some plant species affect the growth of other roots, usually of other species. This can be very noticeable at the seeding stage, and may be the explanation of the observation so frequently made in the field, that even small weeds can interfere with a germinating crop more than one would expect from their power of competing for light and nutrients."

prohibition against plowing with a mixed team of animals.[17] Once the farmer started guarding against mixing seeds of two species and was able to observe the beneficial effects on the soil, crop rotation followed as a natural development.

The observation of the *kilʾayim* prohibition regarding sowing is evident in the Proverb of the Farmer in Isa 28:24–29. Here, the prophet calls the people to listen to the words of YHWH, who is great in wisdom and teaches the farmer all that he knows. Although the meanings of some of the terms in this story are uncertain,[18] the overall theme is very clear: that different species should not be mixed together and should be sown in their appointed place, *gĕbūlātô*.[19] The appointed plots are, probably, those determined by the farmer according to the crop cycle he practiced.

Although there are no specific references in the OT to crop rotation, I suggest that the biblical farmer could see the effects of mixing species and of sowing the same crop continuously in the same field. The biblical farmer, merely by observing his field, was probably aware of the fact that wheat exhausts the soil and legumes enrich it. The taboo against mixing crops and its reflection in the Proverb of the Farmer are our only evidence for the practice of crop rotation in Iron Age Israel.

A hypothetical crop rotation cycle in biblical Eretz-Israel could have been: first, third, and fifth year—cereals (wheat, barley); second, fourth, and sixth year—legumes (lentils, bitter vetch, chick-pea, peas); seventh year—fallow. Summer crops, spices, and crops such as flax could have been added to increase the yearly agricultural output.

[17] Carmichael (1974: 159–63) interprets 'plowing' as meaning 'cross-breeding' here.

[18] *Śôrâ* and *nismān* have been translated 'row' and 'the appointed place, strip' (Wade 1929: 183–84; Slotky 1949: 133; Dillman 1890: 259; and many others). Other scholars interpret these terms as different kinds of crops (Lidzbarski 1898: 374, 442; Zgorodsky 1930: 373–76). Some say that *śôrâ* means 'excellent' and *nismān*, 'fine' (Jenour 1830: 439). For others these two terms are dittographies for *śĕʿōrâ* and *kussemmet*; see BDB 1972: 702, 965, for bibliography.

[19] The verb used by the prophet for sowing the cereals is *śām*, from the root *śwm*/*śym*, 'put, place, set', and that used for sowing the cumin and black cumin is *hēpîṣ*, from the root *pwṣ*, 'be dispersed, scattered'. The regular verb for sowing is *zrʿ*. The use of *śām* indicates the great care the farmer had to take when sowing different seeds in close proximity. Accuracy may have been achieved by employing the seed-drill; see chap. 5.

12
Pests & Diseases

The OT regards want and plenty as results of reward and punishment for observing or breaking the covenant between Israel and YHWH. This belief is the background of Deuteronomy 28, where the blessings and curses are enumerated, and it is reflected in messages delivered by several of the prophets (Isa 30:19–26; Amos 4:9; Joel 2:13). Punishment for breaking the covenant was, in most cases, the destruction of the agricultural economic system, through agents sent by YHWH. The natural disaster most feared by the Near Eastern farmer was drought, *baṣṣōret*. This subject was recently treated by Shea (1976) and therefore will not be dealt with here. There are many other destructive factors recorded in the OT, such as pests and diseases; some of these will be discussed in this chapter, citing the evidence from the OT and from archaeological finds.

Pests

This category includes insects, rodents, and other organisms whose activity causes damage to agriculture and reduces crop yield.

Locust

The earliest mention of the locust, a migratory grasshopper, in the OT is in Exod 10:4–6 and 12–19, where it appears as the eighth plague sent by YHWH against Egypt. Here, the locust is called *ʾarbeh*, which appears twenty-four times in the OT. In some passages *ʾarbeh* describes a certain species of grasshopper (Lev 11:22; Nah 3:15), while in others it serves as a general reference to swarms of devouring grasshoppers (Exod 10:4, 12–14; Job 39:20).[1] These insects belong to the order Orthoptera, which also includes cockroaches, mantids,

[1] According to BDB 1972: 915, the term *ʾarbeh* is from the root *rbh*, 'be, become much, many, great'. Koehler and Baumgartner (1953: 82) relate *ʾarbeh* to Akkadian *aribū, arbū, erbū, erebū,* all of which describe the migratory locust, *Schistocerca gregaria* Forskål.

crickets, etc. Grasshoppers are included in the family Locustidae (Whitewell 1963: 376; Rodriguez 1966: 7–9).

Damage to vegetation by locust occurs when they band into swarms, *gēbîm* (Isa 33:4; *gôbāy*, Nah 3:17; *gōbay*, Amos 7:1). When in swarms, the locust creates a terrible noise (Isa 33:4; Job 39:20) with its constant movement and nibbling. There are three species of grasshoppers in the Near East which, when conditions are right, tend to change from a solitary state into a flock state. These species are the desert locust, *Schistocerca gregaria* Forsk.; the European locust, *Locusta migratoria* L.; and the Moroccan locust, *Dociostraurus maroccanus* Thnbg. (Bodenheimer 1950–51). All documented major invasions of locusts into Eretz-Israel have been identified as invasions of the desert locust, originating in the Sudan—with three exceptions. A locust invasion which occurred in 1838 has been attributed by Bodenheimer (1950–51: 148) to the European locust; an invasion reported in 1897 has been attributed to the Moroccan locust. A more recent invasion of Moroccan locusts into the Jordan Valley was reported in 1959 (*Eternity* 1959: 33).

Locust swarms appear in late winter or early spring, when the late crops sprout, *bitḥillat ʿălôt halleqeš* (Amos 7:1). They fly with the help of the wind (Exod 10:13, 19). Flight is possible only when the insects reach the last of five stages of development and grow wings. It has been suggested that the terms appearing in Joel 1:4 and 2:25 are references to different stages in the development of the locust (Palmoni 1955: 520–21). Accordingly, *yeleq* is the first stage; *ḥāsîl* refers to the second and third stages; and *gāzām* refers to the fourth and fifth stages. Although this theory is attractive, it should be pointed out that (1) it does not deal at all with the term *ʾarbeh*, which appears in Joel 1:4 in second place and in 2:25 in first place; (2) in 1:4 *gāzām* appears in first place and in 2:25 in the last place; (3) in Nah 3:16 the prophet says: "*yeleq* raided and flew away"; this proves that *yeleq* cannot be the first stage.

It seems more reasonable that the terms enumerated in Joel designate different species of grasshoppers that can band into swarms. This suggestion is supported by other OT passages. First, the *ʾarbeh* appears in two different positions in the two passages in Joel. The term *gāzām* also appears in different positions in these passages. If the prophet wanted to express complete agricultural destruction by locusts in different stages of development, one would expect that the prophet would have done so by using a progressive order starting with the first stage. Second, *ḥāsîl* and *ʾarbeh* appear elsewhere in poetic parallelism: "If there is famine in the land, if there is pestilence or *šiddāpôn* or *yērāqôn*[2] or *ʾarbeh* or *ḥāsîl*" (1 Kgs 8:37 = 2 Chr 6:28).[3] This parallelism suggests that *ḥāṣîl* is another pest or another species of grasshoppers which can swarm since Lev 11:21–22 seems to indicate that *ʾarbeh* is a species of grasshopper. Third, the term *yeleq* also appears in parallelism with *ʾarbeh*: "There fire will devour you, the sword will cut you off, it will devour you like *yeleq*; multiply like *yeleq*, multiply like *ʾarbeh* (Nah 3:15).[4] The last passage suggests that *yeleq* is another species which can swarm. From the passages cited above it appears that the Hebrew terms under discussion designate different species rather than stages of development.[5]

Another term referring to a species of locust is *ṣĕlāṣal* (Deut 28:42). Hebrew *ṣlṣl* is related to Akkadian *ṣarṣaru* (Koehler and Baumgartner 1953: 805; Davidson n.d.: 1145), which also probably denotes a kind of locust. The phrase *ṣilṣal kĕnāpayim* (Isa 18:1) shows that this insect has wings (Koehler and Baumgartner 1953: 805).

There is not enough information in the OT to permit a definite scientific identification of the species mentioned there. Nevertheless, attempts have been made to identify the types of locusts enumerated in Lev 11:21–22. On the basis of Mishnaic passages and comparative study of Arabic terminology, the following identifications have been proposed: *ḥāgāb*—*Calliptamus palaestinesis* Ramme; *ḥargōl*—the type *Saga* of the Tettigoniidae family (long-horned grasshoppers); *sālʿām*—*Acridella grandis* Klug. (short-horned grasshoppers; Palmoni 1955: 520–21).

Before the availability of crop dusting and spraying, locusts were fought by burning fields (Robinson and Smith 1874: 155) and by creating noise to scare the insects away (Palmoni 1955: 522). These methods, in addition to prayer, fasting, and blowing the shofar (Joel 2:12–18), might have been used also during the Iron Age.

In biblical literature the locust was used as a symbol for hordes of attacking armies (Judg 6:5; Isa 33:4; Jer 46:23; 51:27; Nah 3:16). In Israelite glyptic art a representation of one locust appears on a seal

[2] See below, Diseases.

[3] See also Ps 78:46: "He gave their crops to the *ḥāsîl* and the fruit of their labor to the *ʾarbeh*."

[4] See also Ps 105:34: "He spoke and the *ʾarbeh* came, and *yeleq* without number."

[5] It has been suggested that *ḥănāmāl* (Ps 78:47) is another species of locust, but it has been pointed out by Bilik (1958) that one of the trees which is not damaged by locusts is sycamore, and the psalm cites the sycamores as the object of destruction by *ḥănāmāl*. Therefore, the term refers to something else, possibly a plant louse which attacks sycamore trees. Otherwise, there is no mention in this psalm of the plague of lice, while all the other plagues are enumerated.

bearing the inscription *lᶜzryw hgbh*, 'belonging to Azaryahu [of] the locust [family]' (Avigad 1966).

Worm

The different kinds of crop-damaging worms are designated in the OT by the general term *tôlaᶜat* or *tôlēᶜâ*. The worm is mentioned twice in the OT as a crop-damaging agent. In Deut 28:39 the worm is described as harmful to vineyards: "You shall plant vineyards and dress them, but you shall neither drink nor store wine, for the worm [*hattôlaᶜat*] shall eat them." In Jonah 4:7 the *tôlaᶜat* damaged the *qîqāyôn*-tree, under which Jonah found shelter from the sun. It has been suggested that in the latter case the worm was a larva of the order Lepidoptera, which includes moths and butterflies. Such larva are often voracious feeders and cause much harm (Whitewell 1963: 378).

In extra-biblical documents the *twlᶜh* appears together with *ᵓrbh* (locust), *twy* (?), *ss* (moth), and *qml* (louse) as a crop-damaging insect (Tawil 1977: 59–60).

Mouse

The mouse, *ᶜakbār*, is a rodent belonging to the Muridae family, which is very prolific. In Eretz-Israel alone there are twenty-five species, most of which are vegetarian, although a few are carnivorous. Some species cause great damage to agricultural products. In years when climatic conditions are right, they multiply tremendously and destroy crops. In addition, they are harmful to humans since they carry germs such as *Pasteuretta pestis*, which causes bubonic plague (Bilik 1971).

As an agricultural menace, mice are mentioned only once in the OT (1 Sam 6:5), where it seems that hordes of mice damaged the crops and spread disease among the Philistines after the capture of the Ark at ᵓEben-haᶜezer.

The modern way of fighting this pest is by spreading poisonous grain, a method unavailable in antiquity. Iron Age farmers could not fight mice in the fields, but they could protect the harvest once it was gathered by building closed storage facilities, storing grain in closed jars, plastering subterranean storage facilities, and fumigating (Stager 1975: 160–61, n. 4).

Bat

There are twenty species of bats, *ᶜăṭallēpîm* (sg. *ᶜăṭallēp*), in Eretz-Israel (order Chiroptera). All eat insects except the fruit-eating bat, *Rousettus aegyptiacus* or *Cynonycteris aegyptiaca*, commonly known as the flying fox. The flying fox, which is very common in Eretz-Israel, devours different kinds of fruit, especially ripe grapes.

Tur-Sinai (1959: 4–5; 1962: 2) and Lieberman (1965) identify the flying fox with the *ḥĕpōr pērôt* of Isa 2:20. The passage is a description of the Day of Judgment: "In that day men will cast forth their idols of silver and their idols of gold, which they made for themselves to worship, to the fruit bat [*ḥĕpōr pērôt*] and the bats [*ᶜăṭallēpîm*]." Tur-Sinai (1962: 2) based his identification on the similarity of the biblical term with the Arabic term for bat, *ḫafdûd*, suggesting that the resh is a mistake for dalet and the phrase should be *ḥapad pērôt*, i.e., fruit bat. Lieberman (1965) reached the same conclusion about the meaning of *ḥpr prwt*, but without recourse to textual emendation. On the basis of Mishnaic and Talmudic passages, he explains that *ḥpr* is not derived from the root *ḥpr*, 'to dig', but from *ḥpr*, 'to search'; hence, the reference is not to a 'mole' but to the 'fruit searcher'. It should also be pointed out that on the Day of Judgment "men shall enter the caves of the rock and the holes of the ground . . . the caverns of the rocks and the clefts of the cliffs" (Isa 2:19, 21)—all of which are places where bats take shelter.

In addition, Lieberman suggests that the "little foxes that spoil the vineyards" in Cant 2:15 are *Rousettus aegyptiacus*. The poet is saying that the flying foxes should be caught before they can spoil the *sĕmādar*-vineyards. This identification is strengthened by the juxtaposition of the beautiful bird "my dove, in the cleft of the rock" in Cant 2:14 and the flying fox (a menacing "bird") in v 15 (Lieberman 1965: 134–35).

There is no reason to doubt that many more pests were in existence during the Iron Age, but unfortunately they have left no trace in the OT. Archaeological evidence is also very scant. In a sample of seeds found in Iron I levels in Afula "some of the kirsenne seeds were found to contain the characteristic hole eaten by an insect pest of the genus *Bruchus*, which is still the chief pest of the seeds of this legume" (Zaitschek 1955: 74). Iron II barley samples from Tel Arad yielded a carbonized, but well-preserved weevil, *Calandria granaria* (family Curculionidae), with its proboscis and legs broken. This type of weevil is presently a common pest of bread grain. "The female deposits one egg per grain, the larva developing and pupating in the grain; the mature weevil finally bores a hole through the seed shell as an exit" (Hopf and Zachariae 1971: 63–64, pl. 6:3). Whether this pest was referred to in biblical times as *tôlaᶜat* cannot be determined with the presently available information.

It is possible that a closer study of organic remains from Iron Age levels will reveal more information concerning pests during that period.

Diseases

Diseases can substantially lower crop yields. In twentieth-century agriculture, crop diseases are prevented by the thermochemical treatment of seeds and through the development of new disease-resistant species. These methods were not available to Iron Age farmers. One preventive technique that they did use was the burning of leftover seeds and straw which they thought were contaminated. This activity left layers of ash in storage areas and threshing floors, e.g., in the Philistine house at Gezer and the storage pits or silos at Tell el-Hesi (Stager 1975: 160–61, n. 4, 196). There are no certain traces of contaminated grain in samples recovered archaeologically, but there are several biblical passages which can be interpreted as references to crop diseases.

Šiddāpôn and *Yērāqôn*

Šiddāpôn and *Yērāqôn* appear in the OT together. In Deut 28:22 they are included in a list of diseases, some of which are clearly identified as human sicknesses with high fever as one of the symptoms. Although in this list *šiddāpôn* and *yērāqôn* could have been names of human diseases, other passages in the OT clearly identify the terms as crop diseases (1 Kgs 8:37 = 2 Chr 6:28; Amos 4:9; Hag 2:17).

Some dictionaries translate *šiddāpôn* as "blight" (Fohrer 1973: 278), on the basis of the phrase *šĕdûpōt qādîm* (Gen 41:6), 'scorched by a sirocco' (BDB 1972: 995). According to the *Webster's Third New International Dictionary*, blight is

> any disease, symptom of disease, or injury of plants characterized by or resulting in withering, cessation of growth, and a more or less general death of parts (as leaves, flowers, and stems) without rotting and caused by fungi or bacteria, viruses, unfavorable climatic conditions or insect attack. . . .

Westcott (1950: 95) makes the observation that

> the term [blight] is somewhat loosely used by pathologists and gardeners to cover a wide variety of diseases, some of which may have rotting as secondary symptom; but in general, the chief characteristic of blight is sudden and conspicuous leaf and shoot damage in contradistinction to leaf spotting where dead areas are delimited and to wilt due to toxin or other disturbance of the vascular system.

(See also Agrios 1969: 583.) Westcott distinguishes at least seventy types of blight, with many varieties, none of which affect cereals (Westcott 1950: 95–142). Dickson (1947: 21–25) recognizes a bacterial blight, *Xanthomonas transluscens*, which according to Rodriguez (1966:74) can occur in barley, wheat, and rye. This type of blight occurs under particularly wet conditions (Dickinson 1947: 21–25). If the sirocco of the phrase *šĕdûpōt qādîm* has any relationship to *šiddāpôn*, then blight, if it exists at all in cereals, has to be ruled out, and another disorder has to be identified.

To identify the disorder expressed by *šiddāpôn* the phrase *daqqôt ûšĕdûpōt qādîm* should be examined. This expression puts the blame for the disorder on the easterly wind. There is a possibility that the reference is simply to thin grain, the result of an easterly wind or drought. But such a disorder could have been expressed by the general term for drought and did not need a special term. A second possibility is that *šiddāpôn* is a disorder which manifests itself in blackened grain, a phenomenon which could have been attributed by the biblical farmer to the easterly wind or the sun. The term *šiddāpôn* could be a result of a *d/z* interchange. The original term might have been *šizzāpôn*, expressing blackness caused by the sun, as expressed in Cant 1:6 (see Koehler-Baumgartner 1953: 959).

There is a disorder known as smut, brand, or charbon; it is caused by fungus, attacking cereals, mostly barley. It is characterized by masses of dark, powdery spores (Agrios 1969: 583) and takes two forms: (1) loose smut, *Ustilago nuda* (Jens.) Rostr.; and (2) covered smut, *Ustilago hordei* (Pers.) Lagreh. The former appears usually in plants which form heads early and, therefore, is more noticeable in the field; the latter infects barley in the seedling stage and is evident only during harvest (*CPD* 1959: 186, pl. 90). Smuts are impossible to eradicate. Some control is achieved today by seed treatment and the use of seeds of certified resistant varieties. During the Iron Age these measures were not available, and the terrible damage the smuts caused was, most likely, attributed to punishment for breaking the covenant.[6]

The term *yērāqôn*, when referring to a plant disease, always follows *šiddāpôn*. Some dictionaries translate this term as 'mildew, paleness, rust' (BDB 1972: 439; Fohrer 1973: 115).[7] Mildew is a fungal disease producing spores which appear as a whitish growth on the host surface (Agrios 1969: 583), a condition not compatible with the root of *yērāqôn*.[8] Therefore, another condition has to be identified, and the

[6] For more details regarding smuts see, Butler and Jones 1949: 367–72, 426–29.

[7] *Yērāqôn* is mentioned once clearly as a human disease affecting the color of the skin (Jer 30:6), may be jaundice.

[8] From the root *yrq*, 'green' (BDB 1972: 438–39).

most appropriate is rust, the effects of which produce colors from yellow to red. There are two prominent varieties of rust: (1) stem rust, *Puccinia graminis tritici*; and (2) leaf rust, *Puccinia triticina* or *Puccinia recondita*. Stem rust produces reddish-brown spores on stems, necks, and heads, and causes shriveled, lightweight grain, reducing crop yield (*CPD* 1959: 206, pl. 100). Leaf rust produces yellowish-orange pustules which develop mostly on leaves, usually appearing first on the lower leaves and progressing upward (*CPD* 1959: 204, pl. 99). This disease can cause a loss of up to 30% of the yield by reducing the number of kernels and shriveling the grain, resulting in low weight and protein content. Leaf rust causes more serious damage than stem rust (Westcott 1950: 349; *CPD* 1959: 206). The color of leaf rust pustules is compatible with that expressed by the root *yrq*.[9]

Leaf rust is most severe in moist and warm seasons and thus may have been attributed by the biblical farmer to excess water or rain. Smut is more common in hot weather and could have been attributed to the hot wind. Both rust and smut are transmitted by the wind, and the reference to the easterly wind in Gen 41:6 may indicate knowledge of this on the part of the biblical farmer.

If the identification of *šiddāpôn* and *yērāqôn* with smut and rust, respectively, is correct, then as punishments for breaking the covenant they are most severe. Rust attacks wheat and smut attacks barley; punishment with rust and smut can result in almost complete destruction of grain crops and thus can attack the very basis of a solid agricultural economy.[10]

Boʾšâ and *Bĕʾūšîm*

In the OT, *boʾšâ* is connected with barley (Job 31:40), and *bĕʾūšîm* with grapes (Isa 5:2, 4). BDB (1972: 92–93) translates *boʾšâ* as "(stinking things) stinking or noxious weeds" and *bĕʾūšîm* as "stinking or worthless things, wild grapes." Fohrer (1973: 28) translates **bāʾūš* as "rotting berry" and *boʾšâ* as "darnel (noxious weeds)." Koehler and Baumgartner (1953: 106) translate *boʾšâ* as "malodorous plants (plants oftenly termed according to their smell) . . . *Mercurialis annua* L. (Dhorme); cockle *Solium temulentum* L." They translate *bĕʾūšîm* as "putrid, rotten berries (of grapes)." All dictionaries agree that these terms stem from the root *bʾš*, 'have a bad small, stink'. To identify

[9] Although this is not a strong argument; but in my view a yellow to red condition is more compatible with the root *yrq* than a whitish condition.

[10] Such punishments as expressed in the curses of Deut 28:22 could have been attributed by the biblical farmer to all the powers of nature, including too much rain resulting in rust and great heat waves resulting in smut.

these conditions properly one has to find similar disorders in barley and grapes, or, at least, disorders which have some similarities.

In the case of *boʾšâ* the most appropriate disease is bunt, or stinking smut, *Tilletia caries* (DC) Tul., described as "spores formed in the grain, more or less concealed by the glumes, blackish and 'oily' mass, with fish-like odor" (Brooks 1953: 253)—hence, the English and Hebrew names.[11]

Běʾūšîm should be identified with the results of black rot, *Guignardia bidwellii* (Ellis) Viala & Ravaz, the most virulent disease of grapes. Black rot causes more damage than all other diseases combined (Westcott 1950: 297, pl. 81). "When fruit is half grown rot starts as a pale spot, soon turning brown and involving the entire berry, which shrivels and becomes a black wrinkled mummy, dropping or remaining in the cluster" (Westcott 1950: 297; see also, *CPD* 1959: 142, pl. 68). The characteristic end result of bunt and black rot is a blackened grain or grape. Both conditions develop late in the growing season: bunt is detected in cereals only during harvest or threshing, and black rot is detected only when the grapes are half-grown.

The identification of *běʾūšîm* with black rot explains the parable in which Israel and Judah are described as the vineyard of YHWH (Isa 5:2–7). YHWH, the vinedresser, looked forward to the vineyard yielding grapes (justice and righteousness) and was disappointed to find, belatedly, black rot (bloodshed and outcry). He did not discover that the grapes coming up were bad until they were half-grown.

One other plant disease is alluded to in the OT by the description of the damage it caused: "You shall have olive trees throughout all your territory, but you shall not anoint yourself with the oil for your olives shall drop off" (Deut 28:40). This condition can only be the result of peacock eyespot, *Cyclonium oleaginum* cal., characterized by "the formation of small, grayish spots on the leaves" (*CPD* 1959: 152, pl. 73). The spots are composed of a series of concentric rings in different shades, resembling the "eye" of a peacock's feather. Infected leaves wither and drop off quite rapidly; the tree itself is weakened, with a consequent reduction in fruit yield. "The disease may also develop on the young peduncle, in which case fruit drop may be considerable" (*CPD* 1959: 152). Control of this disease is achieved by fungicides and with the planting of resistant varieties. Other measures—which were available to the biblical farmer—are proper pruning and correct agricultural practices to assure the maintenance of a healthy tree (*CPD* 1959: 152).

[11] "These masses are about the same size as the original kernels and are composed of dark brown spores which give off a fishy, musty odor" (*CPD* 1959: 202).

Weeds

Another cause of reduced crop yields which has to be mentioned here is weeds. The OT recognizes weeds as an agricultural menace: "Cursed is the ground . . . thorn and thistles it shall bring forth to you" (Gen 3:17–18). Many weeds are mentioned in the OT, in most cases connoting desolation and destruction of the economy as a result of war. Some of these weeds are *qôṣ* (Jer 4:3; 12:13); *dardar* (Gen 3:18; Hos 10:8); *śikkîm* (Num 33:55); *ḥedeq* (Mic 7:4; Prov 15:19); *šāmîr* and *šayit* (Isa 7:23–25; 10:17); *sîrîm*, *qîmôš*, and *ḥôaḥ* (Isa 34:13, Hos 9:6); *sirpād* (Isa 55:13); *sārābîm* and *sallônîm* (Ezek 2:6); *barqānîm* (Judg 8:7); *naᶜăṣûṣîm* (Isa 7:19; 55:13). The OT does not offer sufficient information to enable identification of these weeds.[12]

Some weeds are present in archaeological samples. *Galium tricorne* Stokes of the family Rubiaceae and *Cephalaria syriaca* (L.) Schard of the family Dipsaceae were found among kirsenne (bitter vetch) seeds from the Iron I layer in Afula. Both contaminate kirsenne and other crops throughout Eretz-Israel today (Zaitschek 1955: 74). The leguminous weed caterpillar, *Scorpiurus subvillosa* L., still commonly found in fields, was present in EB specimens from Lachish; Iron Age grain samples from Lachish contained numerous darnel seeds, *Lolium temulentum* L., a plant which has poisonous fruit (Helbaek 1958: 309–17). Darnel is a hardy grass resembling wheat and rye very closely and is very difficult to distinguish from them in its early stages. If not eradicated before harvest, it gets mixed with the grain and is ground for flour. It is believed that the poisonous properties are not due to the plant but to "a fungus growing beneath the seed-coat. . . . Since this fungus seems to be generally associated with the darnel, the net result is virtually the same" (Moldenke and Moldenke 1952: 134).

Several samples from Taᶜannek yielded weeds from levels dated to MB IIC, LB I, LB II–Iron I, Iron II, and Arab. Weeds found in Iron II samples are *Echium judaeum* and *Capparis spinosa.*

Weeding of fields, orchards, vineyards, and gardens was a very important activity for the farmer. The effects of letting weeds grow in cultivated areas are expressed in Isa 5:6: "I will make it [the vineyard] a waste; it shall not be pruned or hoed, and briers and thorns shall grow up." One of the months in the Gezer Manual was named *yrḥ ᶜṣd pšt*, 'a month of hoeing weeds'. Weeding was done with the *maᶜdēr*, 'hoe', the *maᶜăṣad*, 'reaping-hook', and by hand. Some of the weeds were probably used for human and animal consumption.

[12] For attempts to identify some of these weeds, see Hareᵓuveni 1930; Zohary 1958c; Moldenke and Moldenke 1952: 153, 248.

Conclusion

Agriculture was the mainstay of Israelite economy, and its influence on different facets of daily life has been recognized for quite some time. Noth (1966: 163) states that "the chief occupations in ancient Palestine were always animal husbandry and farming. . . . Horticulture has always occupied the attention of the settled inhabitants of Palestine." In the preceding investigation I examined information from literary and archaeological sources in order to try to shed light on the agricultural aspects of life in ancient Israel, so that statements such as Noth's can be substantiated or refuted. From the outset of my investigation I hoped that the study would lead to a comprehensive description of agriculture in Iron Age Israel. I also hoped that the result would produce a better understanding of Israelite daily life and of the influence agriculture had on the economy, laws, and cultic practices (chaps. 1, 3, 4).

At first glance it appears that Israelite agriculture continued the tradition of Canaanite agriculture; i.e., no new species were introduced by the biblical farmer. Palaeobotanical studies show that all the species cultivated by the biblical farmer were already known during the Bronze Age. The biblical farmer inherited a large variety of food plants to choose from, and he chose those which were most suitable for him. The repertoire of plants cultivated by the biblical farmer included several types of cereals, legumes, and vegetables, and a host of fruit trees (chaps. 8–10). The literary evidence shows that the biblical farmer learned to use these plants in a variety of ways, producing not only for himself and his family but also creating surplus for trade.

In the beginning, Israelite society was based on a village-type that was suitable for the hill-country (Stager 1981; Stager, "Highland Villages," forthcoming; see also chap. 2). The necessity of settling in the hill-country brought about a new development in ancient agricultural practices. Although, according to Stager ("Highland Villages," forthcoming), agricultural terraces originated in Late Bronze Phoenicia (as Ugaritic texts suggest), terracing became common during the Iron I period in the Palestinian hill-country and enabled occupation of this inhospitable region. Deforestation and agricultural terracing created enough land to support the newly established villages. Agricultural terracing of slopes in the hill-country led to the innovation of runoff farming, which provided the Israelites with the means of settling the arid Negev. Apparently, the settlements in the Negev were charged with the defense of the southern border of the United, and later the Judean, Kingdom and were required to support themselves with agricultural produce mostly from their own fields (chap. 2). Both innovations, terracing on a large scale and runoff farming, were utilized successfully by succeeding generations of farmers and are still in use today.

Another set of innovations which I attribute to the Israelite farmer is related to restoration of soil fertility. Continuous exploitation of land without care leads to the depletion of its nutritional resources and thus to a reduction in crop yield that can be severe enough to force the farmer to leave the land. Although organic fertilizing may have been practiced before the Iron Age, it seems that the biblical farmer learned to utilize an additional source of minerals—namely, ash, especially that of sacrifical animals (chap. 11). Another important innovation which my investigation leads me to believe was introduced in the Iron Age by the Israelite farmer is that of limited crop rotation. The practice of crop rotation on a small scale is hinted at in the *kilʾayim* laws (Lev 19:19; Deut 22:9) and in the Proverb of the Farmer (Isa 28:24–29). Fallowing was also practiced and apparently was systematized by the Israelites according to the law in Exod 23:10–11. By using crop rotation and fallowing, the first systematic agricultural cycle was created (chap. 11). With the introduction of iron tools, which at first were of poor quality, more grain could be produced and harvested. Iron tools, crop rotation, and fertilizing led to the creation of large surpluses for export and for the support of large cities.

A contribution to food-processing techniques was made by the biblical farmer with the invention of the beam oil-press. Until the Iron II period, pressing oil was done in primitive installations, where pressure was applied by placing heavy stones on top of baskets filled with crushed olives. The beam-press, utilizing leverage, could exert more pressure, thus producing larger quantities of oil in shorter periods (chap. 9).

All the aforementioned innovations resulted in a large surplus of foodstuffs. This situation led to the introduction of a new type of storage facility, the pillared storehouse, which was an Israelite innovation and was used only in Eretz-Israel (chap. 8). I should mention here that the debate concerning these pillared structures and their function as storehouses (Herzog 1973; Pritchard 1970) or stables (Holladay, forthcoming; Stager, "Highland Villages" forthcoming) has not subsided or been resolved.

The preceding investigation is concerned with a long time period, stretching over more than six hundred years. It is only to be expected that during such a long period many changes took place, especially in social and cultural matters. In ancient Israel, society and culture were influenced by agriculture; thus changes in agricultural practices should be reflected in changes in the social structure and cultural life. These changes must be gleaned from the literary evidence, which is very limited, and from archaeology. The latter is now only starting to look at such issues.

Understanding the agricultural background of ancient Israel relies heavily on the availability of seed samples. Today, many archaeologists purposefully retrieve organic samples, using methods such as sifting and flotation. Archaeologists have also started studying whole regions and the interrelationships between sites rather than just excavating an isolated site without paying attention to its regional role and function. More and more, archaeologists are willing to look at tools and installations from the mundane agricultural point of view rather than seeing in everything something cultic.

Archaeology together with literary studies of ancient documents, biblical and extra-biblical, can help us re-create the agricultural life of ancient Israel, and in so doing, other aspects of daily life, including the social, cultural, and religious, will be illuminated.

Bibliography

Agrios, N.
1969 *Plant pathology*. New York: Academic.

Aharoni, Y.
1956 A survey of the Galilee: Israelite settlements and their pottery. *EI* 4:56–64.
1962 The Samaria ostraca—An additional note. *IEJ* 12:67–69.
1966 Hebrew ostraca from Tel Arad. *IEJ* 16:1–7, pl. 1:A, B, C.
1966 The use of hieratic numerals in Hebrew ostraca and the shekel weights. *BASOR* 184:13–19.
1967 *The land of the Bible: A historical geography*. Philadelphia: Westminster.
1968 Arad: Its inscriptions and temple. *BA* 31:2–32.
1970 Three Hebrew ostraca from Arad. *BASOR* 197:16– 42.
1975 Excavations at Tel Beer-sheba, 1973–1974. *Tel Aviv* 2:146–68.

Aharoni, Y., ed.
1973 *Beer-sheba 1*. Tel Aviv: Tel Aviv University/Institute of Archaeology.

Aharoni, Y., Evenari, M., Shanan, L., and Tadmor, N. H.
1960 The ancient desert agriculture of the Negev, V: An Israelite agricultural settlement at Ramat Matred. *IEJ* 10:23–35, 97–111.

Aharoni, Y., and Amiran, R.
1963 The first season of excavations at Tell Arad. *Yediot* 27:217–34. (In Hebrew.)

Aharoni, Y., Fritz, V., and Kempinski, A.
1975 Excavations at Tel Masos (Khirbet el-Meshash). *Tel Aviv* 2:97–124.

Aḥiṭuv, S.
1968 *Sĕmādar*. In *EB* 5, ed. B. Mazar, col. 1052.

Albenda, P.
1974 Grapevines in Ashurbanipal's garden. *BASOR* 215:5–17.

Albright, W. F.
1924. *Excavations and results at Tell el-Ful (Gibeah of Saul)*. AASOR 4.
1943a. The Gezer Calendar. *BASOR* 92:16–26.
1943b. *The excavations of Tell Beit Mirsim*. AASOR 21–22.
1958 The archaeology of Palestine. London: Pelican.

Alt, A.
1925 Judas Gaue unter Josia. *PJB* 21:100–116.

Amiran, R.
1956 The millstones and the potter's wheel. *EI* 4:46–49.
1958 *Ḥermesh.* In *EB* 3, ed. N. H. Tur-Sinai, S. Yeivin, and B. Mazar, cols. 297–99.
1963 *Ancient pottery of the Holy Land.* Jerusalem: Mosad Bialik and Israel Exploration Society. (In Hebrew.)

Amiran, R., and Eitan, A.
1964 The first two seasons of excavation at Tell Nagila (1962–1963). *Yediot* 28:193–203. (In Hebrew.)

Amiran, R., and Van Beek, G. W.
1975 Jemmeh, Tell. In *Eaehl* 2, ed. M. Avi-Yonah, 545–48.

Amit, D.
1979. Of dyeing vats and olive presses. *Israel—Land and nature* 4:114–17. (Reprinted from *Salᶜit* 6 [1977]: 2.)

Amusin, J. D., and Heltzer, M. L.
1964 The inscription from Meṣad Ḥashavyahu. *IEJ* 14:148–57.

Anderson, A. W.
1957 *Plants of the Bible.* New York: Philosophical Library.

Andrew, H. N.
1964 *Ancient plants and the world they lived in.* Ithaca: Comatock.
1970 *Atlas of Israel.* Climatic regions, radiation, evaporation, wind, sharav, IV/3. Jerusalem: Survey of Israel/Ministry of Labour.

Auerbach, E.
1958 Die Feste im alte Israel. *VT* 8:1–18.

Avigad, N.
1966 A Hebrew seal with a family emblem. *IEJ* 16:50–53, pl. 4c.
1972 Two Hebrew inscriptions on wine-jars. *IEJ* 22:1–9.

Avitsur, S.
1972 *Daily life in Iretz* [sic] *Israel in the XIX century.* Tel Aviv: Am Hassefer. (In Hebrew.)
1976 *Man and his work.* Jerusalem: Carta and the Israel Exploration Society. (In Hebrew.)

Balfour, J. H.
1857 *The plants of the Bible.* London: T. Nelson and Sons.

BAR
1976 Megiddo stables or storehouses? *BAR* 2(3): 1, 12–18, 22.
1978 The four-room house found at Izbet Sartah—A typical Israelite dwelling from about the 12th century B.C. *BAR* 4(3): 26–27.

BDB
1972 *See* Brown, Driver, and Briggs.

Beit Arieh, I.
1973 An iron plough-share. In *Beer-sheba I*, ed. Y. Aharoni, 43–44. Tel Aviv: Tel Aviv University/ Institute of Archaeology.

Ben-Dor, E.
1955 *ʾĀsām.* In *EB* 1, ed. E. L. Sukenik, cols. 478–80.

Ben-Hayim, Z.
1943 Back to old glory. *Leshonenu* 12:98–92. (In Hebrew.)

Ben Tor, A.
1977a Excavations at Tell Qiri in Kibbutz Hazorea. *Qadmoniot* 37:24–27. (In Hebrew.)
1977b Letter to author, 6 November.
1977c Letter to author, 29 November.

Bevan, A. A.
1892 *Commentary on the book of Daniel.* Cambridge: Cambridge University Press.

Bewer, J. A.
1942 Notes on I Samuel 13:21; II Samuel 23:1; Psalms 48:8. *JBL* 61:45–49.

Bilik, E.
1958 *Ḥănāmāl.* In *EB* 3, ed. N. H. Tur-Sinai, S. Yeivin, and B. Mazar, col. 217.
1971 *ᶜAkbār.* In *EB* 6, ed. B. Mazar and H. Tadmor, cols. 223–24.

Biran, A.
1974 Tel Dan. *BA* 37:26–51.
1980 Two discoveries at Tel Dan. *IEJ* 30:89–98.

Bodenheimer, F. S.
1950–51 Note on the invasions of Palestine by rare locusts. *IEJ* 1:146–48.

Borowski, O.
1981 Field III, 1980 Season. *Lahav Newsletter* 18:1–4.
1982a On the Dan cultic installation—Is it an olive press? *BAR* 8 (March/Apr): 56–57.
1982b A note on the "iron age cult installation" at Tel Dan. *IEJ* 32:58.
1983 The identity of the biblical *ṣirᶜâ*. In *The word of the Lord shall go forth: Essays in honor of David Noel Freedman in celebration of his sixtieth birthday*, ed. C. L. Meyers, and M. O'Connor. Philadelphia: American Schools of Oriental Research, pp. 315–19.

Bowman, J.
1959 Is the Samaritan calendar the old Zadokite one? *PEQ* 91:23–37.

Breasted, J. H.
1906 *Ancient records of Egypt*, 2 vols. Chicago: University of Chicago Press.

Bright, J.
1974 *A history of Israel.* 2d ed. Philadelphia: Westminster.

Brooks, F. T.
1953 *Plant diseases.* 2d ed. London: Oxford University Press.

Broshi, M.
1962 *Kĕvarâ.* In *EB* 4, ed. B. Mazar, col. 11.

Brown, F., Driver, S. R., and Briggs, C. A.
[1907] 1972 *A Hebrew and English lexicon of the Old Testament.* Reprint. Oxford: Clarendon. (BDB.)

Butler, E. J., and Jones, S. G.
1949 *Plant pathology*. London: Macmillan.

Butzer, K. W.
1971 Agricultural origins in the Near East as a geographical problem. In *Prehistoric agriculture*, ed. S. Struever, 209–35. Garden City: Natural History Press.

Callaway, J. A.
1968 New Evidence on the Conquest of Ai. *JBL* 87:312–20.

Callcott, M. G.
1842 *A Scripture Herbal*. London: Longman, Brown, Green and Longman.

Carmichael, C. M.
1974 *The laws of Deuteronomy*. Ithaca: Cornell University Press.

Cassuto, M. D.
1954 Gezer, the Gezer calendar. In *EB* 2, ed. E. L. Sukenik, cols. 471–74.

Charles, R. H., trans.
1917 *The book of Jubilees or the little Genesis*. London: Society for Promoting Christian Knowledge.

Cohen, A.
1965 The identification of the ᵓ*et*. *Leshonenu* 29:63–64. (In Hebrew.)

Cohen, R.
1970 ᵓ*Atar Haro*ᶜ*ah*. *Atiqot* (Hebrew Series) 6:6–24, 1*–3*.
1976 Excavations at Ḥurvat Ḥaluqim. *Atiqot* (English Series) 11:34–50.
1979a Notes and news: The Negev archaeological emergency project. *IEJ* 29:250–51.
1979b Notes and news: Rescue excavations in the Negev. *IEJ* 29:251–54.
1979c The iron age fortresses in the central Negev. *BASOR* 236:61–79.
1982 Notes and news: Kadesh-Barnea, 1980. *IEJ* 32:70–71.

Cohen, R., and Dever, W. G.
1979 Preliminary report of the second season of the "central Negev highland project." *BASOR* 236:41–60.

Cook, H. N.
1846 *The trees, fruits, and flowers of the Bible*. New York: American Tract Society.

CPD
1959 *Compendium of plant diseases*. Philadelphia: Rohm and Haas.

Cross, F. M., Jr.
1962 Epigraphic notes on Hebrew documents of the eighth–sixth century B.C.: II. The Murabbaᶜât papyrus and the letter found near Yabneh-Yam. *BASOR* 165:34–46.

Cross, F. M., Jr., and Freedman, D. N.
1952 *Early Hebrew orthography*. New Haven: American Oriental Society.

Cross, F. M., Jr., and Wright, G. E.
1956 The boundary and province lists of the kingdom of Judah. *JBL* 75:202–26.

Crowfoot, J. W., Kenyon, K. M., and Sukenik, E. L.
1942 *The buildings at Samaria*. London: Palestine Exploration Fund.

Cziżik, B.
1943 About the *kîššût* and *mĕlafĕfôn*. *Leshonenu* 11:302–3. (In Hebrew.)

Dahood, M.
1968 *The Anchor Bible: Psalms II*. Garden City: Doubleday.

Dalman, G.
1932–35 *Arbeit und sitte in Palästina*. Vols. 2–4. Gütersloh: C. Bertelsmann. Reprint 1964. Hildesheim: Georg Olms.

Dar, S.
1980 Khirbet Jemaᶜin—A village from the period of the monarchy. *Qadmoniot* 13:97–100. (In Hebrew.)

Davidson, B.
n.d. *The analytical Chaldee lexicon*. London: Samuel Bagster and Sons.

Davis, D. R.
1976 Peas. In *Evolution of crop plants*, ed. N. W. Simmonds, 172–74. London: Longman.

de Geus, C. H. J.
1975 The importance of archaeological research into the Palestinian agricultural terraces, with an excursus on the Hebrew word *gbi**. *PEQ* 107:65–74.

Demsky, A.
1972 A "dark wine" from Judah. *IEJ* 22:233–34.
1979 A note on "smoked wine." *Tel Aviv* 6:163.

de Vaux, R.
1961 *Ancient Israel: Its life and institutions*. Trans. J. McHugh. New York: McGraw-Hill.

Dever, W. G.
1972 Notes and news: Tel Gezer. *IEJ* 22:158–60.
1975 Gezer. In *Eaehl* 2, ed. M. Avi-Yonah, 428–43.

Dickson, J. G.
1974 *Diseases of field crops*. New York: McGraw-Hill.

Dillman, A.
1890 *Der prophet Jesaia*. Leipzig: S. Hirzel.

Dimbleby, G. W.
1967 *Plants and archaeology*. London: John Barker.

Diringer, D.
1934 *Le iscrizioni antico-ebraiche palestinesi*. Florence: Felice le Monnier.

Dothan, M.
1955 Excavations at Afula. *Atiqot* (English Series) 1.

Edelstein, G., and Gat, Y.
1980–81 Terraces around Jerusalem. *Israel - Land and Nature* 6(2): 72–78.

Edelstein, G., and Gibson, S.
1982 Ancient Jerusalem's rural food basket. *BAR* 8(4): 46–54.

Edelstein, G., and Kislev, M.
1981 Mevasseret Yerushalayim: Ancient terraces farming. *BA* 44:53–56.

Eiselen, F. C., Lewis, E., and Downey, D. G., eds.
1929 *The Abingdon Bible commentary.* New York: Abingdon.

Eitam, D.
1979 Olive presses of the Israelite period. *Tel Aviv* 6:146–55.

Erdman, A.
1966 *The ancient Egyptians.* Trans. A. M. Blackman. New York: Harper Torchbooks.

Eternity.
1959 Plagues of locusts. *Eternity* (July): 33.

Evenari, M., Aharoni, Y., Shanan, L., and Tadmor, N. H.
1958 The ancient desert agriculture of the Negev, III: Early beginnings. *IEJ* 8:231–53.

Evenari, M., Shanan, L., Tadmor, N., and Itzhaki, Y.
1971 *The Negev: The challenge of a desert.* Cambridge: Harvard University Press.

Felix, J.
1960 *Kělê Habbâqâr Wěhammaḥărēšâ* and their names in Mishnaic times. *Leshonenu* 24:137–56. (In Hebrew.)

Finkelstein, I., Bunimowitz, S., and Lederman, Z.
1984 Excavations at Shiloh, 1981–1983. *Qadmoniot* 65:15–25. (In Hebrew.)

Flannery, K. V.
1973 The origin of agriculture. *Annual Review of Anthropology* 2:271–310.

Fohrer, G., ed.
1973 *Hebrew and Aramaic dictionary of the Old Testament.* Trans. W. Johnston. Berlin: Walter de Gruyter.

Franken, H. J.
1975 Deir ᵓAlla, Tell. In *Eaehl* 1, ed. M. Avi-Yonah, pp. 321–24.

Free, J. P.
1958 The fifth season at Dothan. *BASOR* 152:10–18.
1959 The sixth season at Dothan. *BASOR* 156:22–29.
1960 The seventh season at Dothan. *BASOR* 160:6–15.

Freedman, D. N.
1978 Letter to author, 30 July.

Fussell, G. E.
1971 *Crop nutrition: Science and practice before Liebing.* Lawrence: Coronado.

Galil, J.
1968 An ancient technique for ripening sycomore fruit in East Mediterranean countries. *Economic Botany* 22:179–90.

Galil, J., and Eisikowitch, D.
1968 Flowering cycles and fruit types of *Ficus sycomorus* in Israel. *New Phytology* 67:745–58.

Galling, K.
1937 *Biblisches Reallexikon Handbuch zum Alten Testament.* Tubingen: J. C. B. Mohr.

Garbini, G.
1978 **Parzon* "iron" in the Song of Deborah. *JSS* 23:23–24.

Garsiel, M., and Finkelstein, I.
1978 The western expansion of the house of Joseph in the light of the ʾIzbet Ṣarṭa excavations." *Tel Aviv* 5:192–98.

Gitin, S.
1976 Letter to author, 8 December.
1985 Dramatic finds in Eknon. *ASOR Newsletter* 36(3):2–3.

Goldsmith, M. O.
1960 *A Bible garden.* New York: Abingdon.

Goor, A.
1965 The history of the fig in the Holy Land from ancient times to the present day. *Economic Botany* 19:124–35.
1966a The history of the grapevine in the Holy Land. *Economic Botany* 20:46–64.
1966b The history of the olive in the Holy Land and its history through the ages. *Economic Botany* 20:223–43.
1967a The history of the pomegranate in the Holy Land. *Economic Botany* 21:215–30.
1967b The history of the date through the ages in the Holy Land. *Economic Botany* 21:320–40.

Gophna, R.
1966 Iron Age I *ḥăṣērîm* in southern Philistia. *Atiqot* (Hebrew Series) 3:44–51, 5*–6*.
1970 Some iron age II sites in southern Philistia. *Atiqot* (Hebrew Series) 6:25–30, 3*.

Goudoever, J. Van
1959 *Biblical calendars.* Leiden: Brill.

Grant, E.
1931 *Ain Shems excavations* (*Palestine*) *1928–1929–1930–1931.* Pt. 1. Haverford: Haverford College.
1932 *Ain Shems excavations* (*Palestine*) *1928–1929–1930–1931.* Pt. 2. Haverford: Haverford College.
1934 *Rumeilah, being Ain Shems, excavations* (*Palestine*). Pt. 3. Haverford: Haverford College.

Grant, E., and Wright, G. E.
1938 *Ain Shems excavations* (*Palestine*). Pt. 4, *Pottery.* Haverford: Haverford College.

1939 *Ain Shems excavations (Palestine)*. Pt. 5, *Text*. Haverford: Haverford College.

Gras, N. S. B.
1925 *A history of agriculture in Europe and America*. New York: S. F. Crofts.

Gressmann, H.
1909 *Altorientalische Texte und Bilder zum Alten Testament*. Tubingen: J. C. B. Mohr.
1927 *Altorientalische Bilder zum Alten Testament*. Berlin and Leipzig: de Gruyter.

Gvaryahu, H. M. I.
1954 *Gālāl, gĕlālîm*. In *EB* 2, ed. E. L. Sukenik, col. 510.

Haker, M.
1956 Water supply in antiquity. In *Sefer Yerushalayim I*. Jerusalem and Tel Aviv: Mosad Bialik and Dvir. (In Hebrew.)

Hamilton, R. W.
1934–35 Excavations at Tell Abu Hawam. *QDAP* 4:1–69.

Hammer, R.
1976 *The Cambridge Bible commentary: The book of Daniel*. Cambridge: Cambridge University Press.

Haran, M.
1962 Food and drinks. In *EB* 4, ed. B. Mazar, cols. 543–60.

Hareʾuveni, E.
1930 Studies regarding the names of Palestinian plants. *Leshonenu* 2:177–83. (In Hebrew.)

Hareʾuveni, N.
1974 *Ecology in the Bible*. Kiryat Ono: Neot Kedumim.

Harlan, J. R.
1972 Crops that extend the range of agricultural settlement. In *Man, settlement and urbanism*, ed. P. J. Ucko, T. Tringham, and G. W. Dimbleby, 239–43. Cambridge, Mass.: Schenkman.
1975 *Crops and man*. Madison: American Society of Agronomy/ Crop Science Society of America.

Harlan, J. R., and Zohary, D.
1966 Distribution of wild wheats and barley. *Science* 153:1074–80.

Hayes, J.
1980 *An introduction to Old Testament study*. Nashville: Abingdon.

Helbaek, H.
1958 Plant economy in ancient Lachish. In *Lachish 4*, ed. O. Tufnell, 309–17. London: Oxford University Press.
1963 Paleo-ethnobotany. In *Science in archaeology*, ed. D. R. Brothwell, 177–85. Bristol: Thames and Hudson.

Henrey, K. H.
1954 Land tenure in the Old Testament. *PEQ* 86:5–15.

Herzog, Z.
1977 Notes and news: Tel Beer-sheba, 1976. *IEJ* 27:168–70.

Hestrin, R.
1975 Beth Yeraḥ. In *Eaehl* 1, ed. M. Avi-Yonah, 253–62.
Hestrin, R., and Yeivin, Z.
1977 Oil from the presses of Tirat-Yehuda. *BA* 40:29–31.
Holladay, J. S.
Forth-coming The stables of ancient Israel: Functional determinants of stable construction and the interpretation of pillared building remains of the Palestinian iron age. In *The archaeology of Jordan and other studies* (*Siegfried Horn Festschrift*), ed. L. T. Geraty.
Hopf, M.
1969 Plant remains and early farming in Jericho. In *The domestication and exploitation of plants and animals*, ed. P. J. Ucko and G. W. Dimbleby, 355–59. Chicago: Aldine.
Hopf, M., and Zachariae, G.
1971 Determination of botanical and zoological remains from Ramat Maṭred and Arad. *IEJ* 21:60–64; pls. 5:B–C, 6:A–E.
Hort, A., Sir, ed.
1916 *Enquiry into plants.* Vol. 2. London: Heinemann; Cambridge: Harvard University Press.
Hyams, E.
1971 *Plants in the service of man: 10,000 years of domestication.* Philadelphia and New York: J. B. Lippincott.
Irgun Ovdey Ha-Falha
1960–61 *Annual calendar.* Israel. (In Hebrew.)
James, F.
1966 *The iron age at Beth Shan.* Philadelphia: The University Museum.
Jarman, H. N.
1972 The origins of wheat and barley cultivation. In *Papers in economic prehistory*, ed. E. S. Higgs, 15–26. Cambridge: Cambridge University Press.
Jenour, A.
1830 *The book of the prophet Isaiah.* London: R. B. Seeley and W. Burnside.
Jerusalem American Colony
1907 *The plants of the Bible.* Jerusalem: F. Vester.
Kedar, Y.
1956 The ancient problem of the Hillocks (Tuleilat el-ᶜAnab) in the Negev. *Yediot* 20:31–43. (In Hebrew.)
1957a Ancient agriculture in the Nisa-Beʾerotayim region. *Yediot* 21:161–72. (In Hebrew.)
1957b Ancient agriculture at Shivta in the Negev. *IEJ* 7:178–89.
1957c Water and soil from the desert: Some ancient agricultural achievements in the central Negev. *The Geographical Journal* 123:179–87.
1967 *The ancient agriculture in the Negev.* Jerusalem: Mosad Bialik.

Kelm, G. L., and Mazar, A.
1983 Notes and news: Tel Batash (Timna), 1982. *IEJ* 33:126.

Kelso, J. L.
1968 *The excavation of Bethel (1934–1960)*. AASOR 39.

Kenyon, K. M.
1970 *Archaeology of the Holy Land.* 3d ed. New York: Praeger.

King, E. A.
1941 *Bible plants for American gardens.* New York: Macmillan.
1948 *Plants of the Holy Scripture.* New York: New York Botanical Garden.

Kislev, M.
1973 The identification of *Ḥiṭṭâ* and *Kussemet*. *Leshonenu* 37:83–95, 243–52. (In Hebrew.)

Kochavi, M.
1977 An ostracon from the period of the Judges from ᶜIzbet Ṣarṭa. *Tel Aviv* 4:1–11.

Kochavi, M., ed.
1972 *Judaea, Samaria and the Golan, archaeological survey (1967–1968)*. Jerusalem: The Archaeological Survey of Israel and Carta (In Hebrew.)

Koehler, L., and Baumgartner, W.
1953 *Lexicon in Veteris Testamenti Libros.* Leiden: Brill.

Lamon, R. S., and Shipton, G. M.
1939 *Megiddo I: Seasons of 1925–34, Strata I–V.* Oriental Institute Publications, vol. 42. Chicago: University of Chicago Press.

Lance, D. H.
1971 The royal stamps and the kingdom of Josiah. *HTR* 64:315–32.

Landsberger, B.
1967 *The date palm and its by-products according to the cuneiform sources.* Graz: Im Selbstverlage des Herausgebers.

Langdon, S. H.
1935 *Babylonian menologies and semitic calendars.* London: British Academy.

Lapp, P. W.
1960 Late royal seals from Judah. *BASOR* 158:11–22.
1964 The 1963 excavation at Taᶜannek. *BASOR* 173:4–44.

Laustrup, M.
1982 Summary: 1979 ethnobotanical material. *Lahav Research Project Internal Communication.*

Leible, D.
1958 *Ḥadashâ - Ḥerev, Barzel. Leshonenu* 22:124–25. (In Hebrew.)

Lemaire, A.
1975 *Zāmīr* dans la tablette de Gezer et le Cantique des cantique. *VT* 25:15–26.
1980 A note on inscription XXX from Lachish. *Tel Aviv* 7:92–94.

Lidzbarski. M.

1898 *Handbuch der nordsemitischen Epigraphik* Vol. 1. Weimar: Felber.

1915 *Ephemeris für semitische epigraphik.* Vol. 3. Giessen: Alfred Töpelmann.

Lieberman, S.

1965 *Laḥĕpor pērôt vĕlāᶜătallēpîm* (Isa. 2:20). *Leshonenu* 29:132–35. (In Hebrew.)

Liphschitz, N., and Waisel, Y.

1973 Dendroarchaeological investigations in Israel (Tel Beersheba and Arad in the northern and eastern Negev). *IEJ* 23:30–36.

1980 Dendroarchaeological investigations in Israel (Taanach). *IEJ* 30:132–36.

Loud, G.

1948 *Megiddo II.* Oriental Institute Publications, vol. 52. Chicago: University of Chicago Press.

Löw, I.

1924–34 *Die Flora der Juden 2.* Vienna: R. Löwit.

Lupu, A.

1973 Metallurgical analysis and manufacture of the iron ploughshare. In *Beer-sheba 1*, ed. Y. Aharoni, 45–46. Tel Aviv: Tel Aviv University/Institute of Archaeology.

Macalister, R. A. S.

1912 *The excavation of Gezer, 1902–1905 and 1907–1909.* Vols. 1–3. London: John Murray.

MacKay, A. I.

1950 *Farming and gardening in the Bible.* Emmaus: Rodale.

Malherbe, I. de V.

1953 *Soil fertility.* 3d ed. London: Oxford University Press.

Mayerson, P.

1956 *Arid zone farming in antiquity: A study of ancient agricultural and related hydrological practices in southern Palestine.* Ph.D. diss., New York University.

1960 *The ancient agricultural regime of Nessana and the central Negev.* London: Colt Archaeological Institute.

Mazar, A.

1981 Giloh: An early settlement site near Jerusalem. *IEJ* 31:1–36.

Mazar, A., and Kelm, G. L.

1980 Canaanites, Philistines, and Israelites at Timna/Tel Batash. *Qadmoniot* 13:89–97.

Mazar [Maisler], B.

1950–51 Excavations at Tell Qasile: Preliminary report. *IEJ* 1:61–76, 125–40, 194–218.

1981 The early Israelite settlement in the hill country. *BASOR* 241:75–85.

Mazar, B., Dothan, T., and Dunayevsky, E.
1963 ᶜEn-gedi: The first and second seasons of excavations, 1961–1962. *Yediot* 27:12–38. (In Hebrew.)

McCown, C. C.
1947 *Tell en-Nasbeh I.* Berkeley: Palestine Institute of Pacific School of Religion; New Haven: American Schools of Oriental Research.

McCreery, D. W.
1978 A report from ASOR's Albright fellow. *ASOR Newsletter* 2:1–3.

Mendenhall, G. E.
1962 The Hebrew conquest of Palestine. *BA* 25:66–87.

Meshel, Z.
1976 Kuntilat ᶜAjrud—An Israelite site on the Sinai border. *Qadmoniot* 9:119–24. (In Hebrew.)
1977 Horvat Ritma—An iron age fortress in the Negev highlands. *Tel Aviv* 4:110–35.

Meshel, Z., and Cohen, R.
1980 Refed and Hatira: two iron age fortresses in the northern Negev. *Tel Aviv* 7:70–81.

Meshel, Z., and Meyers, C.
1976 The names of God in the wilderness of Zin. *BA* 39:6–10.

Meyer, B. S., and Anderson, D. B.
1952 *Plant physiology*. 2d ed. New York: D. Van Nostrand.

Meyers, C.
1976 Kadesh Barnea: Judah's last outpost. *BA* 39:148–51.

Miller, J. M.
1977 The Israelite occupation of Canaan. In *Israelite and Judaean history*, ed. J. H. Hayes and J. M. Miller, 213–84. Philadelphia: Westminster.

Moldenke, H. N., and Moldenke, A. L.
1952 *Plants of the Bible*. Waltham: Chronica Botanica.

Morgenstern, J.
1924 The three calendars of ancient Israel. *HUCA* 1:13–78.
1926 Additional notes on "the three calendars of ancient Israel." *HUCA* 3:77–107.
1935 Supplementary studies in the calendars of ancient Israel. *HUCA* 10:1–148.

Naveh, J.
1960 A Hebrew letter from the seventh century B.C. *IEJ* 10:129–39, pls. 17–18.
1962 The excavations at Meṣad Ḥashavyahu—Preliminary report. *IEJ* 12:89–113.

Nayar, N. M.
1976 Sesame. In *Evolution of crop plants*, ed. N. W. Simmonds, 231–33. London: Longman.

Nayar, N. M., and Mehra, K. L.

1970 Sesame: Its uses, botany, cytogenetics and origin. *Economic Botany* 24:20–31.

Negev, A.

1972 *An archaeological lexicon of Eretz Israel.* Jerusalem: Sifriat Maᶜariv. (In Hebrew.)

Nicholson, E. W.

1967 *Deuteronomy and tradition.* Philadelphia: Fortress.

Noth, M.

1966 *The Old Testament world.* Trans. V. I. Gruhn. Philadelphia: Fortress.

Oren, E. D.

1973 Notes and news: Bir el-ᵓbd (northern Sinai). *IEJ* 23:112–13.

Owen, D. I.

1978a Aphek-Antipatris: Late Bronze/Iron Age and Roman period. Paper read at Society of Biblical Literature Annual Meeting at New Orleans.

1978b Letter to author, 7 December.

Palmoni, J.

1955 *ᵓArbeh.* In *EB* 1, ed. E. L. Sukenik, cols. 520–26.

Paul, S.

1968 *Nismān.* In *EB* 5, ed. B. Mazar, cols. 886–87.

Paul, S. M., and Dever, W. G.

1974 *Biblical archaeology.* New York: Quadrangle and New York Times.

Peelman, N.

1975 *The plants of the Bible.* New York: Morehouse-Barlow.

Petrie, M. W. F.

1928 *Gerar.* London: British School of Archaeology in Egypt.

1930 *Beth-pelet (Tell Fara) I.* London: British School of Archaeology in Egypt.

Philips, A.

1973 *Deuteronomy.* Cambridge: Cambridge University Press.

Porath, J.

1974 A fortress of the Persian period. *Atiqot* (Hebrew Series) 7:43–55, 6*–7*.

Pritchard, J. B.

1954 *The ancient Near East in pictures.* Princeton: Princeton University Press.

1958b *Hebrew inscriptions and stamps from Gibeon.* Philadelphia: University Museum.

1970 The Megiddo stables: A reassessment. In *Near Eastern archaeology in the twentieth century: Essays in honor of Nelson Glueck*, ed. J. A. Sanders, 268–76. Garden City, N.Y.: Doubleday.

1950 *Ancient Near Eastern texts relating to the Old Testament.* Princeton: Princeton University Press.

1958a *The ancient Near East: An anthology of texts and pictures.* Princeton: Princeton University Press.

Puchačevsky, M.

1924 Explanation of biblical words related to agriculture. In *Sefer hashana shel Eretz Israel*, 43–45. Tel Aviv: Agudat Hasofrim Ha[c]ivriyim and Dvir. (In Hebrew.)

Rabin, C.

1971 *Pannag.* In *EB* 4, ed. B. Mazar, col. 509.

Rainey, A. F.

1962 Administration in Ugarit and the Samaria ostraca. *IEJ* 12:62–63.

1970 Semantic parallels to the Samaria ostraca. *PEQ* 102:45–51.

Ramanujam, S.

1976 Chickpea. In *Evolution of crop plants*, ed. N. W. Simmonds, 157–59. London: Longman.

Reifenberg, A.

1955 *The struggle between the desert and the sown.* Jerusalem: The Jewish Agency.

Reisner, G. A.

n.d. *Israelite ostraca from Samaria.* Boston: Harvard University Press.

Renfrew, J. M.

1973 *Palaeoethnobotany: The prehistoric food plants of the Near East and Europe.* New York: Columbia University Press.

Reviv, H.

1975 *A commentary on selected inscriptions from the period of the monarchy in Israel.* Jerusalem: The Historical Society of Israel. (In Hebrew.)

Robinson, E., and Smith, E.

1874 *Biblical researches in Palestine and the adjacent regions.* 11th ed. Boston: Crocker and Brewster.

Rodriguez, M. M.

1966 *Lexicon of plant pests and diseases.* Amsterdam: Elsevier.

Ron, Z.

1966 Agricultural terraces in the Judean mountains. *IEJ* 16:33–49, 111–22.

Russell, E. W.

1973 *Soil conditions and plant growth.* 10th ed. London: Longman.

Salonen, A.

1968 *Agricultura Mesopotamic nach sumerisch-akkadischen Quellen.* Helsinki: Suomalaisen Tiedeakatemian Toimituksia.

Schaub, R. T., and Rast, W. E.

1978 Bab edh-Dhra[c] and numeira. *ASOR Newsletter* 6:1–5.

Segal, J. B.

1957 Intercalations and the Hebrew calendar. *VT* 7:250–307.

Seger, J. D., and Borowski, O.
1977 The first two seasons at Tell Halif. *BA* 40:156–66.

Sellers, O. R., Funk, R. W., McKenzie, J. L., Lapp, P., and Lapp, N.
1968 *The 1957 excavation at Beth Zur.* AASOR 38.

Shea, W. H.
1976 Famines in the early history of Egypt and Palestine. Ph.D. diss., University of Michigan.

Shewell-Cooper, W. E.
1962 *Plants and fruits of the Bible.* London: Longman and Todd.

Shiloh, Y.
1970 The four-room house: Its situation and function in the Israelite city. *IEJ* 20:180–90.
1973 The four-room house—The Israelite type-house. *EI* 11:277–85.
1976 New proto-Aeolic capitals found in Israel. *BASOR* 222:67–77.
1977 New proto-Aeolic capitals—The Israelite "*timorah*" (palmette) capital. *PEQ* 109:39–52.
1978 Elements in the development of town planning in the Israelite city. *IEJ* 28:36–51.
1981 *The proto-Aeolic capital and Israelite ashlar masonry. Qedem* 11.

Simmonds, N. W., ed.
1976 *Evolution of crop plants.* London: Longman.

Sinclair, L. A.
1960 *An archaeological study of Gibeah (Tell el-Ful).* AASOR 34–35.

Singer, J.
1929 *Taboos in the Hebrew Scripture.* Chicago: Open Court.

Slotky, I. W.
1949 *Isaiah.* London: Soncino.

Smith, W. R.
1894 *The religion of the Semites.* London: Adam and Charles Black.

Stager, L. E.
1972–73 Ancient irrigation agriculture in the Buqeiᶜah Valley. *ASOR Newsletter* 2:1–4.
1975 Ancient agriculture in the Judean desert: A case study of the Buqeᶜah Valley in the iron age. Ph.D. diss., Harvard University.
1976 Farming in the Judean desert during the Iron Age. *BASOR* 221:145–58.
1981 Highland village life in Palestine some three thousand years ago. *The Oriental Institute News & Notes* 69:1–3.
1982 The archaeology of the east slope of Jerusalem and the terraces of the Kedron. *JNES* 41:111–21.
1983 The finest olive oil in Samaria. JSS 28:241–45.
Forthcoming First fruits of civilization. In *Palestine in the Bronze and Iron Ages* (Olga Tufnell Festschrift), ed. J. M. Tubb. Palestine Exploration Fund.

Forthcoming Highland villages in 12th–11th centuries B.C. Palestine. In *Ai/et-Tell: A case study in archaeology and the Bible*, ed. J. A. Callaway.

Stager, L. E., and Wolff, S. R.
1982 Production and commerce in temple courtyards: An olive press in the sacred precinct at Tel Dan. *BASOR* 243:95–102.

Talmon, S.
1958 Divergences in calendar-reckoning in Ephraim and Judah. *VT* 8:48–74.
1961 *Yrḥ ᶜṣd pśt. Leshonenu* 25:199–200. (In Hebrew.)

Tawil, H.
1977 A curse concerning crop-consuming insects in the Sefire treaty and in Akkadian: A new interpretation. *BASOR* 225:59–62.

Thiele, E. R.
1965 *The mysterious numbers of the Hebrew kings*. Grand Rapids: Eerdmans.

Thompson, L. M.
1952 *Soils and soil fertility*. New York: McGraw-Hill.

Thompson, T. L.
1974 *The historicity of the patriarchal narratives*. Berlin and New York: de Gruyter.

Toombs, L. E., and Wright, G. E.
1963 The fourth campaign at Balâṭa (Shechem). *BASOR* 169:1–60.

Tufnell, O.
1953 *Lachish III (Tell ed-Duweir): The Iron Age*. London: Oxford University Press.

Tur-Sinai [Torczyner], N. H.
1947 *The language and the book*. Jerusalem: Mosad Bialik. (In Hebrew.)
1962 Following the language and the book. *Leshonenu* 26:2–12. (In Hebrew.)

Tushingham, A. D.
1971 A royal Israelite seal(?) and the royal jar handle stamps. *BASOR* 201:23–35.

Ussishkin, D.
1975 Dothan. in *Eaehl* 1, ed. M. Avi-Yonah, 337–39.
1976 Royal Judean storage jars and private seal impressions. *BASOR* 223:1–13.
1977 The destruction of Lachish by Sennacherib and the dating of the royal Judean storage jars. *Tel Aviv* 1–2:28–60.

Van Beek, G. W.
1972 Notes and news: Tell Gamma. *IEJ* 22:245–46.
1974 Notes and news: Tel Gamma. *IEJ* 24:138–39.

Vincent, H.
1909 Un calendrier agricole israelite. *RB* 18 (n.s. 6): 243–69.

von Soden, W.
1965–81 *Akkadisches Handwörterbuch*. 3 vols. Wiesbaden: Otto Harrassowitz.

Wade, G. W.
1929 *The book of the prophet Isaiah.* London: Methuen.

Waldbaum, J. C.
1978 *From bronze to iron: The transition from the Bronze Age to the Iron Age in the eastern Mediterranean.* Göteborg: Paul Aströms.

Walker, W.
1957 *All the plants of the Bible.* New York: Harper.

Weippert, M.
1971 *The settlement of the Israelite tribes in Palestine: A critical survey of recent scholarly debate.* Studies in Biblical Theology, n.s. 21. London: S.C.M. Press.

Westcott, C.
1950 *Plant disease handbook.* New York: D. Van Nostrand.

Whitewell, W. M.
1963 Insects in the Bible. In *Zondervan Pictorial Bible Dictionary,* ed. M. C. Tenney, 375–80. Grand Rapids: Zondervan.

Wilkinson, J. G.
1841 *Manners and customs of the ancient Egyptians.* Vol. 1. London: John Murray.

Wirgin, W.
1960 The calendar tablet from Gezer. *EI* 6:9*–12*.

Wright, G. E.
1955 Israelite daily life. *BA* 18:50–79.

Yadin, Y.
1958 Excavations at Hazor, 1957: Preliminary communique. *IEJ* 8:1–14.
1961a Ancient Judaean weights and the date of the Samaria ostraca. 9–25 in *Scripta Hierosolymitana 8.* Jerusalem: Magnes Press.
1961b The fourfold division of Judah. *BASOR* 163:6–12.
1962 A further note on the Samaria ostraca. *IEJ* 12:64–66.
1966 *Masada: Herod's fortress and the zealots' last stand.* Trans. M. Pearlman. New York: Random House.
1975a The Megiddo stables. *EI* 12:57–62.
1975b Hazor. In *Eaehl* 2, ed. M. Avi-Yonah, 474–95.
1976 In defense of the stables at Megiddo. *BAR* 2(3): 18–22.

Yadin, Y., Aharoni, Y., Amiran, R., Dothan, T., Dunayevsky, I., and Perrot, J.
1958 *Hazor 1.* Jerusalem: Hebrew University and Magnes Press.

Yadin, Y., Aharoni, Y., Amiran, R., Dothan, T., Dunayevsky, I., Perrot, J., and Augress, S.
1960 *Hazor 2.* Jerusalem: Hebrew University and Magnes Press.

Yadin, Y., Aharoni, Y., Amiran, R., Dothan, T., Dothan, M., Dunayevsky, I., and Perrot, J.
1961 *Hazor 3–4.* Jerusalem: Hebrew University and Magnes Press.

Yaffe, S. D.
1943a *Mĕlafĕfôn*—What does it mean? *Leshonenu* 11:42– 44. (In Hebrew.)

1943b More on the meaning of *mĕlafĕfôn*. *Leshonenu* 12:85–88. (In Hebrew.)

Yeivin, S.

1971 *The Israelite conquest of Canaan*. Uitgaven van het Nederlands historisch-archaeologisch institute te Istanbul 27. Istanbul: Nederlands historisch-archaeologisch institute in het Nabije Oosten.

1975 El-ʾAreini, tell. In *Eaehl* 1, ed. M. Avi-Yonah, 89–97.

Zaitschek, D. V.

1955 Remains of cultivated plants from ʿAfula. *Atiqot* (English Series) 1:71–74.

1959 Remains of cultivated plants from Ḥorvat Beter (Beersheba): Preliminary report. *Atiqot* (English Series) 2:49–50.

1961 Remains of cultivated plants from the caves of Naḥal Mishmar. *IEJ* 11:70–72.

1962 Remains of plants from the Cave of the Pool. *IEJ* 12:184–85.

Zgorodsky, M.

1930 *Ḥiṭṭâ, śôrâ, śĕʿorâ, nîsmān wĕ-kussemet*. *Leshonenu* 2:373–76. (In Hebrew.)

Zohary, D., and Hopf, M.

1973 Domestication of pulses in the Old World. *Science* 182:887–94.

Zohary, D., and Spiegel-Roy, P.

1975 Beginning of fruit growing in the Old World. *Science* 187:319–27.

1978 Fruit from the old world. *Madaʿ* 22:16–21, 50. (In Hebrew.)

Zohary, M.

1954a *Gad*. In *EB* 2, ed. E. L. Sukenik, col. 429.

1954b *Doḥan*. In *EB* 2, ed. E. L. Sukenik, col. 649.

1954c *Boṭnîm*. In *EB* 2, ed. E. L. Sukenik, col. 50.

1954d *Bāṣāl*. In *EB* 2, ed. E. L. Sukenik, cols. 306–7.

1955 *ʾĂbaṭṭîaḥ*. In *EB* 1, ed. E. L. Sukenik, cols. 21–22.

1958a *Ḥiṭṭâ*. In *EB* 3, ed. N. H. Tur-Sinai, S. Yeivin, and B. Mazar, cols. 104–6.

1958b *Ḥāṣîr*. In *EB* 3, ed. N. H. Tur-Sinai, S. Yeivin, and B. Mazar, cols. 270–71.

1958c *Ḥôaḥ*. In *EB* 3, ed. Tur-Sinai, S. Yeivin, and B. Mazar, col. 45.

1967 *The cultivated plants of Israel*. Israel: Hakkibbutz Hammeʾuchad. (In Hebrew.)

1971a *ʿĂdāšîm*. In *EB* 4, ed. B. Mazar, cols. 95–96.

1971b *Pištâ, Pištîm*. In *EB* 6, ed. B. Mazar and H. Tadmor, cols. 635–36.

1976 Lentil. In *Evolution of crop plants*, ed. N. W. Simmonds, 163–64. London: Longman.

1982 *Plants of the Bible*. Cambridge: Cambridge University Press.

Bibliography: Updated and Annotated

The interest among scholars and lay people in topics related to agriculture has increased since the first publication of this book. In re-issuing this work, it became necessary to update the bibliography with new materials that have appeared since its initial publication, and with older materials that were not included in the first publication. For ease of use, the following bibliography is arranged by categories and is briefly annotated. In doing so I realized that several of the entries can be listed under more than one category, but in order to save space a determination had to be made where to place them. Although this list is not all-inclusive, I do hope that it will make my attempt useful.

Agriculture: General

Many new studies related to the general topic of agriculture have been published recently, among them some that relate to periods later than the Iron Age. They are included here for comparative purposes.

Adams, R. M.

1978 Strategies of Maximization, Stability, and Resilience in Mesopotamian Society, Settlement, and Agriculture. *Proceedings of the American Philosophical Society* 122: 329–35.

Agricultural practices in early Mesopotamia for comparative purposes with Palestinian practices.

Borowski, O.

1988 "He who tills his land will have plenty": What Archaeology Reveals. In *Mysteries of the Bible: The Enduring Questions of the Scriptures*, ed. A. E. Guiness, 95–98. Pleasantville, NY: Reader's Digest.

A brief description of agricultural practices in ancient Israel.

1992 Agriculture. *Anchor Bible Dictionary* Vol. 1, ed. D. N. Freedman, 95–98. New York: Doubleday.
A brief description of agricultural practices in biblical times.

Brawer, M.
1991 The Supply of Food to Jerusalem from Its Rural Environment during the Late 19th and Early 20th Centuries. *Eretz Israel* 22: 45–51 (Hebrew), 34*–35*.
Pre-industrial practices in Palestine for comparative purposes.

Broshi, M.
1992 Agriculture and Economy in Roman Palestine: Seven Notes on the Babatha Archive. *IEJ* 42(3–4): 230–40.
Agricultural practices in late antiquity for comparison.

Gottwald, N.
1979 *The Tribes of Yahweh: A Sociology of the Religion of Liberated Israel, 1250–1050 B.C.E.* Maryknoll, NY: Orbis.
Deals in places with the role of agriculture, crops, and agricultural technology in the ancient societies of Canaan.

Harrison, R. K.
1983 Agriculture. In *The New International Dictionary of Biblical Archaeology*, ed. E. M. Blaiklock and R. K. Harrison, 11–13. Grand Rapids, MI: Zondervan.
Brief description of agricultural practices in biblical times.

Healy, J. F.
1984 Ancient Agriculture and the Old Testament (with Special Reference to Isaiah 28:23–29). In *Prophets, Worship and Theodicy*, ed. J. Barton, 108–19. Leiden: E.J. Brill.
Relationship between agriculture and the text.

Hopkins, D. C.
1983 The Dynamics of Agriculture in Monarchical Israel. *Society of Biblical Literature Seminar Papers* 22: 177–202.
The role of agriculture in the economy of monarchical Israel.

1987 Life on the Land: The Subsistence Struggle of Early Israel. *BA* 50: 178–91.
Farming in the highlands.

1997 Agriculture. In *The Oxford Encyclopedia of Near Eastern Archaeology*, Vol. 1, ed. E. M. Meyers, 22–30. Oxford: Oxford University.
Brief description of agricultural practices in biblical times.

Howayej, B. A.
1973 *Agricultural Atlas of Jordan*. Amman: Ministry of Agriculture.
Study of the agricultural practices in Jordan. For comparative purposes with pre-industrial and ancient practices in Palestine.

Mattingly, G. L.
1985 Farming. In *Harper's Bible Dictionary*, ed. P. J. Achtemeier. San Francisco: Harper and Row: 303–4.
Brief study of agricultural practices in biblical times.

Nesbitt, M.
1995 Plants and People in Ancient Anatolia. *BA* 58: 68–81.
Study of agriculture in a neighboring region for cross-influences.

Stager, L. E.
1976 Agriculture. In *Interpreter's Dictionary of the Bible: Supplementary Volume*, 11–13. Nashville, Abingdon.
Brief description of agricultural practices in biblical times.

Weitz, J. and Z. Lif
1953 The Extent of Cultivable Land in Palestine. *Eretz Israel 2*: 11–19 (Hebrew).
Description of cultivable lands in pre-industrial Palestine.

Agricultural Resources

Ahituv, S.
1978 Economic Factors in the Egyptian Conquest of Canaan. *IEJ* 28: 93–105.
A glimpse at the agricultural resources of Palestine.

Finkelstein, I.
1989 The Emergence of the Monarchy in Israel: The Environment and Socioeconomic Aspects. *JSOT* 44: 43–74.
Environmental and social conditions influencing the economy of ancient Israel.

Zertal, A.
1988 The Water Factor during the Israelite Settlement Process. In *Society and Economy in the Eastern Mediterranean (c. 1500–1000 B.C.)*, ed. M. Heltzer and E. Lipinski, 341–52. Leuven: Peeters.

Agricultural Economy

Eitan-Katz, H.
1994 Specialized Economy in Judah in the Eighth-Seventh Centuries B.C.E. Ph.D. Dissertation, Tel Aviv University.
Study of the economy of Judah during the Iron Age II, including the role of agriculture.

Holladay, J. S.
1995 The Kingdoms of Israel and Judah: Political and Economic Centralization in the Iron Age IIA–B (ca. 1000–750 BCE). *The Archaeology of Society in the Holy Land*, ed. T. E. Levy, 368–98. New York: Facts on File.
The role of agriculture in the economy of the monarchy.

McGovern, P. E.
1987 Central Transjordan in the Late Bronze and Early Iron Ages: An Alternate Hypothesis of Socio-Economic Transformation and Collapse. In *Studies in the History and Archaeology of Jordan III*, ed. A. Hadidi, 267–73. Amman: Department of Antiquities of Jordan.
A socio-economic study of Jordan in the LB and Iron Ages.

Na'aman, N.
1981 Economic Aspects of the Egyptian Occupation of Canaan. *IEJ* 31: 172–85.
The early economy of Canaan before the appearance of the Israelites.

Animal Use

The first edition of this book made reference to animal use only in passing. The following entries deal with this subject in depth.

Borowski, O.
1998 *Every Living Thing: Daily Use of Animals in Ancient Israel.* Walnut Creek, CA: AltaMira.
Animal use in agriculture.

Pullen, D. J.
1992 Ox and Plow in the Early Bronze Aegean. *AJA* 96: 45–54.
Use of animals in agriculture.

Food Production

Brothwell, D. R. and P. Brothwell
1998 *Food in Antiquity: A Survey of the Diet of Early Peoples.* Baltimore, MD: Johns Hopkins University.
Detailed discussion of the history of food and its consumption.

Geraty, L. T. and fl . S. LaBianca
1985 The Local Environment and Human Food Procuring Strategies in Jordan: The Case of Tell Hesban and Its Surrounding Region. In *Studies in the History and Archaeology of Jordan*

II, ed. A. Hadidi, 323–30. Amman: Department of Antiquities of Jordan.

Hirschfeld, Y.
1992 Bread and Its Place in the Diet of Judean Desert Monks. In *New Studies on the Agriculture and Economy of the Land of Israel in Antiquity: The 12th Annual Conference of the Department of Land of Israel Studies*, ed. S. Dar, 41–51 (Hebrew). Ramat Gan: Bar Ilan University.
Bread as a component in the diet of ancient Palestine.

Hoffmann, M.
1956 *5000 Jahre Bier*. Frankfurt: Metzner.
The production and use of beer through history.

LaBianca, fl. S.
1990 *Sedentarization and Nomadization: Food System Cycles at Hesban and Vicinity in Transjordan*. Berrien Springs, MI: Andrews University.
Modes of food production east of the Jordan.

Food Remains

Eshel, H.
1992 Agriculture in Jericho during the Bar Kokhba Rebellion Period in Light of the Excavations at Avior Cave. In *New Studies on the Agriculture and Economy of the Land of Israel in Antiquity: The 12th Annual Conference of the Department of Land of Israel Studies*, ed. S. Dar, 41–51 (Hebrew). Ramat Gan: Bar Ilan University.
Food remains from the Roman period for comparative purposes with earlier periods.

Food Storage

Borowski, O.
1997 Food Storage. In *The Oxford Encyclopedia of Near Eastern Archaeology*, Vol. 2, ed. E. M. Meyers, 217–19. Oxford: Oxford University.
Brief study of storage of food commodities.

Herzog, Z.
1992 Administrative Structures in the Iron Age. In *The Architecture of Ancient Israel from the Prehistoric to the Persian Period*, ed. A. Kempinski and R. Reich, 223–30. Jerusalem: Israel

Exploration Society.
Study of a certain type of storage facility.

Holladay, J. S.
1992 Stable, Stables. In *Anchor Bible Dictionary*, Vol. 6, ed. D. N. Freedman, 178–83. New York: Doubleday.
Study of tripartite buildings not as storage but as stable facilities.

Food Systems

LaBianca, fl. S.
1989 Intensification of the Food System in Central Transjordan During the Ammonite Period. *Andrews University Seminary Studies* 127: 169–78.
Food production during the Iron Age II.

LaBianca, fl. S.
1991 Food Systems Research: An Overview and a Case Study from Madaba Plains, Jordan. *Food and Foodways* 4(3–4): 221–35.
Food resources and production in Central Transjordan.

Grain Production

Aranov, M. M.
1977 The Biblical Threshing-Floor in the Light of the Ancient Near Eastern Evidence: Evolution of an Institution. New York: Ph.D. dissertation, New York University.

Avitsur, S.
1985 *The Threshing Floor*. Tel Aviv: Ha'aretz Museum. (Hebrew).

Borowski, O.
1992 Harvest, Harvesting. In *Anchor Bible Dictionary*, Vol. 3, ed. D. N. Freedman, 63–64. New York: Doubleday.
Brief description of harvest of grains and fruits.

Gonen, R.
1979 *Grain*. Jerusalem: Shikmona.

Hopkins, D. C.
1977 Cereals. In *The Oxford Encyclopedia of Near Eastern Archaeology*, Vol. 1, ed. E. M. Meyers, 479–81. Oxford: Oxford University.
Summary of grain crops and ways of consumption.

Grain Storage

Borowski, O.

1997 Granaries and Silos. In *The Oxford Encyclopedia of Near Eastern Archaeology*, Vol. 2, ed. E. M. Meyers, 231–33. Oxford: Oxford University.
Brief study of grain storage facilities.

Currid, J. D.

1985 The Beehive Granaries of Ancient Palestine. *ZDPV* 101: 151–64.
Study of a certain type of storage facility.

1986 The Beehive Buildings of Ancient Palestine. *BA* 49: 20–24.
Study of a certain kind of storage facility.

1993 Rectangular Storehouse Construction during the Israelite Iron Age. *ZDPV* 108: 99–121.
Study of a certain kind of storage facility.

Currid, J. D. and J. Gregg

1988 Why Did the Early Israelites Dig All Those Pits. *BAR* 14(5): 54–57.
Study of a certain kind of storage facility.

Currid, J. D. and A. Navon

1989 Iron Age Pits and the Lahav (Tel Halif) Grain Storage Project. *BASOR* 273: 67–78.
Study of a certain type of storage facility.

Kemp, C.

1979 Large Middle Kingdom Granary Buildings (and the Archaeology of Administration). *ZAS* 113: 120–36.
Egyptian grain storage installations for comparison.

Van Beek, G. W.

1986 Are There Beehive Granaries at Tell Jemmeh? A Rejoinder. *BA* 49: 245–47.
Storage facilities in Palestine in Late Iron Age.

Grape, Viticulture, Wine and Wine Making

Allen, H. W.

1962 *A History of Wine: Great Vintage Wine from the Homeric Age to the Present Day*. London: Faber and Faber.

Altbauer, M.

1971 More on "Semadar" on the Jar from Hazor. *Eretz Israel 10*: 64–66. (Hebrew).
Study of a particular term related to wine.

Bacchiocchi, S.

1989 *Wine in the Bible: A Biblical Study on the Use of Alcoholic Beverages.* Berrien Springs, MI: Biblical Perspectives.

Barash, I.

1998 Survey of Wine Presses and Agricultural Installations: Ramat Bet Shemesh Excavation Project (Stage A). *Excavations and Surveys in Israel* 17: 132–37.
Installations for wine making.

Beck, P. and M. Kochavi

1983 The Egyptian Governor's Palace in Aphek. *Qadmoniot* 16(62–63): 47–51. (Hebrew).
Installations for wine making (LB) and grain storage (IA).

Borowski, O.

1996 Viticulture. In *Dictionary of Judaism in the Biblical Period*, Vol. 2, ed. J. Neusner, 660–61. New York: Macmillan.

Broshi, M.

1985 *Wine in Ancient Eretz Israel.* Tel Aviv: Ha'aretz Museum. (Hebrew).

Eisenstein, J. D.

1964 Wine. In *The Jewish Encyclopedia*, 532–35. New York: Funk and Wagnalls.

Frankel, R.

1984 The History of the Production of Wine and Oil in Galilee during the Period of the Bible and the Mishna and the Talmud. Tel Aviv, Ph.D. dissertation. Tel Aviv University. (Hebrew with English summary).
Thorough study of wine and oil making.

1988 *Grape Vine, Wine Presses and Wine in Antiquity.* Tel Aviv: Eretz Israel Museum. (Hebrew).

Grace, V.

1979 *Amphoras and the Ancient Wine Trade.* Princeton, NJ: American School of Classical Studies at Athens.

Herzog, Z.

1997 Michal, Tel. In *The Oxford Encyclopedia of Near Eastern Archaeology*, Vol. 4, ed. E. M. Meyers, 20–22. Oxford: Oxford University.
Wine presses from the Iron age.

Hirschfeld, Y.

1981 Ancient Wine Presses in the Area of the Ayalon Park. *Eretz Israel* 15: 383–90.
Remains of wine industry.

Johnson, B. L. and L. E. Stager

1994 Ashkelon: Wine Emporium of the Holy Land. In *Recent*

Excavations in Israel: A View to the West, ed. S. Gitin, chapter 6. Boston: AIA.
Ashkelon as center of wine trade and shipping.

Mayerson, P.
1985 The Wine and Vineyards of Gaza in the Byzantine Period. *BASOR* 257: 75–80.
Viticulture in the Gaza region in late antiquity for comparison.

McGovern, P. E., S. J. Fleming, *et al.*, eds.
1995 *The Origins and Ancient History of Wine.* Philadelphia: Gordon and Breach.

Miller, N. F.
1997 Viticulture. In *The Oxford Encyclopedia of Near Eastern Archaeology*, Vol. 5, ed. E. M. Meyers, 304–6. Oxford: Oxford University.
Brief description of the topic.

Palmer, R.
1994 *Wine in the Mycenaean Palace Economy.* Austin: University of Texas at Austin.

Poo, M.-c.
1995 *Wine and Wine Offering in the Religion of Ancient Egypt.* New York: Kegan Paul International.

Rainey, A. F.
1982 Wine from the Royal Vineyards. *BASOR* 245: 57–62.
Study of wine making and distribution in Judah based on *lmlk* seal impressions.

Seltman, C. T.
1957 *Wine in the Ancient World.* London: Routledge and Paul.

Walsh, C. E.
2000 *The Fruit of the Vine: Viticulture in Ancient Israel.* Winona Lake, IN: Eisenbrauns.

Land Ownership

Demsky, A.
1982 The Genealogies of Manasseh and the Location of the Territory of Milcah Daughter of Zelophehad. *Eretz Israel 16*: 70–75 (Hebrew), 254*.
Relationship between the Samaria ostraca and historical geography.

Dybdahl, J. L.
1981 Israelite Village Land Tenure: Settlement to Exile. Fuller Theological Seminary. Ann Arbor: University Microfilm.
Study in land ownership.

Na'aman, N.
1981 Royal Estates in the Jezreel Valley in the Late Bronze Age and Under the Israelite Monarchy. *Eretz Israel 15*: 140–44 (Hebrew), 81*.

Land Use

Avner, U.
1990 Ancient Agricultural Settlement and Religion in the Uvda Valley in Southern Israel. *BA* 53: 125–41.
Agriculture in arid zone.

Borowski, O.
1997 Irrigation. In *The Oxford Encyclopedia of Near Eastern Archaeology*, Vol. 3, ed. E. M. Meyers, 181–84. Oxford: Oxford University.
Irrigation methods in the ancient Near East.

Edelstein, G. and Y. Gat
1980–81 Terraces around Jerusalem. *Israel-Land and Nature* 6(2): 72–78.
Terracing in the hill-country.

Finkelstein, I.
1995 The Great Transformation: The 'Conquest' of the Highlands Frontiers and the Rise of the Territorial States. In *The Archaeology of Society in the Holy Land*, ed. T. E. Levy, 349–65. New York: Facts on File.
The role of agriculture in the settlement process of the highlands.

Gibson, S. and G. Edelstein
1985 Investigating Jerusalem's Rural Landscape. *Levant* 17: 139–55.
Terracing in the hill-country.

Gleason, K. L.
1997 Gardens: Gardens in Preclassical Times. 349–65*The Oxford Encyclopedia of Near Eastern Archaeology*, Vol. 2, ed. E. M. Meyers, 383–85. Oxford: Oxford University.

Golomb, B. and Y. Kedar
1971 Ancient Agriculture in the Galilee Mountains. *IEJ* 21(2–3): 136–40.
Agriculture in the Galilee region.

Haiman, M.
1995 Agriculture and Nomad-State Relations in the Negev Desert in the Byzantine and Early Islamic Periods. *BASOR* 297:

29–53.
Agriculture in arid region in late antiquity for comparison.

Hillel, D.
1982 *Negev - Land, Water, and Life in a Desert Environment.* New York: Praeger.
Study of land use in arid environment.

Hopkins, D. C.
1985 *The Highlands of Canaan: Agricultural Life in the Early Iron Age.* Sheffield: Almond.
Study of the nature of Israelite settlement in the highlands from socio-economic point of view.

Kloner, A.
1973 Dams and Reservoirs in the North-Eastern Mountains of the Negev. *Eretz Israel* 11: 248–57 (Hebrew), 30*.
Use of runoff water in arid region.
1975 Ancient Agriculture at Mamshit and the Dating of the Water-Diversion Systems in the Negev. *Eretz Israel* 12: 167–70 (Hebrew), 124*.
Instructive concerning agriculture in arid zones.

LaBianca, fl . S., D. C. Hopkins, *et al.*
1988 *Early Israelite Agriculture: Reviews of David C. Hopkins' Book* The Highlands of Canaan. Berrien Springs, MI: Institute of Archaeology and Andrews University.
A panel discussion of land use in the highlands.

Maitlis, Y.
1989 Agricultural Settlement in the Vicinity of Jerusalem in the Late Iron Age. M.A. Thesis. Hebrew University of Jerusalem.
Study of agricultural land use in the Jerusalem region.
1992 Farmsteads around Jerusalem in the Late First Temple Period. In *New Studies on the Agriculture and Economy of the Land of Israel in Antiquity: The 12th Annual Conference of the Department of Land of Israel Studies*, ed. S. Dar, 3–13 (Hebrew). Ramat Gan: Bar Ilan University.
Study of agricultural land use in the Jerusalem region.

Mayerson, P.
1960 The Ancient Agricultural Remains of the Central Negeb: Methodology and Dating Criteria. *BASOR* 160: 27–37.
Agriculture in arid region in late antiquity for comparison.
1967 A Note on Demography and Land Use in the Ancient Negeb. *BASOR* 185: 39–43.
Agriculture in arid region in late antiquity for comparison.

Moody, J. and A. T. Grove
1990 Terraces and Enclosure Walls in the Cretan Landscape. In

Man's Role in Shaping the Eastern Mediterranean Landscape, ed. S. Bottema, G. Entjes-Nieborg and W. Van Zeist. Rotterdam, Balkama.
Terracing in neighboring countries.

Prausnitz, M. W.
1959 The First Agricultural Settlements in Galilee. *IEJ* 9(3): 166–74.
Farming in Galilee in early times.

Zohary, D.
1953 Ancient Agriculture in the Central Negev. *Eretz Israel* 2: 94–97. (Hebrew).
Agriculture in the Negev highlands.
1954 Notes on Ancient Agriculture in the Central Negev. *IEJ* 4(1): 17–25.
Agriculture in arid region.

Olive, Oil Production

Avitsur, S.
1986 *The Traditional Olive Press*. Tel Aviv: Ha'aretz Museum. (Hebrew).

Ben David, H.
1992 Olive Cultivation and Oil Production During the Mishnaic and Talmudic Periods: Geographical and Economical Considerations. In *New Studies on the Agriculture and Economy of the Land of Israel in Antiquity: The 12th Annual Conference of the Department of Land Israel Studies*, ed. S. Dar, 14–24. (Hebrew). Ramat Gan: Bar Ilan University.
Study of oil production in late antiquity for comparative purposes.

Eitam, D.
1980 The Production of Oil and Wine in Mt. Ephraim in the Iron Age, Ph.D. Dissertation. Tel Aviv University.
Regional study of oil production.
1987 Olive Oil Production during the Biblical Period. In *Olives Oil in Antiquity*, ed. M. Heltzer and D. Eitam, 16–43. Haifa: Haifa University.
Study of oil production in biblical times.

Eitam, D. and M. Heltzer, eds.
1996 *Olive Oil in Antiquity: Israel and Neighbouring Countries from the Neolithic to the Early Arab Period*. Padova: Sargon.

Frankel, R.
1986 *The Ancient Oil Press.* Tel Aviv: Ha'aretz Museum. (Hebrew).
1997 Olives. In *The Oxford Encyclopedia of Near Eastern Archaeology*, Vol. 4, ed. E. M. Meyers, 179–84. Oxford: Oxford University.
Brief description of olive cultivation and oil pressing.

Frankel, R., S. Avitsur, *et al.*
1994 *History and Technology of Olive Oil in the Holy Land.* Tel Aviv: Eretz Israel Museum.
Survey of olive oil production.

Gitin, S.
1990 Ekron of the Philistines: Olive Oil Suppliers to the World. *BAR* 16(2): 32–42, 59.
Oil production center at the end of Iron Age at Ekron.

Kelm, G. L. and A. Mazar
1983 Notes and News: Tel Batash (Timna), 1982. *IEJ* 33: 126.
Description of oil industry at the site.

Stager, L. L.
1990 Shemer's Estate. *BASOR* 277/78: 93–107.
Study of the wine and oil industries in early Iron Age Samaria.

Pests and Diseases

Bodenheimer, F. S.
1953 Rare Species of Locust in Israel. *Eretz Israel* 2: 93 (Hebrew).
Factors in crop yield.

Plant Identification

Hareuveni, N.
1980 *Nature in our Biblical Heritage.* Kiryat Ono: Neot Kedumim.
1984 *Tree and Shrub in Our Biblical Heritage.* Kiryat Ono: Neot Kedumim.

Omer, Z.
1998 Identifying the Plants of the Bible in Light of Koran Commentary. *Beit Mikra* 43(152): 67–77 (Hebrew).

Sussman, J.
1982 The Inscription in the Synagogue at Rehob. In *Ancient Synagogues Revealed*, ed. L. I. Levine, 146–51. Jerusalem: Israel Exploration Society.
Study of the inscription which mentions cultivated plants.

Younker, R. W.
1990 Present and Past Plant Communities of the Tell el-'Umeiri Region. *Madaba Plains Project 1 :The 1984 Season at Tell el-'Umeiri and Vicinity and Subsequent Studies*, ed. L. T. Geraty, L. G. Herr, Ø. S. LaBianca and R. W. Younker, 32–40. Berrien Springs, MI: Andrews University.

Plants: Medical

Duke, J. A.
1983 *Medical Plants in the Bible*. New York: Trado-Medic Books. Plants used for medical purposes.
Merrillees, R. S.
1989 Highs and Lows in the Holy Land: Opium in Biblical Times. *Eretz Israel* 20:148*–53*.

Plant Remains

Garfinkel, Y., I. Carmi, *et al.*
1987 Dating of Horsebean and Lentil Seeds from the Pre-Pottery Neolithic B Village of Yiftah'el. *IEJ* 37(1): 40–42.
Seed remains.
Liphschitz, N. and G. Birger
1991 Cedar of Lebanon (*Cedrus libani*) in Israel during Antiquity. *IEJ* 41: 167–75.
Liphschitz, N. and Y. Waisel
1973 Analysis of the Botanical Material of the 1969–70 Seasons and the Climatic History of the Beer-Sheba Region. In *Beer-Sheba I: Excavations at Tel Beer-sheba, 1969–1971 Seasons*, ed. Y. Aharoni, 97–105. Tel Aviv: Tel Aviv University/ Institute of Archaeology.
1983 Analysis of the Botanical Material. In *Ergebnisse der Ausgrabungen auf der Hirbet el-msas (Tel Masos) 1972–1975*, ed. V. Fritz and A. Kempinski. Wiesbaden: Harrassowitz.
1985 Analysis of Wood Remains from Tell Qasile. In *Excavations at Tell Qasile; Part Two, The Philistine Sanctuary: Various Finds, The Pottery, Conclusions, Appendixes*, ed. A. Mazar, 139. Jerusalem: Hebrew University/Institute of Archaeology.
Mayerson, P.
1997 The Role of Flax in Roman and Fatimid Egypt. *JNES* 56: 201–7. The use of flax in Egypt in Late Antiquity for comparative purposes.

McCreery, D.
1983 Ancient Plant Remains. In *The Excavations at Araq el-Emir, Vol. 1*, ed. N. L. Lapp, 103–4. AASOR 47. Philadelphia: American Schools of Oriental Research.

Population Estimates

Demographic studies are highly pertinent to the study of ancient agriculture. The following entries deal with the role of the population in the development of the economy and the practice of agriculture by different groups in different periods.

Broshi, M.
1993 Methodology of Population Estimates: The Roman-Byzantine Period as a Case Study. In *Biblical Archaeology Today, 1990: Proceedings of the Second International Congress on Biblical Archaeology*, ed. A. Biran and J. Aviram, 420–25. Jerusalem: Israel Exploration Society.
Study in population estimates in late antiquity for comparison with Iron Age.

Broshi, M. and I. Finkelstein
1992 The Population of Palestine in Iron Age II. *BASOR* 287: 47–60.

Broshi, M. and R. Gophna
1984 The Settlements and Population of Palestine During the Early Bronze Age II–III. *BASOR* 253: 41–53.
Study in population estimates for comparison with Iron Age.

Harmon, G. E.
1983 Floor Area and Population Determination: A Method for Estimating Village Population in the Central Hill Country During the Period of the Judges (Iron Age I). Ph.D. Dissertation, University Microfilm International.
Study of population in the early history of Israel.

Rural Sites

Many rural sites yielded remains of agricultural activities in the form of architecture, installations and tools.

Alpert Nakhai, B., J. P. Dessel, *et al.*
1993 Wawiyat, Tell el-. In *The New Encyclopedia of Archaeological*

Excavations in the Holy Land, Vol. 4, ed. E. Stern, 1500–1. Jerusalem: Israel Exploration Society.

Amit, D.

1991 Khirbet Jarish. *Excavations and Surveys in Israel* 9: 157–58.

1992 Farmsteads in Northern Judea (Betar Area), Survey. *Excavations and Surveys in Israel* 10: 147–48.

Beit Arieh, I.

1992 Horvat Radum. *Eretz Israel* 23: 106–112 (Hebrew), 150*. Study of a rural site.

Ben-Tor, A., M. Avisar, *et al.*

1987 A Regional Study of Tel Yoqne'am and Its Vicinity. *Qadmoniot* 20(1–2): 2–17. (Hebrew). Study of an agricultural site in its regional context.

Ben-Tor, A. and Y. Portugali

1987 *Tell Qiri*. Jerusalem: The Hebrew University.

Braun, E.

1993 Avot, Horvat. In *The New Encyclopedia of Archaeological Excavations in the Holy Land*, Vol. 1, ed. E. Stern, 122–23. Jerusalem: Israel Exploration Society.

Covello-Paran, K.

1996 H. Malta. *Hadashot Arkheologiot* 106: 39–41. (Hebrew). Site with agricultural character.

Dar, S.

1986 Hirbet Jemein - A First Temple Village in Western Samaria. *Shomron Studies*, ed. S. Dar and Z. Safrai, 13–73 (Hebrew). Tel Aviv: Hakibbutz Hameuchad. Site with remains of agricultural character.

Edelstein, G.

1988/89 Manahat - 1987/1988. *Excavations and Surveys in Israel* 7–8: 117–23. Site with agricultural remains.

1993 Manhat - A Bronze Age Village in South-western Jerusalem. *Qadmoniot* 26(103–104): 96–102. (Hebrew). Site with agricultural remains.

Eisenberg, E.

1988/89 Nahal Refa'im. *Excavations and Surveys in Israel* 7–8: 84–89. Site with agricultural remains.

Eitam, D.

1992 Khirbet Khaddash - Royal Industry Village in Ancient Israel. In *Judea and Samaria Research Studies: Proceedings of the 1st Annual Meeting - 1991*, ed. Z. H. Erlich and Y. Eshel,

161–82 (Hebrew). Jerusalem: Reuven Mas.
Site with agricultural remains.

Feig, N.
1996 New Discoveries in Rephaim Valley, Jerusalem. *PEQ* 128: 3–7.
Site with agrarian remains.

Finkelstein, I.
1981 Israelite and Hellenistic Farms in the Foothills and in the Yarkon Basin. *Eretz Israel* 15: 331–48 (Hebrew), 86*.
Sites with agricultural remains.
1994 *'Izbeth Sartah: An Early Iron Age Site Near Rosh Ha'ayin, Israel.* Oxford: BAR.
Site with agrarian remains.

Finkelstein, I. and Y. Magen, eds.
1993 *Archaeological Survey in the Hill Country of Benjamin.* Jerusalem: Israel Antiquities Authority.
Sites with agricultural remains.

Gophna, R.
1979 A Middle Age II Village in the Jordan Valley. *Tel Aviv* 6: 28–33.
Site with agricultural remains from MBII for comparative purposes.

Gophna, R. and Y. Porat
1972 The Land of Ephraim and Manasseh. In *Judaea, Samaria and the Golan: Archaeological Survey 1967–1968.* M. Kochavi. Jerusalem: Carta (Hebrew).
Sites with agricultural remains.

Greenberg, R.
1987 New Light on the Early Iron Age at Tell Beit Mirsim. *BASOR* 265: 55–80.
Site with agricultural remains.

Gudovitch, S. and N. Feig
1999 Nahal Yarmut. *Hadashot Arkheologiyot: Excavations and Surveys in Israel* 110: 120 (Hebrew), 97*.
Site with agricultural remains.

Heiman, M.
1992 Farmers and Shepherds in the Negev Highlands during the Byzantine and Early Islamic Periods. In *New Studies on the Agriculture and Economy of the Land of Israel in Antiquity: The 12th Annual Conference of the Department of Land of Israel Studies*, ed. S. Dar, 91–113 (Hebrew). Ramat Gan: Bar Ilan University.

Agricultural remain from late antiquity for comparative purposes.

1999 Surveys in the Forests of the Jewish National Fund. *Hadashot Arkheologiyot: Excavations and Surveys in Israel* 110: 110–11 (Hebrew), 86*.
Sites with agricultural remains.

Hizmi, H.

1996 Horvat Eli. *Hadashot Arkheologiot* 106: 74–75.
Site with agricultural remains.

Kislev, M. E.

1985 References to the Pistachio Tree in Near East Geographical Names. *PEQ* 117: 133–38.
Use of plants in place names.

Kochavi, M.

1989 Zeror, Tel. In *The New Encyclopedia of Archaeological Excavations in the Holy Land*, Vol. 4, ed. E. Stern, 1524–26. New York: Simon and Schuster.
Site with agricultural remains.

Mazar, A.

1982 Three Israelite Sites in the Hills of Judah and Ephraim. *BA* 45: 167–78.
Sites with agricultural remains.

1985 Between Judah and Philistia: Timnah (Tel Batash) in the Iron Age II. *Eretz Israel* 18: 300–24 (Hebrew), 75*–76*.
Site with agricultural remains.

1990 Iron Age I and II Towers at Giloh and the Israelite Settlement. *IEJ* 70: 77–101.
Remains of an agricultural site.

Mazar, A., D. Amit, *et al.*

1983 The "Border Road" between Michmash and Jericho and the Excavations at Horvat Shilhah. *Eretz Israel* 17: 236–50 (Hebrew), 10*.
Site with agricultural remains.

McDonald, B.

1988 *The Wadi el Hasa Archaeological Survey 1979–1983, West-Central Jordan.* Waterloo, Ontario: Wilfrid Laurier University.
Sites with agricultural remains.

McGovern, P. E.

1986 *The Late Bronze Age and Early Iron Age of Central Transjordan: The Beq'ah Valley Project, 1977–1981.* Philadelphia: University of Pennsylvania/The University Museum.
Sites with agricultural remains.

Miller, J. M., Ed.
1991 *Archaeological Survey of the Kerak Plateau.* ASOR Archaeological Reports 1. Atlanta: Scholars.
Sites with agricultural remains.

Riklin, S.
1997 Bet Aryé. *'Atiqot* 32: 7–20 (Hebrew), 37*–38*.
Site with agricultural remains.

Zertal, A.
1984 *Arubboth, Hepher and the Third Solomonic District.* Tel Aviv: Hakkibbutz Hameuchad.
Sites related to the agricultural economy.
1988 The Israelite Settlement in the Hill-Country of Manasseh, Ph.D., Tel Aviv University. (Hebrew).
Sites with agricultural remains.
1992 *The Manasseh Hill Country: The Shechem Syncline.* Tel Aviv: Ministry of Defense. (Hebrew).
Sites with agricultural remains.

Settlement and Land Use

Broshi, M.
1996 Fire, Soil and Water: Three Elements That Enabled the Settlement of the Hilly Regions of Palestine in the Iron Age. *Eretz Israel* 25: 94–98 (Hebrew), 90*–91*.
Study of land acquisition methods in early Israel.

Callaway, J. A.
1985 A New Perspective on the Hill Country Settlement of Canaan in Iron Age I. In *Palestine in the Bronze and Iron Ages: Papers in Honour of Olga Tufnell*, ed. J. N. Tubb, 31–49. London: Institute of Archaeology.
The role of agriculture in the settlement of the hill country.

Currid, J. D.
1984 The Deforestation of the Foothills of Palestine. *PEQ* 116: 1–11.
Study of land acquisition methods in early Israel.

Dar, S. O. and S. Applebaum
1986 *Landscape and Pattern: An Archaeological Survey of Samaria, 800 B.C.E. – 636 C.E.* Oxford: B.A.R.

Dearman, A.
1992 Settlement Patterns and the Beginning of the Iron Age in Moab. In *Early Moab and Edom: The Beginning of the Iron Age in Southern Jordan*, ed. P. Bienkowski, 65–76. Sheffield: J.R. Collins.

Finkelstein, I.
1985 The Iron Age "Fortresses" of the Negev - Sedentarization of Desert Nomads. *Eretz Israel* 18: 366–79 (Hebrew), 78*.
Land use in the Negev highlands in the Iron Age.
1988 *The Archaeology of the Israelite Settlement.* Jerusalem: Israel Exploration Society.
Settlement patterns in early Israel and their impact on the economy.
1996 The Settlement History of the Transjordan Plateau in Light of Survey Data. *Eretz Israel* 25: 244–51 (Hebrew), 97*.
Settlement patterns in Transjordan for comparison with Cisjordan.

Finkelstein, I., Z. Lederman, *et al.*
1997 *Highlands of Many Cultures: the Southern Samaria Survey: The Sites.* Tel Aviv: Institute of Archaeology of Tel Aviv University.

Hart, S.
1992 Iron Age Settlement in the Land of Edom. In *Early Edom and Moab: The Beginning of the Iron Age in Southern Jordan*, ed. P. Bienkowski. Sheffield: J.R. Collins.
Settlement patterns in Transjordan for comparison with Cisjordan.

Herr, L. G.
1992 Shifts in Settlement Patterns of Late Bronze and Iron Age Ammon. In *Studies in the History and Archaeology of Jordan IV*, ed. M. Zaghloul *et al.*, 175–77. Amman: Department of Antiquities of Jordan.
For comparison between Cis- and Transjordan.

Hutteroth, W.
1975 The Pattern of Settlement in Palestine in the Sixteenth Century. In *Studies on Palestine during the Ottoman Period*, ed. M. Ma'oz, 2–22. Jerusalem: Magness.
For comparison purposes with pre-industrial Palestine.

Joffe, A. H.
1993 *Settlement and Society in the Early Bronze Age I and II, Southern Levant: Complementarity and Contradiction in a Small-Scale Complex Society.* Sheffield: Sheffield Academic.
Study of ancient settlement patterns in Palestine.

Mazar, B.
1981 The Process of Israelite Settlement in the Hill-Country. *Eretz Israel* 15: 145–50 (Hebrew), 82*.
How did the Israelites establish themselves in the hill-country?

Meshel, Z. and A. Goren
1992 "Aharoni Fortress" - Another "Israelite Fortress" in the Negev and the Problem of These "Fortresses". *Eretz Israel* 23: 196–215 (Hebrew), 153*.
Continuing the study of the settlement of the Negev highlands in the Iron Age.

Ofer, A.
1994 "All the Hill Country of Judah": From a Settlement Fringe to a Prosperous Monarchy. In *From Nomadism to Monarchy: Archaeological and Historical Aspects of Early Israel*, ed. I. Finkelstein and N. Na'aman, 92–121. Jerusalem: Israel Exploration Society.
How did the Israelites establish themselves in the hill-country?

Shiloh, Y.
1980 The Population of Iron Age Palestine in the Light of a Sample Analysis of Urban Plans, Areas, and Population Density. *BASOR* 239: 25–35.
Land use during the Iron Age.

Yadin, Y.
1979 The Transition from a Semi-nomadic to a Sedentary Society in the Twelfth Century B.C.E. In *Symposia Celebrating the Seventy-Fifth Anniversary of the Founding of the American Schools of Oriental Research*, ed. F. M. Cross, 57–68. Cambridge, MA: American Schools of Oriental Research.
How did the Israelites settle the hill-country?

Social Structure

The social structure of early Israel was tightly related to the agricultural economy either by influencing it or being influenced by it. The following entries highlight this relationship.

Bendor, S.
1996 *The Social Structure of Ancient Israel*. Jerusalem: Simor.
The make up of Israelite society and its relationship to the economy.

Blenkinsopp, J.
1997 The Family in First Temple Israel. In *Families in Ancient Israel*, ed. L. G. Purdue, 48–103. Louisville, KY: Westminster John Knox.
The role of the family in the rural economy of ancient Israel.

Bunimovitz, S.

1994 Socio-Political Transformations in the Central Hill Country in the Late Bronze-Iron I Transition. In *From Nomadism to Monarchy: Archaeological and Historical Aspects of Early Israel*, ed. N. Na'aman and I. Finkelstein, 179–202. Jerusalem: Yad Izhak Ben-Zvi.
Study of the population in the heart of the Israelite hill country. Important to the understanding of the rise of Israelite society in the region.

Chaney, M. L.

1983 Ancient Palestinian Peasant Movements and the Formation of Premonarchic Israel. In *Palestine in Transition*, ed. D. N. Freedman and D. F. Graf, 39–90. Sheffield: Almond.
Socio-economic forces in the formation of Israel.

Coote, R. B. and K. W. Whitlam

1987 *The Emergence of Early Israel in Historical Perspective.* Sheffield: Almond.

Dever, W. G.

1995 Social Structure in Palestine in the Iron II Period on the Eve of Destruction. In *The Archaeology of Society in the Holy Land*, ed. T. E. Levy, 416–31. New York: Facts on File.

Finkelstein, I.

1993 The Sociopolitical Organization of the Central Hill Country in the Second Millennium BCE. In *Biblical Archaeology Today, 1993: Proceedings of the Second International Congress on Biblical Archaeology, Pre Congress Symposium Supplement*, ed. A. Biran and J. Aviram, 98–118. Jerusalem: Israel Exploration Society.
The role of society in the economy.

Freedman, D. N. and D. F. Graf, eds.

1983 *Palestine in Transition: The Emergence of Ancient Israel.* Sheffield: Almond.
Peasantry and politics on the eve of the Israelite emergence.

Frick, F. S.

1989 Ecology, Agriculture and Patterns of Settlement. In *The World of Ancient Israel: Sociological, Anthropological and Political Perspectives*, ed. R. E. Clements, 67–93. Cambridge: Cambridge University.

Gottwald, N. K.

1986 The Participation of Free Agrarians in the Introduction of the Monarchy to Ancient Israel: An Application of H.A. Landsberger's Framework for the Analysis of Peasant

Movements. *Semeia* 37: 77–106.
Economics as a catalyst for social-political change.

Lemche, N. P. and F. H. Cryer
1985 *Early Israel: Anthropological and Historical Studies on the Israelite Society Before the Monarchy.* Leiden: E.J. Brill.
A look at early Israelite society in its rural setting.

Marmorstein, E.
1953 The Origins of Agricultural Feudalism in the Holy Land. *PEQ* 85: 111–17.
The history and role of feudalism in Palestine.

McNutt, P. M.
1999 *Reconstructing the society of ancient Israel.* Louisville, KY: Westminster John Knox.

Meyers, C.
1983 Procreation, Production, and Protection: Male-Female Balance in Early Israel. *JAAR* 51: 569–93.
Women's role in the economy of early Israel.
1988 *Discovering Eve: Ancient Israel Women in Context.* Oxford: Oxford University.
Place of women in the agrarian economy.
1992 Everyday Life: Women in the Period of the Hebrew Bible. *The Women's Bible Commentary*, ed. C. Newsome and S. H. Ringe, 244–51. Louisville, KY: Westminster John Knox.
Women's place in the agrarian economy.
1997 The Family in early Israel. In *Families in Ancient Israel*, ed. L. G. Perdue, J. Blenkinsopp, J. J. Collins and C. Meyers, 1–47. Louisville, KY: Westminster John Knox.
How the family functioned in the agrarian economy.

Perdue, L. G., J. Blenkinsopp, *et al.*, eds.
1997 *Families in Ancient Israel.* Louisville, KY: Westminster John Knox.
The role of the family in the Israelite (mostly agrarian) economy.

Stager, L. E.
1985 The Archaeology of the Family in Ancient Israel. *BASOR* 260: 1–35.
The role of the family in the agrarian economy of early Israel.

Tools

Avitsur, S.
1986 *Inventors and Adopters.* Jerusalem: Yad Ben-Zvi. (Hebrew).

1988 *Selected Papers on the History of Eretz Israel: Industrial Processes and Ways of Life*. Jerusalem: Ariel. (Hebrew).

Boraas, R. S.
1985 Plow. In *Harper's Bible Dictionary*, ed. P. J. Achtmeier, 804. San Francisco: Harper and Row.
Brief description of the farming implement.

McNutt, P. M.
1989 The Symbolism of Ironworking in Ancient Israel. Ph.D. Dissertation. Vanderbilt University.
1990 *The Forging of Israel: Iron Technology, Symbolism, and Tradition in Ancient Society*. Sheffield: Almond.
Discussion of Iron-made farm implements.

Mully, J. D.
1984 The Beginning of Iron Metalurgy in Antiquity. *Qadmoniot* 17(65): 2–11. (Hebrew).
Iron-made farm implements.

Rosen, S. A.
1997 *Lithics after the Stone Age: A Handbook of Stone Tools from the Levant*. Walnut Creek, CA, AltaMira.
Stone tools, especially sickle blades.

Stein, A.
1991 *Felaheen, Machines and Peasants: The History of Agricultural Technique from the Beginning to the End of the Nineteenth Century*. Tel Aviv: Sifriat ha-Poalim. (Hebrew).
Study of agricultural technology and technics through the ages.

Ussishkin, D.
1983 Excavations at Tel Lachish. *Tel Aviv* 10: 97–175.
Farm tools discovered at Lachish.

Zorn, J.
1988 The Badé Institute of Biblical Archaeology. *BA* 51: 36–45.
Display of farm implements from Tell en-Nasbeh.

Urban Planning

Agriculture influenced also city planning and the design of certain structures.

Aufrecht, W. E., N. A. Mirau, *et al.*, eds.
1997 *Urbanism in Antiquity: From Mesopotamia to Crete*. Sheffield: Sheffield Academic.
Several articles on the role of agriculture in the urban economy.

deGeus, C. H. J.
1993 Of Tribes and Towns: The Historical Development of the

Israelite City. *Eretz Israel* 24: 70*–76*.
The role of the city in the history and economy of ancient Israel.

Finkelstein, I., S. Bunimovits, *et al.*
1993 *Shiloh : the archaeology of a biblical site.* Tel Aviv: Institute of Archaeology of Tel Aviv University Publications Section.

Herzog, Z.
1984 *Beer-Sheba II: The Early Iron Age Settlements.* Tel Aviv: Tel Aviv University Institute of Archaeology/Ramot Pub. Co.

Reich, R.
1992 Palaces and Residences in the Iron Age. In *The Architecture of Ancient Israel from the Prehistoric to the Persian Periods*, ed. A. Kempinski and R. Reich, 202–22. Jerusalem: Israel Exploration Society.
Structures as a reflection of urban economy.

Shiloh, Y.
1987 The Casemate Wall, the Four-Room House, and Early Planning in the Israelite City. *BASOR* 268: 3–15.
The house as a unit in urban society and economy.

Village Economy

Callaway, J. A.
1984 Village Subsistence: Iron Age Ai and Raddana. *The Answers Lie Below: Essays in Honor of Lawrence Edmund Toombs*, ed. H. O. Thompson, 51–66. Lanham, MD: University Press of America.

Edelstein, G. and S. Gibson
1983 Food Production and Water Storage in the Jerusalem Region. *Qadmoniot* 16(61): 16–23. (Hebrew).
Rural economy in the Judean Mountains.

Falconer, S. E.
1987 *Heartland of Villages: Reconsidering Early Urbanism in the Southern Levant.* Ph.D. Dissertation, University of Arizona.
Study of early villages for comparison with Iron Age villages.
1995 Rural Responses to Early Urbanism: Bronze Age Household and Village Economy at Tell el-Hayyat, Jordan. *Journal of Field Archaeology* 22: 399–419.
Village economy in the ancient Levant.

Faust, A.
1995 The Rural Settlement in the Land of Israel During the Period of the Monarchy. M.A. Thesis, Bar Ilan University. (Hebrew with English abstract).

Hopkins, D. C.
1987 Life on the Land: The Subsistence Struggles of Early Israel. *BA* 50: 178–91.
Economy of village life.

Rosen, B.
1986 Subsistence Economy of Stratum II. In *'Izbet Sarta: An Early Iron Age Site near Rosh Ha'ayin, Israel*, ed. I. Finkelstein, 156–85. Oxford: British Archaeological Reports.
Rural economy of early Israel.

Schwartz, G. M. and S. E. Falconer, eds.
1994 *Archaeological Views from the Countryside: Village Communities in Early Complex Societies.* Washington, DC: Smithsonian Institution.
For comparison purposes with village life in the Iron Age.

Steinberg, N. A.
1993 *Kinship and Marriage in Genesis: a Household Economics Perspective.* Minneapolis: Fortress.

Village Planning

The physical appearance of the Israelite village was due to pre-planning and/or needs dictated by the agricultural nature of the economy practiced by its inhabitants.

Dar, S.
1996 The Relationship Between the Dwelling Place and the Family in Ancient Israel. *Eretz Israel* 25: 151–57 (Hebrew), 93*–94*.
The house and its use by the family.

Daviau, P. M. M.
1993 *Houses and Their Furnishings in Bronze Age Palestine: Domestic Activity Areas and Artefact Distribution in the Middle and Late Bronze Ages.* Sheffield: JSOT.
The dwelling house in Palestine.

Hardin, J. W.
2001 An Archaeology of Destruction: Households and the Use of Domestic Space in Iron II Tell Halif. Ph.D. Dissertation. Tucson: The University of Arizona.

Herzog, Z.
1992 Settlement and Fortification Planning in the Iron Age. In *The Architecture of Ancient Israel from the Prehistoric to the Persian Periods*, ed. A. Kempinski and R. Reich, 231–74.

Jerusalem: Israel Exploration Society.
How sites were adapted to their agricultural nature.

Holladay, J. S.
1992 House, Israelite. In *Anchor Bible Dictionary*, Vol. 3, ed. D. N. Freedman, 308–18. New York: Doubleday.
The house as a reflection of agrarian economy.
1997a House: Syro-Palestinian Houses. In *The Oxford Encyclopedia of Near Eastern Archaeology*, Vol. 3, ed. E. M. Meyers, 94–114. Oxford: Oxford University.
The house as a reflection of the agrarian economy.

1997b Four-Room House. In *The Oxford Encyclopedia of Near Eastern Archaeology*, Vol. 2, ed. E. M. Meyers, 337–42. Oxford: Oxford University.
The house as a reflection of agrarian economy.

Hopkins, D. C.
1997 Farmsteads. In *The Oxford Encyclopedia of Near Eastern Archaeology*, Vol. 2, ed. E. M. Meyers, 306–7. Oxford: Oxford University.
Type-sites with agricultural character.

Kotter, W. R.
1997 Settlement Patterns. In *The Oxford Encyclopedia of Near Eastern Archaeology*, Vol. 5, ed. E. M. Meyers, 6–10. Oxford: Oxford University.
Theoretical discussion of the reasons behind settlement patterns.

Kramer, C.
1979 An Archaeological View of a Contemporary Kurdish Village: Domestic Architecture, Household size, and Wealth. In *Ethnoarchaeology: Implications of Ethnography for Archaeology*, ed. C. Kramer, 139–63. New York: Columbia University.
Study of present-day living for comparison purposes.
1982 *Village Ethnoarchaeology: Rural Iran in Archaeological Perspective*. New York: Academic.
For comparison purposes.

Lev, N.
1999 Two Iron Age Industrial Villages in the Central Highland. In *Judea and Samaria Research Studies: Abstracts of the Ninth Annual Meeting, 1999*, 5 (Hebrew). Ariel, Judea and Samaria College.

Mazar, A., D. Amit, *et al.*
1996 Hurvat Shilhah: An Iron Age Site in the Judean Desert. In

Retrieving the Past: Essays on Archaeological Research and Methodology in Honor of Gus W. Van Beek, ed. J. D. Seger, 193–211. Winona Lake, IN: Eisenbrauns.
Rural site with village remain.

Moore, A. M. T.
1997 Villages. In *The Oxford Encyclopedia of Near Eastern Archaeology*, Vol. 5, ed. E. M. Meyers, 301–3. Oxford: Oxford University.
The village as a focal point for the economy and social life.

Netzer, E.
1992 Domestic Architecture in the Iron Age. In *The Architecture of Ancient Israel from the Prehistoric to the Persian Periods*, ed. A. Kempinski and R. Reich, 193–201. Jerusalem: Israel Exploration Society.
The house as a reflection of the agrarian economy.

Ohata, K., Ed.
1970 *Tel Zeror*. Tokyo: Society for Near Eastern Studies in Japan.
Remains of a rural site.

Portugali, Y.
1983 'Arim, Banot, Migrashim: Spacial Organization of Eretz-Israel in the 12th–10th Centuries BCE According to the Bible. *Eretz Israel* 17: 282–90 (Hebrew),12*.
Study of terminology and its application to spatial analysis and utilization.

Riklin, S.
1994 Bet Arye. *Excavations and Surveys in Israel* 12: 39.
Remains of a rural village.

Seligman, J.
1994 A Late Iron Age Farmhouse at Ras Abu Ma'aruf, Pisgat Ze'ev A. *'Atiqot* 25: 63–75.
Remains of an agricultural site.

Singer-Avitz, L.
1996 Household Activities at Beersheba. *Eretz Israel* 25: 166–74 (Hebrew), 94*.
The house as a reflection of agrarian economy.

Village Social Structure

Antoun, R. T.
1972 *Arab Village: A Social Structure Study of a Transjordanian Peasant Community*. Bloomington: Indiana University.
Study of a pre-industrial village for comparison with Iron Age village structure.

Diakonoff, I. M.
1975 The Rural Community in the Ancient Near East. *JESHO* 18: 121–33.
Comparison between village communities in the Ancient Near East.

Faust, A.
1997 The Family Structure in Iron Age II Villages. In *The Village in Ancient Israel*, ed. S. Dar and Z. Safrai, 131–46. (Hebrew). Tel Aviv: Eretz.
The family and its role in the village.
2000 The Rural Community in Ancient Israel during the Iron Age II. *BASOR* 317: 17–39.
The rural community and its role in ancient Israelite society.

Index of Archaeological Sites

Index of Biblical References

General Index

Glossary of Hebrew Terms*

ʾăbaṭṭîaḥ/ʾăbaṭṭîḥîm	melon	137
ʾābîb	name of month	11, 33, 38
ʾābîb	stage in cereal ripening	88
ʾăguddôt môṭâ	ropes for yoke	52
ʾĕgôz	walnut	133
ʾădāmâ	cultivated land	145
ʾôpan ʿăgālâ	wheel-thresher	65
ʾôṣārôt	storage facilities	83
ʾōṣĕrôt haššemen	storage facilities for oil	125
ʾēzôr pištîm	belt made of flax	98
ʾăḥuzzâ	landed property	22
ʾêpâ	measure	60–61
ʾikkār	farmer	47
ʾallôn	oak	131
ʾalmug	red sandalwood	133
ʾălummâ	sheaf	60
ʾălāpîm	oxen	52
ʾāsîp	ingathering	8, 31, 38, 40
*ʾāsām/ʾăsāmîm**	grain-pit	71, 83
ʾăsuppîm	storage facilities	83
*ʾāpîl/ʾăpîlōt**	late crop	88
ʾēper	ash	146–47
ʾarbeh	migratory locust	153–54
ʾărūḥat yārāq	meal of vegetables	135
ʾōrōt	herbs	136
ʾăšîšâ/ʾăšîšôt	raisin cake	113
ʾăšîšê ʿănābîm	raisin cakes	113
ʾeškôl or *ʾeškōl/ʾaškōlôt*	bunch of grapes	110
ʾēt/ʾittîm	digging tool	108–9
boʾšâ	bunt	160–61
bĕʾūšîm	black rot	160–61

* The Hebrew terms are alphabetized according to Hebrew consonantal order (including final *hē* and the *matres lectionis*); vowels are ignored.

bûl	name of month	33, 40
bôlēs śiqmîm	piercer of sycamore figs	129
boṭnîm	pistachio nuts	132
bākāʾ/bĕkāʾîm	black mulberry(?), aspen(?), balsam tree(?)	130
bikkûrâ/bakkūrôt	early fig	115
bikkūrîm	early fruit	115
bĕlîl	mixed fodder	69, 96
bāmâ/bāmâh	high-place	81
bnh	build	105
bōser	unripe grapes	110
bĕṣēʾt haššānâ	at the end of the year	40
bāṣîr	vintage	31, 36, 109–10
bāṣāl or *bāṣēl/bĕṣālîm*	onion	138
bôṣēr/bôṣĕrîm	grape harvester	110
baṣṣōret	drought	153
bqʿ	plow	48
bqq	be luxuriant	104
bāqār	cattle	52
bār	clean grain	68, 89
bĕrōʾš ʾāmîr	at the top of the tree	119
barzel	iron	65
barqānîm	thorns	162
bāšal	(grain) ripen	57, 110
hibšîl	(grapes) ripen	110
bitḥillat ʿălôt halleqeš	at the beginning of the growth of late crops	31, 154
*gĕbûlâ**	boundary, territory	151
gēbîm/gôbāy or *gōbay*	swarms of locust	154
gad	coriander	98
gĕdûd	deep part of furrow	48
gādîš	heap of sheaves	61
gādēr	stone wall	105–6
gādēr ʾăbānîm	stone wall	105
gôʾēl	redeemer	23–24
gôdēr	*gādēr*-builder	105
gāzām	species of locust	154
gālāl/gĕlālîm	dry dung	145–46
gan	orchard, garden	101
gan bêtô	the garden of his house	136
gan hammelek	the royal garden	136
*ginnâ** or *gannâ*	garden	101, 136
ginnat ʾĕgôz	walnut garden	133
gepen	grapevine	103
gepen ʾadderet	climbing grapevine	104, 108
gepen bôqēq	variety of grapevine	104

gepen sĕdōm	wild vine	105
gepen sôraḥat	spreading grapevine	107
gepen śibmâ	variety of grapevine	104
gepen śādeh	poisonous wild vine	105
gargĕrîm	olives	119
gērîm	sojourners	25
gōren	threshing floor	62, 69, 111
gereś	crushed grain	88
gešem	rain	54
gat	type of wine press	63, 111–12
dĕbēlâ / dĕbēlîm	fig cake	115
dĕbelet tĕʾēnîm	fig cake	115
dĕbāš	date honey	127
dāgān	cereals	57, 87, 113, 126
dōḥan	millet	93
dayiš	threshing, threshing time	31
*dālît**	tendril	103
dam ʿēnāb	wine (poetic)	104
dam ʿănābîm	wine (poetic)	104
dōmen	dung	145–46
dărbān or *dărbōnâ*	goad	52
dardar	thornbush	162
drk	tread, tread grapes	112
dôrēk baggat	tread in wine press	112
dôrēk ʿănābîm	tread grapes	112
tidrōk zayit	tread (press) olives	119
dešen	ash of burnt animals	147–48
dĕšēnîm	well fertilized with *dešen*	148
hbr (hiphil of *brr*)	cleanse (grain)	65–66
hêdād	noise made by wine treaders	112
hillûlîm	rejoicing (during grape harvest)	110
hanniṣṣāb ʿal haqqôṣĕrîm	person in charge of the cereal harvesters	59
hpṣ	broadcast seeds	53
zāg	grape skin	103
zhh	be bright, splendid	118
zhr / ṣhr (*ṣhl*)	shine	126
ziw	brightness	118
zayit / zêtîm	olive tree, olive	117
zêt yiṣhār	olive for oil	125
zalzallim	tendrils	109
zĕmôrâ	vine branch	103, 109
zāmîr	grape harvesting	38

zāmîr	pruning of vines	109
zmr	grape harvest in the Gezer Manual	36, 109
zmr	pruning	109
zimrat hāʾāreṣ	fruit of the land	38, 101
zrh	broadcast seeds, winnow	53
zērûaᶜ zērûᶜîm	vegetables	135
zērōᶜîm or *zērᶜōnîm*	vegetables	135
zrᶜ	sow	53, 151
zôrēaᶜ	sower	54
zeraᶜ	seed	31, 51
zrq	broadcast seeds	53
ḥbṭ	beat out (grain, olives)	63, 119
ḥag	feast	39
ḥag haqqāṣîr	harvest festival	39
ḥāgāb	carob tree(?)	131
ḥāgāb	type of grasshopper	155
ḥedeq	thornbush	105, 162
ḥōdeš	month	32
ḥôaḥ	thornbush	162
ḥiṭṭâ/ḥiṭṭîm	wheat	88, 89, 91
ḥōṭer	shoot (of a plant)	119
ḥēleb	animal fat	148
ḥll	defile; convert vineyard from forbidden to permitted	110
ḥallāmîš	flint	61
ḥelqat haśśādeh	tract of land	95
ḥămôr	ass	52
ḥāmîṣ	chickpeas(?)	96
ḥōmeṣ	vinegar	61, 113
ḥemer	type of wine (red?)	113
ḥnṭ	become ripe	115
ḥănāmāl	plant louse(?)	128, 155
ḥāsîl	species of locust	154–55
ḥpr	dig, search	157
ḥĕpōr pērôt	fruit bat	157
ḥēṣen or *ḥōṣen*	fold of garment	60
ḥāṣîr	a vegetable (leeks?)	138
ḥṣr	be green	138
ḥăṣērîm	unwalled settlements	24
ḥargōl	type of grasshopper	155
ḥārîṣ or *ḥārûṣ*	iron tooth for threshing sledge	65
ḥārîš	plowing	54
ḥermēš	flint sickle	59, 61
ḥăšaš	straw	69

yôbēl	Jubilee	24
yôgēb	agriculturalist	18
yôreh	early rain	47, 54
yayin	wine	112–13
yyn ḥelbōn	type of wine	113
yyn ḥemer or ḥāmar	type of wine	113
yyn lĕbānôn	type of wine	113
yyn mezeg	type of wine	113
yyn ʿāsîs	pomegranate wine	113, 117
yyn reqaḥ	type of wine	113
yeleq	species of locust	154–55
yĕmê bikkûrê ʿănābîm	time of early grapes	31
yiṣhār	olive oil	113, 125–26
yeqeb	rock-hewn wine press	111, 123
yeraḥ	month	32
yrḥ ʿṣd pst	month of hoeing weeds	32–36, 38, 136
yrḥ qṣ	month of ingathering summer fruit	32, 38
yrḥ qṣr wkl	month of harvesting wheat and measuring grain	32, 36, 38, 40, 43, 57, 68, 88
yrḥ qṣr śʿrm	month of harvesting barley	32, 36, 38, 43, 57, 91
yrḥw ʾsp	two months of ingathering (olives)	32–34, 38, 119
yrḥw lqš	two months of late sowing	32, 34, 38, 47
yrḥw zmr	two months of grape harvesting	32, 34, 36–38, 109
yrḥw zrʿ	two months of sowing	32, 34, 47, 88
yrq	be green	159
yārāq	vegetables	135
yērāqôn	plant rust	155, 158–59
yātēd	digging tool	145
kĕbārâ	sieve	66
kayil	measure	38
klʾ	shut up, imprison	150
kilʾayim	mixture of two kinds	54, 149–51
kĕlê habbāqār	yoke	51
kammōn	cumin	97
kussemet/kussĕmîm	emmer	88, 91
kerem	vineyard	103, 106
kerem zayit	olive grove	119
kôrēm/kôrĕmîm	vinedresser	104
karmel	stage in cereal ripening	88
karmel	raw grain	88
kātît	crushed olives	120

lěhāběr	See *hbr*	
lûz	almond tree	132
lizrôt	See *zrh*	
leḥem	bread, food	90, 115
leḥem śěᶜorîm	barley bread	92
leqeṭ	gleaning	11, 61
leqeš	late crop	31, 154
migdāl	watchtower	106
měgûrâ	storage facility	83
maggāl	sickle	59, 61–62
*magrēpâ**	agricultural implement	53
migrāš	Levitical (common) land	30
mědōkâ	mortar	89
madmēnâ	compost hill	146
madrēgâ	terrace	17
mědūšâ	threshed matter	63, 69
môṭ or *môṭâ*	yoke	51–52
môsērôt	ropes	52
môrāg	threshing sledge	64
môrag ḥārûṣ	threshing sledge with iron teeth	65
mazmērâ / mazmērôt*	pruning knife	38, 109
mizreh	winnowing fork	65, 96
maḥărēšâ or *maḥărešet*	plow, plowshare	48
maṭṭeh	(threshing) stick	63
maṭṭāᶜ	orchard, planting place	101
mělûnâ	watchman's hut	106, 136
*mělîlâ**	dry ear of grain	58
malmēd	goad	52
malqôš	late rain	34, 54
*mamměgūrâ**	storage facility	83
miskěnôt	storehouses	79, 83, 99
mispôʾ	fodder	69
maᶜdēr	hoe	54, 108, 162
měᶜammēr	*ᶜāmîr*-gatherer	60
maᶜănâ or *maᶜănît*	marking-furrow	48, 53
maᶜăṣād	reaping tool, type of hoe	34, 162
maᶜăśēr	tithe	126
mōṣ	chaff	66, 69
měqôm haddešen	*dešen*-place	147
māqôm ṭāhôr	pure place	147
miqšâ	field of cucumber	136–37
měśûkâ or *měśūkâ*	thorn hedge	105
mešî	silk(?)	130
māšîaḥ	anointed	126

mešek hazzeraʿ	seed bag	54
môšēk hazzeraʿ	sower (poetic)	54
mišʿôl hakkĕrāmîm	path between vineyards	106
mišpaṭ haggĕʾullâ	law of redemption	24
mišat ʿănābîm	syrup	113
matbēn	heap of straw	69
nēbel yayin	skin-bottle of wine	115
nôṭĕrîm or *nôṣĕrîm*	(vineyard) guards	107
nāzîd	pottage	95
nāzîr	one who is consecrated, a Nazirite	113
naḥălâ/naḥălâh	land inheritance	10, 22
nĕṭîšâ/nĕṭîšôt	spreading branches	103, 109
nṭʿ	plant	104
nṭš	leave	58, 144–45
nîr	furrow in virgin land	48
nismān	sesame(?), millet(?)	93, 99, 151
naʿăṣûṣîm	thorns	162
naʿărôt	maidens	59
nĕʿārîm	young men	59
*nāpâ**	sieve	66
niṣṣâ	petals	119
nĕṣîbîm	governors	27
nēṣer	sprout	119
nōqep zayit	beating olive (branches)	119
sĕʾâ/sĕʾîm	a measure	115
sîrîm	thorns	162
sukkâ	watchman's hut	106
sukkôt	Feast of Tabernacles	11, 38
sallônîm	thornbush	162
*salsillâ**	tendril	103
sālʿām	type of grasshopper	155
sĕmādar	variety of grapevine	104, 157
sāpîaḥ	aftergrowth	144
sql	clear stones away (piel)	104
saqqĕlû mēʾeben	clear the stones!	104
sārābîm	thorns	162
sirpād	weed	162
ʿōbĕdê pištîm	processors of flax	98
ʿăbôt	rope	52
ʿeglâ	young cow	52
ʿăgālâ	wagon	62

ᶜūgat śĕᶜōrîm	baked good made from barley	92
ᶜădāšîm	lentils	94–95
ᶜzq	uproot the *ᶜajjaq*-bush	104
ᶜăṭallēp / *ᶜăṭallēpîm*	bat	156–57
ᶜîr hattĕmārîm	city of date palms	127
ᶜăyārîm	young donkeys	52
ᶜakbār	mouse	156
ᶜōl	yoke	51
ᶜōl barzel	iron yoke	52
ᶜll	glean (grapes)	110
ᶜōlēlôt or *ᶜôlēlôt*	gleaning	11, 110, 119
ᶜāmîr	cut cereal	60, 146
ᶜōmer	cut cereal	60, 61, 62, 40
ᶜōmer	a measure	60
ᶜēnāb / *ᶜănābîm*	grapes	103
ᶜinnĕbê nāzîr	grapes of unpruned vine	110
ᶜănābîm lāḥîm	fresh grapes	113
ᶜāsîs	pomegranate wine	113, 117
ᶜāpār	loose soil, dust	146
ᶜēṣ	tree	
ᶜēṣ hayyaᶜar	cultivated tree	102
ᶜēṣ haśśādeh	cultivated tree	101
ᶜēṣ šemen	oleaster	117
ᶜărēlîm	forbidden grapes	110
ᶜărēmâ	heap	68
ᶜēt hazzāmîr	time of the grape harvest	38, 109

pēʾâ	side, edge (of field)	11, 61
*pēʾēr**	glean olives	119
*pōʾrâ** / *pōʾrōt*	branch	119
pag or *paggâ**	unripe fig	115
pôl	broad beans	94
pwṣ	scatter, broadcast seeds	151
pûrâ	portable(?) wine press	111, 123
plḥ	plow	48
pelaḥ hārimmôn	slice of pomegranate	117
pannag	a food (made of millet?)	93
pessaḥ / *maṣṣôt*	Passover	11, 36, 38, 57, 9
pardēs	orchard	101
pereṭ	small bunch of grapes	11, 110
pśt	weeds	35
pištâ / *pištîm*	flax, linen, wick	98
pištê ᶜēṣ	flax stalks	98
pat	bread	61
ptḥ	open; plow	48

pattiaḥ	first plowing	53
pĕtîl pištîm	rope	98
ṣēʾâ or *ṣōʾâ*	human excrement	145
*ṣebet**	bundle of harvested cereal	59
ṣĕlāṣal	species of locust	155
ṣilṣal kĕnāpayim	migratory locust	155
ṣemed	pair, team of oxen	51–52
ṣemed bāqār	team of oxen	52
ṣimdê kerem	area measurement	52
ṣemed śādeh	area plowed per day by a *ṣemed*	52
ṣimmûqîm	raisins	113, 115
ṣpwʿy (ṣpyʿy) hbqr	cattle dung	145
ṣappaḥat haššemen	vessel for oil	126
qôṣ	thornbush	162
qîmôš	weed	162
qayiṣ	summer; summer fruit	31, 38
qayiṣ	second crop of figs	115
qîqāyôn	type of tree	156
qālî	parched grain	61, 88, 94, 115
qāmâ	standing (uncut) cereal	57
qemaḥ	flour	90
qemaḥ solet	fine flour	90
qemaḥ śĕʿōrîm	barley flour	92
qeṣaḥ	black cumin	97
qāṣîr	harvest, harvest time	31, 36, 54
qĕṣîr ḥiṭṭîm	wheat harvest	31, 57
qĕṣîr śĕʿōrîm	barley harvest	31, 36, 57
qōṣēr/qōṣĕrîm	reaper	59
qaš	straw	66
*qiššūʾâ** or *qiššût**/ *qiššūʾîm*	cucumber	137
rbq	tie fast	64
ribqâ	row of animals	64
rēḥayim	grinding stones	90
raḥat	winnowing shovel	66, 96
rimmôn	pomegranate	116
ripôt	product of grain	90
raqqâ	cheek or temple	117
reqaḥ	type of wine	113
śdd	leveling the ground	53
śiddûd	activity related to ground preparation	53

śwm/śym	put, place	151
śôrâ	cultivated crop	151
śîkîm	thornbush	162
śākîr	day-laborer	25
śĕᶜōrâ/śĕᶜōrîm	barley	91
śār	official	28
śārê hārĕkûš	officials in charge of royal property	28
śārîg	tendril	103
śōrēq or *śōrēqâ*	variety of red grapes	104
*śārōq**	variety of grapes	104
šebeṭ	(threshing) stick	63
šibbōlet	ear of grain	57, 63, 88
šābūᶜôt	Pentecost	11, 36, 38, 57
šĕdēmâ	terrace	17, 18
šĕdēpâ	disease	17
šiddāpôn	smut	154, 158–60
šĕdûpôt qādîm	crop hit by smut (as if by sirocco)	158–59
*šûm** or *šûmâ**/*šûmîm*	garlic	138
šôr	ox, bull	52
šĕḥîn	skin infection	115
šayit	weeds	162
šēkār	beer	92
šālōš rĕgālîm	Three Pilgrimages	11
šmṭ	forsake	144
šĕmiṭṭâ	remission of debts, year of fallowing	24, 145
šāmîr	weed	162
šemen	oil	118
šemen hammišḥâ	anointing oil	126
šemen zayit zāk kātît lammāʾôr	pure oil of crushed olives for lighting	119–20
šaᶜaṭnēz	mixture of wool and flax	150
šqd	watch, wake	131
šāqēd/šĕqēdîm	almond	131
šiqmîm or *šiqmôt*	sycamore	128
šĕtīlê zêtîm	olive suckers	119
tĕʾēnâ/tĕʾēnîm	fig	114
tĕʾēnîm rāᶜôt	bad-tasting figs	115
tĕʾēnîm šōᶜārîm	bad-tasting figs	115
teben	chopped straw	66, 69
tôlēᶜâ or *tôlaᶜat*	worm	156–57
tôšāb	resident	25

tîrôš	wine	113
telem	upper part of furrow	48
tāmār or *tōmer*	date palm	126
timōrâ	pillar capital	12, 128
tōmer miqšâ	scarecrow	136
tappûaḥ	apricot(?), peach(?)	129–30
tappûḥê zāhāb	apricots	130
tōpēś maggāl	reaper (poetic)	59